Design and the Social
Imagination

T0277383

DESIGNING IN DARK TIMES

Responding to the current and wide ranging systemic, social, economic, political, and environmental challenges we face, the aim of this series is to bring together short, polemical texts that address these crises and their inherent possibilities.

Understanding that the old division between the theoretical focus of the social sciences and the practical stance integral to designing, making and shaping the world is dissolving, *Designing in Dark Times* explores new ways of acting and knowing concerning the artificial. Identified by the refusal of resignation to what-is and by the equal necessity and urgency of developing new models of the possible, the series presents both modes of thought (models, concepts, arguments) and courses of action (scenarios, strategies, proposals, works) at all levels from the local and the micro (the situation) to the global and the macro.

The aim is to push the boundaries of both design and thought, to make each more capable of opening genuine possibilities for thinking and acting otherwise and thus of better facing, and facing down, the myriad failures of the present.

As the world descends into crisis these books seek to offer, in small ways, a counter view. Against the instrumental they use the fact that design is *also* a means of articulating hitherto unforeseen possibilities—for subjects as much as for the world—to show how at base it offers irreplaceable capabilities for thinking and acting well in the artificial. In so doing, they point us toward ways of reversing some of the negative and destructive tendencies threatening to engulf the world.

TITLES IN THE SERIES

SERIES EDITORS

Clive Dilnot
Eduardo Staszowski

"In this lively and accessible book, Matthew DelSesto argues persuasively for meaningful self-reflection, coupled with practical intervention, to solve social problems. DelSesto's design-theoretic approach, informed by C. Wright Mills's imaginary, shows a way of acting in the social world and of creating possibilities in it that is not only inspiring, but also doable."

— A. JAVIER TREVIÑO, Professor of Sociology,
Wheaton College, USA

"For those of us who have struggled to bring the design and socio-logical traditions together in dialogue, this book is a welcome arrival. In a world where academics and practitioners work in silos and speak only to narrow disciplinary audiences, we see far too few efforts to develop transdisciplinary thinking. This book breaks away from those enduring shackles, offering a grounded historical understanding of how several of the most important urbanists of the twentieth century have re-thought the social world through the lens of design, and vice-versa."

— DIANE E. DAVIS, Charles Dyer Norton Professor
of Regional Planning and Urbanism,
Harvard University, USA

"In *Design and the Social Imagination*, Matthew DelSesto sketches out practices that attempt to blend rigorous social inquiry with creative forms of activism. In the process, he produces a guide to a possible way of thinking for action. While he draws inspiration from historic figures such as Patrick Geddes, Jane Addams, and W.E.B. Dubois, readers of this book will be equally inspired to seek out contemporary practices of social transformation that combine design and activist strategies in highly effective ways. In sum, the book serves two purposes, as an enlightening introduc-tion to awakening the social imagination by examining the fields of sociology and design, and as an inspiring jumping-off point for the 'choreography of beautiful action' by framing approaches that are already well underway in cities around the world."

— ASEEM INAM, Professor and Chair in Urban Design,
Cardiff University, UK

Design and the Social Imagination

Matthew DelSesto

BLOOMSBURY VISUAL ARTS
LONDON • NEW YORK • OXFORD • NEW DELHI • SYDNEY

BLOOMSBURY VISUAL ARTS
Bloomsbury Publishing Plc
50 Bedford Square, London, WC1B 3DP, UK
1385 Broadway, New York, NY 10018, USA
29 Earlsfort Terrace, Dublin 2, Ireland

BLOOMSBURY, BLOOMSBURY VISUAL ARTS and the Diana logo
are trademarks of Bloomsbury Publishing Plc

First published in Great Britain 2022

Copyright © Matthew DelSesto, 2022

Matthew DelSesto has asserted his right under the Copyright,
Designs and Patents Act, 1988, to be identified as Author of this work.

Cover design by Andrew LeClair and Chris Wu of Wkshps

All rights reserved. No part of this publication may be reproduced or transmitted
in any form or by any means, electronic or mechanical, including photocopying,
recording, or any information storage or retrieval system, without prior
permission in writing from the publishers.

Bloomsbury Publishing Plc does not have any control over, or responsibility for, any
third-party websites referred to or in this book. All internet addresses given in this
book were correct at the time of going to press. The author and publisher regret
any inconvenience caused if addresses have changed or sites have ceased
to exist, but can accept no responsibility for any such changes.

Every effort has been made to trace copyright holders of images and to obtain their
permission for the use of copyright material. The publisher apologizes for any errors
or omissions in copyright acknowledgement and would be grateful if notified of any
corrections that should be incorporated in future reprints or editions of this book.

A catalogue record for this book is available from the British Library.

A catalog record for this book is available from the Library of Congress.

ISBN: HB: 978-1-3502-4295-1
         PB: 978-1-3502-4294-4
         ePDF: 978-1-3502-4297-5
         eBook: 978-1-3502-4296-8

Series: Designing in Dark Times

Typeset by Integra Software Services Pvt. Ltd.
Printed and bound in India

To find out more about our authors and books visit www.bloomsbury.com
and sign up for our newsletters.

CONTENTS

FIGURES

PREFACE

The concept of this book emerged as a result of my experiences as a student and educator in a design school and a sociology department. In my graduate work in urban design at Parsons School of Design and later in sociology at Boston College, I was being presented with what initially seemed like two entirely different worlds. It was only through teaching and seeing how students responded to my own presentations of these disciplines—in the context of design at Parsons and sociology at Boston College— that I began to understand the potentials of combining ways of knowing and acting from different traditions in design and social thought.

It was in seeing sociology students' desire for action and change, including my own, that I began to wonder what sociology could offer more concretely. Like many undergraduates, I had been told in my own sociological education that sociology was different than philosophy, because while philosophers attempted to understand the world, the point was to change it (with the implication that sociology is positioned to do this world-changing). As I became more familiar with the discipline, it was clear that the current practices and the conventional disciplinary foundations did not often offer resources for making things happen or participating in social change.

The first sociology class I taught—just a few years after studying and collaborating with different students and faculty at Parsons—was "Introductory Sociology." This was something that I initially dreaded because I had never taken such a course, I did not major in sociology as an undergraduate, and I was not even sure I knew what sociology was. How could I introduce others to something I scarcely knew myself? It turns out this not-knowing provoked some generative searching and reflection.

I began to look for ways of engaging the core concepts and methods of sociology while also maintaining the creative spirit necessary to make interventions. The strange irony to me in this was that, while almost all introductory sociology texts give a nod to the "sociological imagination," most then proceed to present social reality as a series of social facts about a world that is becoming progressively better understood. This historical development—toward ever more complete knowledge of society— is then often presented as conclusions for students to learn for an exam or repeat in an essay. Even beyond the typical textbook, there were few resources that actually showed what difference the sociological imagination would make for actually devising courses of action and intervention—and many were built on a backward-looking historical presentation of figures such as Karl Marx, Emile Durkheim, or Max Weber.

I realized that my students wanted something that I, in some ways, had already begun to develop in my time attempting to use the tools of both design and sociology to understand some of the issues I had been encountering in my work outside of universities. My searching for some alternative foundations for thought and action led me to the worlds of Patrick Geddes, Jane Addams, and W.E.B. DuBois that I present in this book.

While much of sociology, and especially the introductory-level textbook, emphasizes thinkers who contribute to the *profession* of sociology, these three seemed to offer something slightly different. Their hybrid practices blended rigorous social inquiry with creative forms of activism. To me, they offered models for navigating between professional practices and concrete actions. Rather than use thinking to distance themselves from their social world, like many scholars in their time and ours, they employed thought as a means to participate in making and shaping worlds. They used their own lived experiences and social location as a strength—blending the professional, political, and personal realms of life toward actions they thought might respond to the pressing social challenges of their time.

As I thought more about these three figures, I came to see their lives, contexts, and projects—both implicitly and directly—as framing some potentials of social thought, particularly in terms of linking together forms of social understanding and action. Applying this approach created lively discussions and work that was able to cover the topics in Introductory Sociology courses while also, in part, moving beyond "sociology" as only a professional discipline, and into something that we could all apply to our thinking and acting in activism, organizations and institutions, or daily life. What emerged was the beginning of a critical engaged mode of thought and action—albeit, one that was not quite defined in advance.

To be clear: my intention here is not to simply reflect on my own teaching and work, write a sociology textbook, offer a new "cannon" for design, or to tell an alternative history of a professional discipline. I do, however, see this book as a reference or guide to a possible way of thinking and acting. Overall, my hope is that I've brought together arguments, concepts, strategies, and models for the thought and practice that led me to the Geddes-Addams-Du Bois trio. In this, I've attempted to elaborate their ideas further in a way that is relevant to those who are attempting to face down contemporary challenges of today (from the perspective of design, social science, or everyday life).

The book also aims to make a meaningful intervention into design thinking and practice. Like a growing number of design scholars and practitioners, I have become convinced that there is a role for design in responding to the complexity and urgency of our social and environmental crises today. Design can, and must, do more than offer one-off workshops on design thinking, or create consumer spaces, services, and objects for those who have money to pay designers. I have found that students who are interested in design would often like to make and do things that create some sort of positive change—yet they are not often-enough given the histories, theories, and perspectives that encourage them to adequately reflect on the implications and contexts of their interventions. Moreover, the reactionary qualities of professional design practice—which involve responding to requests for proposals or demands of specific clients—too often emphasize the needs of those who already have resources, while ignoring the larger potentials of design to proactively remake society.

It is in this sense that the book contributes to some foundations for reflective and strategic action that also challenge dominant trends in both design and social sciences. It does this by highlighting a broader sense of action than has conventionally been considered in design. By drawing on examples of people who are not necessarily "designers," but are nevertheless exercising a design capacity, the book makes a contribution to better understanding the capabilities of designing today. At the same time, the book shows how, although social thinkers today often consider themselves to be observers of an already-made world, thought has tremendous potential to participate in the making of new worlds.

The book is divided into three parts, which, to an extent, could each stand on their own as a particular contribution, even as they inform each other. Part One describes a way of conceiving the relations between design, the human imagination, and social thought. It makes connections from classical twentieth-century writings such as C. Wright Mills on the "sociological imagination" and Horst Rittel and Melvin Webber on "wicked problems" to contemporary efforts of activists, practitioners, and thinkers address the enduring gap between reflection and action. Part Two centers on the social contexts and projects of Geddes, Addams, and Du Bois. The chapters in this part of the book argue that it is fruitful for both thought and action today to view these three social thinkers *also* as designers or project-makers. Rather than presenting mini-biographies of Geddes, Addams, and Du Bois, the chapters here explore the relevance of their work to the present, including how they might inspire a reimagining of design and social thought today. Finally, in Part Three, an effort is made to draw on the work of the three key thinkers, along with the proposed framework for relating social thought and design from Part One, in order to further elaborate a model for action today. This third part is, at times, less concrete and more open-ended. It is meant to suggest some possible future implications, along with ways of orienting oneself for pursuing forms of reflective action today.

Overall, the urgent underlying theme throughout is reflection, action, and the inter-relationship between the two. While traditional social sciences often see themselves as reflecting "on" social reality, this book conceptualizes reflection itself as an intervention from within social reality. Alternatively, design often sees itself as exclusively intervention-oriented, whereas this book conceptualizes acting as the subject-matter for reflection. It is in this sense that the book explores how designing might begin to be understood a process of reflection on what is possible. To use Herbert Simon's words, the book centers on how "design like [social] science is a tool for understanding as well as for acting."[1]

Most of what I write on the coming pages has been informed by my last ten years of research, teaching, and practice, and I have learned a great deal in reflecting on this period in the course of writing. I am especially grateful to have discovered the *Designing in Dark Times* book series early in its formation. This book and my scholarly work in general have benefited enormously from the guidance of Clive Dilnot, who has been a constant source of support and insight in the development of this project.

I am also grateful to all of those whose ideas, conversations, and mentorship have contributed to the perspective I share here. In particular, much of what I know about the possibilities of design I learned from my professors and advisors at Parsons School of Design, especially Aseem Inam, Miodrag Mitrasinovic, Bill Morrish, Miguel Robles-Duran, and Jilly Traganou. Their ability to reflectively present their own practices, and use their teaching to make spaces for creativity and collaboration has shaped my own scholarly sensibilities. The cohort of urban graduate students in my program at Parsons also taught me a great deal about combining social thought and action, through the incredible diversity of knowledge and experience they brought into our conversations. In my time at Boston College, Stephen Pfohl's intellectual generosity and relentlessly creative thinking has long inspired my own work and perspective on what sociology is and can be. I met Brinton Lykes at just the right moment in my academic career, when she connected me to a larger social imagination of the ways that thoughtful reflection and action can go together in the service of social transformation. Throughout it all, Mike Cermak has always shown me a powerful example of the ways that social thinking can be a process of reflective action—and

[1] Simon further explains an aspiration that is shared by this book: "One can envisage a future, however, in which our main interest in both science and design will lie in what they teach us about the world and not in what they allow us to do to the world. Design like science is a tool for understanding as well as for acting." Herbert Simon, *Sciences of the Artificial* (MIT Press, 1969), page 164.

how what we actually do can often speak more meaningfully than any written text or academic presentation.

Some of the organizations and communities I have been fortunate enough to get to know in the last ten years have offered profound lessons that shape the perspectives presented on the coming pages. My understanding of environmental issues of today is only possible because of the many horticulturalists, urban farmers, activists, and environmental advocates I met through organizations like The Food Project and The New Garden Society in Boston or 596 Acres and the Horticultural Society of New York in New York City. The Jesuit-inspired approach to accompaniment and praxis, a model that I first came to know through Boston College and later through community activists and educators in El Salvador, has profoundly shaped my understanding of reflective action. The students and educators I have met in prisons, most especially those affiliated with the international network of the Inside-Out Prison Exchange Program, continue to reveal the power of the human imagination to make new worlds.

There are of course many more I am thankful for including my persistently caring partner Megan, my family who has inspired me to question conventional wisdom, the anonymous reviewers who gave feedback at multiple stages of this process, and many others whose input has shaped the words on the coming pages.

PART ONE
Awakening the Social Imagination

In 2020, great uncertainty and change characterized life in the United States where I write these words. Unprecedented wildfires and heat waves ravaged the Western states. Species extinctions accelerated at alarming rates. Massive protests about racial injustice and police violence rocked the streets, while the country incarcerated more people per capita than any other nation on Earth. Record numbers of migrants and refugees arrived at the US border. A global pandemic devastated lives and economies. Billionaires and large multinational corporations racked up historic profits, while economic inequality grew, social mobility remained stalled, and unemployment skyrocketed.

It is the main contention of this book that the overlapping challenges of today can all be traced back to a larger failure of public life: a failure of our social imaginations. This is to say that Western societies with historically high levels of industrialization, urbanization, and wealth accumulation are also midst of a larger cultural crisis, where our institutions have been fundamentally unable to reorganize their ways of thinking and making.[1]

[1] Teddy Cruz, "Where Is Our Civic Imagination?" in Miodrag Mitrasinovic (editor), *Concurrent Urbanities: Designing Infrastructures of Inclusion* (Routledge, 2016), pages 9–23.

On a global level, public and private institutions have failed to reexamine the ecologically and socially unsustainable ways we have grown.

This is not because such institutions—from governments to corporations and philanthropic foundations—are completely ignoring the most pressing issues of our time. The failure to imagine differently is ultimately a result of a profound alienation which has been "heavily conditioned by institutions" themselves.[2] We do not need only new policies, laws, buildings, products, services, and systems. We need to radically rethink the challenges we face. In short, we need to reawaken our social imaginations.

Yet the social imagination is neither a switch that can be turned on, nor is it only a change of individual thought patterns. It requires people, communities, organizations, and institutions to grapple with the deepening alienation of today. This alienation stems from the apparent triumph of "rational mastery," where all aspects of the world, including even human thought, are considered valuable only as they are useful to the advancement of economic or scientific progress. In the wake of rational mastery, organizations and institutions seem to become autonomous on their own—with increasing automation of society more broadly, from processes of economic production to the collection and management of "big data."

The political economy and advance of scientific knowledge shape an alienating social context, where people are made to stand alone before a world that they are told is being rationally mastered by ever-increasing economic growth, scientific expertise, and technical management. The social world is said to be fully

---

[2] The understanding of alienation and social imagination here draws on Cornelius Castoriadis, who explains that: "Alienation therefore appears as *instituted*, in any case as heavily conditioned by institutions … once an institution is established it seems to become autonomous, the fact that it possesses its own inertia and its own logic, that, in its continuance and in its effects, it outstrips its function, its 'ends', and its 'reasons for existing'. The apparent plain truths are turned upside-down: what could have been seen 'at the start' as an ensemble of institutions in the service of society becomes a society in the service of institutions." Cornelius Castoriadis, *The Imaginary Institution of Society* (Polity Press, 1987), pages 109–110.

comprehensible and always progressing, yet the process of understanding the world is put largely out of the hands of people in the wider public—who, rather than thinking and acting with/ for themselves, are then left further outside of progress as they simply refuse to consume the knowledge that is being handed down to them.

Leaders then double down on increasing rationalization, where the solution is said to be somehow bringing more people into an already-narrowing vision of scientific, technological, and economic progress. What results is a widespread doubt and uncertainty—in the very possibility of having any sort of shared understanding about societal and ecological challenges. People grow skeptical that human beings have the capacity to alter the course of their societies, which appear to grow increasingly contradictory and complex by the day. Meanwhile, large institutions and organizations portray the present and future as an inevitable outcome of reason, science, and progress.

In the wake of governmental and economic failures of the twentieth century, people no longer seem to believe that "technical-material power, as such, is … the decisive cause or condition for human happiness or emancipation" (whether through neoliberal capitalism or government), yet there is nowhere left to turn because the logic of instrumental rationality and rational mastery of the world presents itself as "unchallengeable reason."[3] This notion of unchallengeable reason is perhaps most evident today in media portrayals of the irrational masses who supposedly allow power-hungry leaders or inaccurate social media pages to convince them to ignore what the science says, misunderstand historical facts, and vote against their own interests. At the same time, there is still a belief in the unchallengeable nature of economic progress, which echoes from the supposed triumph of Western capitalist democracies with the end of the Cold War. There is, the saying goes, no alternative to this model of civilization, as large

---

[3] Cornelius Castoriadis, *World in Fragments: Writings on Politics, Society, Psychoanalysis, and the Imagination* (Stanford University Press, 1986), page 39.

organizations and institutions are said to be lifting people out of poverty through an unprecedented expansion of capitalism, science, and democratic governments.[4]

At the core of the problem is a *crisis of contemporary ways of knowing and being.* As Castoriadis notes, knowledge is indefinitely extending to all aspects of life, even as it is increasingly fragmented. As knowledge accumulates and specializes, it leaves people potentially less able to understand and transform social reality, where the sheer volume of information, that is now so rapidly being produced, outpaces the ability to meaningfully synthesize knowledge and act. A society without a sense of meaningful self-reflection is itself in danger, adrift in a sea of information and media.[5] What is needed, then, is *another relationship to knowledge,* and ultimately perhaps even a new conception of what it means to be a human being today. This is certainly a matter of developing new personal capacities, but it is also a question of remaking power relationships and the "individual's relationship to authority."[6]

How, then, to begin to develop another relationship to knowledge? How might we cultivate sensibilities and dispositions that are oriented toward the remaking of society? At least one way forward is a reawakening of our social imaginations. It is certainly the case that various forms of social imagining are already happening now,

[4] The narrative of wealthy philanthropic organizations, corporations, and governments is that economic "development" and aid has produced record-low poverty levels, when in fact global economic inequality has grown and there are likely more people in poverty than before. Jason Hickel, *The Divide: Global Inequality from Conquest to Free Markets* (W.W. Norton, 2018).

[5] Castoriadis comments that there is "perpetual uncertainty as to *what* knowledge has been ascertained," as the "monstrous tree of knowledge that modern humanity is cultivating" has the potential to "collapse under its own weight and crush its gardener as it falls." Cornelius Castoriadis, "The Anticipated Revolution," in David Ames Curtis (editor and translator), *Political and Social Writings*, volume 3 (University of Minnesota Press, 1993), pages 153–154.

[6] Castoriadis follows: "All of this is obviously inconceivable without an upheaval not only in existing institutions but even in *what we intend by institution.*" Castoriadis, "The Anticipated Revolution," page 154, emphasis added.

and continue to emerge in social movements and other areas of civil society. What distinguishes the social imagination is its inherently plural and dynamic qualities. It is *plural* in the sense that "the social" does not point toward a universal vision of society, but rather to pluriversal futures where many worlds can flourish and continue to be imagined.[7] It is *dynamic* because the imagination is a living process that is constantly circulating among people in virtual and physical communities. The process of thinking and imagining is therefore not only the individual *reaching in* to the deep recesses of the brain, but also *reaching out* to engage local communities and environments.

Although the ways that we think are thoroughly conditioned by schools, from kindergarten to university, such conditioning is relevant to everyone beyond educational institutions. Because we tend to act based on what we know (from both intuitive and credentialed knowledge), the ways that we have learned to think set boundaries around what we see as possible for our lives individually and collectively. The modes of thought we inherit also structure our everyday life, in terms of what we do moment-to-moment and how we relate to the spaces, people, plants, and animals we encounter over the course of a day.

The first part of this book accordingly serves as somewhat of a problem statement, that outlines some features of our contemporary crisis, alongside emerging responses. It begins to set the stage for why and how we might begin to develop another relationship to knowledge, which is meant to demonstrate the need for the histories and projects (explored in Part Two) that model different ways of thinking and acting. Overall, Part One reframes *the social* as a field of reflective action, in the context of the kinds of challenges we face, and in terms of what designing might be capable of in this moment.

The first chapter draws on scholarship related to the "sociological imagination" to introduce the broad significance of social

[7] The Zapatista movement is known for the aspiration toward "a world where many worlds fit," and the notion of the pluriversal imagination being used here is explored in Arturo Escobar's writings, for example: Arturo Escobar, *Pluriversal Politics: The Real and the Possible* (Duke University Press, 2020).

thought. It locates this approach to social thinking as a response to the kinds of challenges we face in the present, and explores what it means to say that the challenges we face are "wicked problems." Finally, the chapter briefly explores the significance of conceiving designing as social action, instead of from the starting point of already existing professional practices. This general approach to designing, as a mode of action, will frame the contributions that the historical thinkers presented in Part Two might make to models for thinking and acting in the present.

The second chapter offers a broad sketch of the enduring chasm between thought and action today. In offering a mutual reflection—which reframes social science knowledge production through the lens of action and critiques designing activities from the perspective of social science—it points to the continuing need for interrogating, bridging, or dissolving the boundaries between reflection and action. The chapter concludes part one by describing how the imagination might be one generative way to approach this task.

1 Another Relationship to Knowledge

As I have listened to students reflect on their experiences at universities over the last decade, it has been especially disheartening to see the extent to which so many have come to view their education as a credential that is a hurdle in the way of their social life or professional advancement. While many do have a broader sense of learning in their lives, countless students report simply "going through the motions," and therefore not investing their full effort in themselves or their communities.

The malaise runs deep. After years of teaching at elite universities, William Deresiewicz came to the conclusion that they are training students to be "excellent sheep"—who are good at meeting requirements, following paths that have been prepared for them, and curating their resumes. A result of this condition is that many universities ultimately fail to facilitate their students' capacities for reflective participation in larger society. It has long been noted that many schools *teach to the test*, to maximize student grades and test scores, but Deresiewicz argues that students at schools and universities today are increasingly *living the test*.[1] More broadly this means that the

---

[1] William Deresiewicz, *Excellent Sheep: The Miseducation of the American Elite* (Free Press, 2014).

progression from childhood to adulthood is approached as a series of exams that must be passed and hoops that must be jumped through to achieve financial stability or upward social mobility.

The core of the problem is that, from a young age, our primary relationship to knowledge is school. In Western societies compulsory schooling is not simply a fact of life that children must submit to, but it conditions our way of knowing, thinking, and being more generally. In schools, grades or credentials are falsely equated with learning, diplomas are used as if they are the best measure of competence, and fluency in speaking or writing is the main evidence used to assess capabilities for human expression. What is ultimately "schooled" in this system is our imaginations, where we come to "accept service in the place of value."[2] That is, we learn to see human dignity, creativity, and potential as things that we perform through our participation (as service provider or recipient) in institutions like universities. This contemporary condition is why Ivan Illich argued for the need to "disestablish school."

For Illich, the "de-schooling" of society is not simply about reforming schools, or even necessarily about the closure of school buildings. It is about recognizing how society has become progressively schooled and what this represents for all of its institutions, including dire implications for our social imaginations. While education is often prized as a universal social good in Western democracies, the deepening institutionalization of education assembles a "hidden curriculum" that potentially constrains democracy, community, and human potential. Through reliance on specialized courses of study—that involve textbooks, exams, library databases, web searches, or carefully planned extra-curricular activities in a highly institutionalized environment—students implicitly learn to be passive consumers of knowledge. Academic disciplines ultimately become forms of self-discipline, where the goal is not learning, but disciplining oneself to focus just long

---

[2] This insight and many of the arguments here are based on Illich's perspective in: Ivan Illich, *Deschooling Society* (Harper & Row, 1972).

enough to produce content, to follow the right procedures, and to mimic the ways of thinking of a particular specialization.

Environmental educator David Orr explains that this hidden curriculum of schools today teaches us to believe a number of myths about knowledge and education. Myths of education today are communicated through schooling, where those in Western societies implicitly learn that increasing formal knowledge and education is a reflection of increasing human goodness, or at least it is assumed to be a good thing. Knowledge is considered a moral good for humanity in Western societies because education is assumed to solve the problem of ignorance, help individuals achieve upward social mobility, and contribute to positive scientific and technological advances.[3] For Orr, however, these things are not the fundamental purpose of education. He argues that there is nothing inherently good about knowledge, technology, or education, and that a society with high levels of formal schooling does not necessarily represent an advancement for humanity. Overall, the valorization of formal and specialized knowledge, above more holistic understandings of the world that include people's lived experience, perpetuates a hierarchical relationship to knowledge.

The result is a society that stifles human capacities for serious thinking and reflection in everyday life, where those whose thinking and acting are said to really matter are the experts or executives in large organizations. Indeed, the conventional model of social and scientific research holds that expert, credentialed scholars pursue truth, using methodologies that have been developed by their peers, and then they "disseminate" their findings through lectures, publications, or media coverage. This dominant way of knowing simultaneously also shapes what counts as legitimate knowledge and practice in the professions.[4]

[3] David Orr, *Earth in Mind: On Education, Environment, and the Human Prospect* (Island Press, 1994).
[4] Pablo Calderón Salazar and Alfredo Gutiérrez Borrero, "Letters South of (Nordic) Design," *NORDES 2017: Design and Power*, Number 7, ISSN 1604-9705.

To some extent, expert knowledge about the problems being faced becomes a "product of the mind" that wider society is meant to consume.[5] And the better trained the minds that produce the knowledge are, the more supposed non-experts are told to accept their conclusions. While learning is certainly expanding beyond schools through the internet and open courses that are theoretically accessible to all, such self-guided learning is also often said to be unreliable—especially when considered in tandem with the deception and alternative facts proliferating on the internet.

The overall result of this disposition toward thinking and knowing is a dispassionate and disembodied relationship to knowledge. It is a relationship to knowledge that, although still functioning for those who benefit, can actually contribute to the deepening the very problems it aims to address. For instance, when researchers at universities study and teach about poverty, they actually tend to entrench the categories and ways of thinking that produce poverty in the first place—as they develop solutions to poverty that begin in academic literature, established professional practices, or communities of credentialed experts, rather than the needs, experiences, and innovations of the poor.[6]

Given this current crisis of knowledge, a main focus of this chapter, and the book overall, is on some possible other ways of knowing. The project to develop another relationship to knowledge is certainly not a new one.[7] In some ways, this book builds on perspectives that have long critiqued conventional ways of knowing in Western societies, or "traditional theorizing," as content to explain society as it is. In contrast to traditional theory,

---

[5] Ann Game and Andrew Metcalfe, *Passionate Sociology* (SAGE Publications, 1996).

[6] For instance, a similar argument is made in: Ananya Roy, Genevieve Negrón-Gonzales, Kweku Opoku-Agyemang, and Clare Talwalker, *Encountering Poverty: Thinking and Acting in an Unequal World* (University of California Press, 2016).

[7] It is the epistemological challenge that Donald Schön's explains, but as will be discussed in the coming pages it is also an ontological challenge, which requires new ways of being in, and relating to, social realities. On Schön's call for a "new epistemology," see especially: Donald Schön, "The New Scholarship Requires a New Epistemology," *Change: The Magazine of Higher Learning*, volume 26, issue 6, 1995, pages 26–34.

critical scholarship is grounded in a social imagination that aims to mobilize thought for transforming our everyday lives and society.[8] Although social thought and the knowledge that social sciences produce is often considered to be an evolving description of society, there is a lineage of critical social thinking that imagines alternatives.[9] This first chapter builds on this work, in presenting the need for and possibilities of another relationship to knowledge. Of particular relevance on the radical potentials of social thought and imagination for this project is C. Wright Mills, whose general approach clarifies the focus of this book and will be explored in the next section.

FROM SOCIOLOGY TO THE SOCIAL IMAGINATION

What I am referring to as the social imagination has been most notably described by sociologist C. Wright Mills, in his writing on the sociological imagination. For Mills, the sociological imagination is a *quality of mind* and a *mode of thought*. It is not just for those who do social research. It is potentially relevant for everyone. At its core, Mills tells us that the sociological imagination is the quality of mind that "enables us to grasp history and biography and the relations between the two in society."[10] He explains that the sociological imagination creatively crosses scales and disciplines, beyond studies within the discipline of sociology. This mode of thought "is the capacity to shift from one perspective to another—political to the psychological; from examination of a single family to the comparative assessment of the national budgets of the world; from the theological school to

[8] In distinguishing critical theory from traditional theory, Max Horkheimer noted the radical potential of critical theory, as opposed to traditional theory, to "liberate human beings from the circumstances that enslave them." Max Horkheimer, "Traditional and Critical Theory," in Matthew O'Connell (translator), *Critical Theory: Selected Essays* (Continuum Publishing, 1972), pages 188–243.

[9] See, for example: Matt Dawson, *Social Theory for Alternative Societies* (Bloomsbury, 2016).

[10] C. Wright Mills, *The Sociological Imagination* (Oxford University Press, 1959), page 6.

the military establishment; from considerations of an oil industry to studies of contemporary poetry."[11]

Someone who is using the sociological imagination makes the familiar strange and the strange familiar. To do this is to question what is seemingly natural everyday life, and to be attentive to how current social realities came to be. Those who cultivate the sociological imagination find that "their capacity for astonishment is made lively again," and "they acquire a new way of thinking."[12] By considering where *personal troubles* or lived experiences connect with larger *public issues* we can come to understand how society operates, and also discern the possible contradictions, communities, and points of intervention that might be starting places for change.

All people are born into a world that they did not personally make—a social context that has unique possibilities and limits, human suffering and flourishing. In an era of global pandemics, racism, inequality, migration, and ecological collapse, it is easy to believe that the individual makes little difference in a world that spins bewilderingly out of control. Some may come to believe that the best option is to carve out a secure individual life, to constrain one's work in response to the school, employer, government, bottom line, or other powers that be.

A more sociological imagination locates our own individual story in history. It invites us to view ourselves as fundamentally *social* creatures, whose lives are situated uniquely within a web of social relations that we shape, even as they shape us. To see oneself as a primarily social being is not to disavow individual freedom and creativity, but rather to empower it. This sort of social thinking and imagining challenges conventional wisdom— not for the sake of being new and different, but to work within the cracks and failures of a social reality that seems as if it is solid and inevitable. Such an imagination is also inherently critical because it does not accept the world as given. It contrasts present social conditions with possible futures, opening toward

[11] Mills, page 7.

[12] Mills also explains that, overall, the sociological imagination "works between the 'personal troubles of the milieu' and the 'public issues of social structure'" (page 7).

all that could be otherwise. In this sense the greatest potential of a sociological imagination is not only the backward-looking deconstruction of present injustices, but also the development of a *relationship to the possible.*

More generally, an imagination that centers *the social* can enrich our lives, making the work and projects that we undertake more meaningful to communities and wider society. When we situate single events—seemingly unique problems or personal troubles—within larger unfolding social worlds, we see that people are neither completely alienated individuals nor all-powerful decision makers. This questioning of our world, to look for new connections between everyday life and the society in which we live, allows us to see how we might participate in society and contribute to confronting injustice or alleviating human suffering.

A desire to critically understand the social has been part of many academic disciplines, but *reflection for and about remaking the social* is important beyond an academic context. This is why, for Mills, the sociological imagination is not merely an academic exercise. He writes that a wide range of people across different professions need to be "raising demands" for other forms of social organization, and "setting forth such alternatives."[13] This is because for Mills the sociological imagination is a future-oriented way of seeing the world, or a form of social thought oriented toward, what he calls, *the possible futures of human affairs.*[14] The goal of such an imagination is to "find points of effective intervention, in order to know what can and must be structurally changed," and "discern the alternatives within which human reason and human freedom can now make history."[15]

Today it has become clear that even if the ideals of critical thought and the sociological imagination are still relevant, in practice the kind of social thinking Mills was arguing for remains relatively marginalized within the field of sociology, academia, and society more broadly. Indeed, a number of sociologists have

[13] Mills, page 183. Note that by describing a public issue in a new way, or engaging different groups of people in defining the problem, new "publics" are potentially created.

[14] Mills, page 174.

[15] Mills, page 176.

pointed out that, as a discipline, sociology has been more inter-ested in cataloging problems than in identifying possible solutions or points of intervention. For instance, Monica Prasad explains that although much social research begins with an interest in solving problems, it ends up describing an identified problem, complaining about the problem, or giving detailed descriptions about how people talk about the problem.[16]

What is also stake is the issue of how to mobilize the social thinking and imagining for specific projects that actually begin to transform systems or address human needs in the present.[17] That is, dominant approaches to sociology, and perhaps social science more broadly, continue to be more interested in the "real" (explainable social conditions) than in the "possible" (desired, preferred, or alternative conditions). Rather than contributing to concepts and practices that might bring people together to imagine and make new social worlds, social problems research can breed conceptions of the world that are rooted in despair—tilting toward inaction which ultimately sustains the status quo.[18]

It also seems that in an age of continuing specialization, the term "sociological imagination" suggests that this type of thinking is the domain of the academic discipline of sociology. The paradox here is that to use what Mills calls a sociological imagination, one must, in some ways, transcend professional disciplines like sociology. If the sociological imagination is a potential quality of mind and a mode of thought, or more directly *a human capacity*, then why describe it with a name that places it within the bounds of a discipline that often fails to represent this capacity? This is a

[16] Monica Prasad, "Problem-Solving Sociology," *Contemporary Sociology*, volume 47, issue 4, 2018, pages 393–398. Duncan Watts similarly argues that social science has emphasized "theory development" over the solution of practical problems for the last 100 years. Duncan Watts, "Should Social Science Be More Solution-Oriented?" *Nature Human Behavior*, volume 1, 2017, article 15.

[17] A. Javier Treviño, "Service Sociology and Social Problems," in A. Javier Treviño (editor), *The Cambridge Handbook of Social Problems* (Cambridge University Press, 2018), pages 133–148.

[18] See, for example: Heather M. Dalmage, "Bringing the Hope Back in: The Sociological Imagination and Dreams of Transformation," *Social Problems*, volume 68, issue 4, 2021, pages 801–808.

main reason why the book will use the term *social imagination* to explore the implications of this mode of thought.[19] One way of seeing how this social imagination can be relevant for today is the influential framework of *wicked problems*, which has long been important in planning and design research.

SOCIAL IMAGINATION FOR (AND BEYOND) WICKED PROBLEMS

Compared to when Mills was writing in the 1950s, the sorts of problems societies were beginning to face in the latter part of the twentieth century, and through today, seem to have evolved. In the present age of high-speed computing and big data, we have social analysis and information about nearly every problem at our fingertips—from academic reports, to journalistic narratives and videos from around the world. At the same time, there has been intensifying systemic critique of public institutions in the twenty-first century—from social movements, courtrooms, and political campaigns.

It might seem that the accessibility of this knowledge makes problems easier to address, but instead, they only grow increasingly complex. For example, racism can now be seen, in part, as an environmental issue, eviction could be viewed as both a cause and effect of poverty, addiction and substance abuse are related to high rates of incarceration, which is related to issues of race and class. These sorts of interconnections can make action seem contradictory or difficult. When groups or organizations do try to act, critiques and retrospective analyses are nearly instant, adding to the vast store of information about social reality.

It is in this context that a social imagination is essential to addressing the challenges of today. A call for a renewed social imagination is not necessarily to suggest a need for more research, data, description, or information about different issues. Especially in the

[19] Mills himself explained that what the quality of mind he was referring to was named is less important than promoting its overall mode of thinking in human societies, for example: Mills, page 19.

face uncertainty and complexity, it can seem as though the solutions to social and policy problems ought to be addressed scientifically through more precise analysis. That is, it can be tempting to buy into the notion that the most enlightened and publicly beneficial decisions will require assembling the right data or knowledge. Especially given a widespread doubt in scientific authority and the willingness of leaders to select their own facts in a "post-truth" politics, some thinkers double down on a scientific approach, calling for ever more research, evidence, and fact-checking.

It is, however, worth remembering what Horst Rittel and Melvin Webber explain in their classic 1973 essay on "Dilemmas in a General Theory of Planning"—that purely scientific bases for confronting social and policy problems are bound to fail. One of the core problems they identify is "professionalism," where thinking and acting are understood as best done through a highly controlled or scientifically managed process, and "each of the professions has been conceived as the medium through which the knowledge of science is applied."[20] Part of the rise of professionalism, they argue, is an optimism that social problems can be solved with the appropriate application of science, technology, and deliberative reasoning. They argue that in the twentieth century, the social professions, from education and human services to urban planning and social policy, were fatally transformed into applied sciences, where professionals were trained to solve problems as if they were scientists.

Clearly with the advance of neo-liberalization and the financialization of every sector of society, exemplified in 1980s critiques of the government "welfare state," much has changed. Even though it might seem that many professions have moved beyond this modernist optimism, its legacy continues to shape design and the social sciences. As David Graeber suggests, the core challenge that Rittel and Webber pointed to—of thought and action becoming professionalized and bureaucratized—has actually deepened. One significant reason is that the advance of the private sector into government and social institutions initiated a larger

[20] Horst W. J. Rittel and Melvin M. Webber, "Dilemmas in a General Theory of Planning," *Policy Sciences*, volume 4, 1973, page 158.

cultural transformation "whereby the bureaucratic techniques ... developed in financial and corporate circles came to invade the rest of society—education, science, government—and eventually to pervade almost every aspect of everyday life."[21] A major sign of this is the use of schooling (and increasingly graduate or professional degrees), as a credentialing, social sorting, and formal training process in fields that previously relied, to a large degree, on learning through doing. Even if some of the twentieth-century belief in rationalistic science and technology has faded, bureaucracies managed by corporate and governmental professionals seem to have invaded all aspects of life.

It is precisely in this context that Rittel and Webber's description of *wicked problems* takes on a renewed importance. They explain that social and policy problems are *wicked* because they are impossible to definitively "solve" due to their complex, contradictory, and constantly changing qualities.[22] They describe the ten characteristics of wicked problems as follows:

— There is no definitive formulation of a wicked problem;
— Wicked problems have no stopping rule;
— Solutions to wicked problems are not true-or-false, but good-or-bad;
— There is no immediate and no ultimate test of a solution to a wicked problem;
— Every solution to a wicked problem is a "one-shot operation";
— Wicked problems do not have an enumerable (or an exhaustively describable) set of potential solutions;
— Every wicked problem is essentially unique;
— Every wicked problem can be considered to be a symptom of another problem;
— The existence of a discrepancy representing a wicked problem can be explained in numerous ways;
— The planner [or social problem solver] has no right to be wrong.

[21] David Graeber, *The Utopia of Rules: On Technology, Stupidity, and the Secret Joys of Bureaucracy* (Melville House, 2015), page 21.
[22] Rittel and Webber, page 158.

Overall, the wicked problems framework shows the limitations of creating social change through increasing applications of science, technology, or professional expertise. That is, more than attempting describe the world as a list of specific problems to be solved, addressing the challenges we face today entails reawakening our social imaginations and radically reframing the role of knowledge and thinking for action more generally. Below I highlight three of these characteristics that are particularly relevant to the need for another relationship to knowledge today.

Wicked Problems Do Not Have a Single or Definitive Formulation. Any solution to a wicked problem has implicit assumptions about the nature of the problem, and from a purely scientific approach, there are potentially endless ways to define the problem. For example, poverty research fragments the problem of poverty into dozens of different variables and possible causes. Accordingly, for social policy on a problem like poverty, there is likely no way to ever have enough information to definitively explain the problem (in terms of how poverty should be defined, what causes poverty, and the effects of poverty). This is evident in endless calls for further research from different social science disciplines that study poverty. In this context, Rittel and Webber remind us that we can only really define the problem when we know what it might look like if the problem were solved. Accordingly, a key need is to frame current challenges in ways that might situate information in terms of the desires, aspirations, and needs of diverse groups. This is precisely where a sense of social imagination is most needed—to engage more people in imagining the kind of world they want to see, especially those who are most impacted by the problems being addressed.

There Is No Way to Test the Solution to a Wicked Problem before Implementation. In scientific activity that takes place in a laboratory, research can learn by trial and error. That is, researchers can manipulate the lab experiment to simulate real-world conditions in a controlled setting. In contrast, any attempt to solve a wicked problem is immensely costly—socially and financially. Creating new social and physical environments for humans can be very expensive, and ethically fraught if it is done experimentally. As Rittel and Weber explain, wicked problems are social and highly context dependent. What occurred in one social intervention is not likely to be fully replicable in other contexts.

Yet the social sciences continue to work toward the documentation of a social world that is said to be fully knowable if only we had enough resources to design the appropriate studies and gather the right amount of evidence. For example, research to develop evidence-based practices aims to build an understanding of "what works" from past interventions, but from the stand point of wicked problems, such backward looking analysis may not always be helpful for actually solving problems in different institutional or community contexts. Although there are increasingly social research "laboratories"—on cities, education, criminal justice, housing, or other social problems—this could exacerbate the problem if social "labs" only intend to gather evidence and publish "research findings" or "policy recommendations" about a particular topic. In this sense, a social imagination is increasingly important to translate across contexts and scales. It's not just about having more data to predict what will "work," but rather discerning and imagining how particular cases or practices might be transfer across time (e.g., inspiration from something that worked in the past) and space (e.g., sharing lessons from one site to another).

There Is No Clear Point at Which a Wicked Problem Is Completely Solved. This characteristic of wicked problems is related to the dynamic and relational quality of society. Rittel and Webber explain that wicked problems are especially difficult because unlike a mathematical problem, which can have one solution, society is always shifting and in flux. In other words, any attempt to solve a wicked problem is unlikely to be a permanent fix. Moreover, the problems themselves may actually be the symptom or effect of other problems (or even the result of attempted solutions). This sets up a related dilemma in wicked problems. On the one hand, an overly specific formulation of the problem may have a more fleeting and limited solution, or have a significant blind spot that does not see potential unintended consequences. At the same time, the more general a problem becomes, the more difficult it is to act. For example, if systemic racism is identified as the problem, action is hampered when some view it as too large of a problem to make concrete interventions. This is why addressing wicked problems today demands a reinvigorated social imagination—so that before getting to work, and while engaged in action, we also seek to reimagine the problems we are facing from multiple perspectives.

Overall, these characteristics of wicked problems point to the need to move beyond a reactionary response to problems after-the-fact, and toward proactive forms of intervention. They underscore the limits of social thought when it is more interested in the "real" than the "possible." A wicked problems framework shows how, when the real is not attuned to the possible, descriptions of the real can be overly narrow, conflicting, or even irrelevant conceptions of social reality that actually impede effective action.

This is to say that our social imaginations, if they are to confront issues of today, must be oriented toward creating courses of reflective action. As some scholars have suggested a new social imagination for the early twenty-first century would be a "creative form of inquiry more than a secure source of definite answers," which "does not aspire to be a corpus of knowledge but, rather, grounded in the service of questioning reality."[23] At the same time, the notion of wicked problems also requires a renewed sensibility toward designing.[24] The necessary sort of designing for today is found not only in established professional design practices, but also as a capability and mode of imaginatively acting and intervening that is potentially accessible to everyone.

[23] Although writing about issues related to academic theory and the discipline of sociology, these lessons Solis-Gadea articulates are relevant for forms of thought and imagination beyond academic contexts as well: Hector Raul Solis-Gadea, "The New Sociological Imagination: Facing the Challenges of a New Millennium," *International Journal of Politics, Culture, and Society*, volume 18, issue 4, 2005, pages 113–122.

[24] Richard Buchanan, for instance, argues that all design problems are essentially "wicked" because of their indeterminacy. Richard Buchanan, "Wicked Problems in Design Thinking," *Design Issues*, volume 8, issue 2, 1992, pages 5–21.

While it can be helpful to view design through the lens of wicked problems, it is also potentially deceiving. The framing of "wicked problems" acknowledges that acting amidst the complexity of the social world requires more than a purely scientific orientation, however, it ultimately can still conceptualize the world as a series of problems to be solved. The real work in a world of wicked problems is imagining possible interventions and trying out courses of action, with recognition that any intervention is part of larger systems that cannot be fully predicted, managed, or controlled.[25] This also requires moving beyond social science or design professions as problem-solving in a narrow sense, and toward *designing as a mode of acting and world-making*—a way of proceeding that can bring thought and action together. Accordingly, it is essential to better clarify what is meant by design, and how it relates to the social imagination.

DESIGNING AS SOCIAL ACTION, OR THE SOCIAL ORIGINS OF DESIGN

Humans are distinct from other species in that we are not born with a biologically imprinted instincts that automatically provide a stable sense of social order. We are almost entirely dependent on language for survival—through words exchanged, laws written down, or policies that are implemented. Language is also more broadly the externalization of human life. Together, human beings regularly transform thoughts, ideas, symbols, and desires, into an "artificial" social and spatial order, which would not exist without human intervention.[26] Language (thought, spoken, and written) is central to understanding how anything is made. This is because making anything—whether that is an object, image, environment, identity, or system—requires representing or articulating *concepts*

[25] Terry Irwin, "Wicked Problems and the Relationship Triad," in Stephan Harding (editor), *Grow Small, Think Beautiful: Ideas for a Sustainable World from Schumacher College* (Floris Books, 2011), pages 232–257.

[26] Stephen Pfohl, "The Reality of Social Constructions," in James A. Holstein and Jaber F. Gubrium (editors), *Handbook of Constructionist Research* (Guilford Press, 2007), pages 645–668.

of what might be.[27] It is in this sense that "all creation begins in praxis," with inventive combinations of thought and action.[28]

We are makers of our social worlds, even as we are made over by them. Zygmunt Bauman refers to this condition as *human praxis*, which is a fundamental basis of human societies.[29] Human praxis is this paradoxical "duality of human experience," where we are both subjects and objects of unfolding social realities. It is the creative or generative capacity in human life—the work to transform existing conditions into something imagined. To recognize human praxis is to see that although social realities can be terribly constraining, they are never totally determined. In this distinction (between constrained and determined), there is a world of difference. If something is already determined, then there is no possibility for intervention, but if it is constrained, then openings persist where a range of tiny shifts or magnificent transformations might begin.[30]

Like the social imagination, design is therefore also explored in this book as a fundamentally human capacity. To design is to invent, mark, or designate through actions and interventions that "transform existing conditions into preferred ones."[31] These interventions are large and physical in the immense urban

---

[27] See, for example: John Heskett's comments on the relationship between design and language in his book: *Design: A Very Short Introduction* (Oxford University Press, 2002), pages 8–12.

[28] Zygmunt Bauman notes that "The first and the most fundamental distinction accomplished by the human-activity-in-the-world is the one between the realm shaped by human praxis and all the rest. Creation begins with praxis." Zygmunt Bauman, *Culture as Praxis* (SAGE Publications, 1998), page 98.

[29] Defined by Bauman (on page 112) as "active creation of an artificially (i.e. with the species' activity) stabilized environment."

[30] This idea was taken up in design in a volume, James Auger and Julian Hanna (editors), *Reconstrained Design* (The Reconstrained Design Group, 2019). Their idea was precisely that in constraints there are possibilities.

[31] Note Herbert Simon's widely used definition of design: "Engineers are not the only professional designers. Everyone designs who *devises courses of action aimed at changing existing situations into preferred ones.* The intellectual activity that produces material artifacts is no different fundamentally from the one that prescribes remedies for a sick patient or the one that devises a new sales plan for a company or a social welfare policy for a state." Herbert Simon, *Sciences of the Artificial* (MIT Press, 1969), page 111, emphasis added.

infrastructures that transform land, and also small and subtle in organizational management charts that shape who has access to resources and power.

The immense power of designing to shape social and spatial realities should not be underestimated. It creates new social realities for better and worse. One powerful example of what design can do is seen in European colonization of the Americas. Ángel Rama explains that the Iberian colonization of South America was not merely spontaneous opportunists looking for resources and new land. The endurance of colonization was the result of carefully designed urban networks, procedures, and geometrical layouts that were imagined as "creations of the human mind," and then carefully mapped out on paper.[32] Rama argues that colonizers and successive generations of elites maintained unequal society precisely through words, records, drawings, documents, and literature that both shaped physical spaces and seeped into culture as literacy expanded.

Just as designing can be destructive social action for the concentration of power, taking of land, or reorganization of society for a specific group's interest, it can also initiate a remaking of society that imagines more reciprocal and life-giving relations. One instance of designing as social action in this way comes from efforts in the twentieth century to transform how societies imagine mental health and disability. By the 1960s, a number of different groups of deinstitutionalization activists were bringing public attention to mental asylums and psychiatric institutions, which often used dangerous and abusive treatments to constrain people against their will. Although not universally successful, the deinstitutionalization movement primarily envisioned community-based systems of mental health care in place of large-scale dehumanizing institutions.

As Liat Ben-Moshe notes, the extent to which deinstitutionalization would be successful hinged on both in its ability to transform laws and its ability to create a new consciousness that involved new ways of thinking, acting, and being.[33] In particular, the movement

---

[32] Ángel Rama, *The Lettered City* (Duke University Press, 1996).

[33] Liat Ben-Moshe, *Decarcerating Disability: Deinstitutionalization and Prison Abolition* (University of Minnesota Press, 2020). As Ben-Moshe and others note, deinstitutionalization happened internationally and was not always completely successful.

around the notion that mental asylums and large institutions should be abolished mobilized an imaginative approach to the problems of human suffering and exclusion that simultaneously envisioned and enacted alternatives. On one level, it could be said that institutions were redesigned, but at the same time, it was also a new way of being that was designed. The key, for contexts where deinstitutionalization succeeded, was not just in mobilizing the managerial and logistical power of governments but in bringing together different groups and resources toward inventive forms of social action.

These two examples, of colonization and deinstitutionalization, portray the relevance of designing, not only as a professional practice, but also as social action more generally. It also demonstrates that designing is not a neutral social act, but that a design imagination can be mobilized for destroying or sustaining life. This conception of designing as social action, which will be the main way that design and designing is discussed in the book, follows a framing of design in the work of John Chris Jones—that defines designing as creativity, participation, and a process of devising systems and environments. As Jones notes, the profound potential of design is its potential to become, "an activity through which we transform our lives."[34]

This is because at its root, designing is how human-made words, ideas, and symbols become new social realities. Although what human beings create (roads, bridges, cities, buildings, systems, services, spaces, or organizations) may be practically useful, human creations also reflect a process of meaning-making, where specific people designate what is meaningful or important in a particular moment of history. Design is therefore not merely something that societies produce; society itself (with its physical artifacts, policies, procedures, and practices) is *an outcome of the ongoing expression of the human design capacity*. In other words, society is the creative result of actions taken in the past. It is how people respond to the waves of accumulated past decisions that crash into the present.

---

[34] John Chris Jones, *Designing Designing* (Bloomsbury/Radical Thinkers in Design, 2021).

Viewing society as the evolving outcome of human design capacity-in-action, it is evident that there is also something fundamentally creative about being human—which may be activated or awakened to a different extent, depending on the person or social context. Contrary to the individualistic and commercialized perception of design (as in the star architect or designer name brand), this is a kind of creativity that has its source in the ongoing dialog and tradition of communities.[35] Society is not purely accidental. It was made by design. Creativity is therefore not about "adapting" to oppressive or difficult situations. It is about acting to remake the conditions under which new situations might arise.

Of course, it is important that such freedom is not given, especially for peoples and communities that have been violently marginalized. It must be actively mobilized and put into practice, or as social activists have long noted, *freedom is a constant struggle*.[36] In most contexts, it can be easier to simply accept the social world as given, living out identities, work, and policies that others have previously formed. The human mind, while full of creative potential to invent and make, is also highly conditioned and habit forming around routines of the status quo. It can be personally, professionally, and politically more comfortable to accept the world as it is. This is why laboring to re-make the very conditions under which new situations (and perhaps

---

[35] Note how this contrasts the ideas that are sometimes prevalent in design communities (e.g., "starchitects" or other individuals whose name become associated with designer brands and design awards), for instance, Bauman, page 95: "The idea of creativity, of active assimilation of the universe, of imposing on the chaotic world the ordering structure of the human intelligent action—the idea built irremovably into the notion of *praxis—is indeed comprehensible only if viewed as an attribute of community*, capable of transcending the natural or 'naturalized' order and creating new and different orders" (emphasis added). Others like Paolo Freire, in his *Pedagogy of the Oppressed* (Continuum International Publishing Group, 1970), view society as fundamentally "dialogical," meaning that society is made in an ongoing contestation of social realities.

[36] See especially: Angela Davis, *Freedom Is a Constant Struggle* (Haymarket Books, 2016).

even new social realities) might come into being is a daring and courageous act.[37]

To work with this approach to design as a form of reflective social action, then, is to *stand on the edge of the real and the possible.* The real is social reality, or the multiple historical, social, and spatial contexts within which people live. This includes some of the most urgent conditions of our time, such as economic inequality, racism, war, and ecological collapse. On the other hand, the possible is all that is emerging, has not happened, and has not yet been recorded and analyzed. It is what *could be* in a future: imaginative projections about what steps could be taken to arrange human affairs differently.

The real and the possible are not simply singular, objective concepts about the past and the future. We are always positioned *in* the real—situated in histories and social realities, oriented toward some future(s). To design or shape new worlds we therefore must draw upon or attune to particular histories and futures with others. To recognize where and how we stand in this way is to be on the edge of human experience. While past decisions that shape the present can weigh on bodies and minds, human experience actually unfolds on a moment-to-moment basis, on the edge of past and future. There are both stubborn continuities with how things unfold, but also, if we pay attention closely, astonishing openings and transformations. It is precisely this dynamic between the real and the possible that the book argues can, and should, be the focus of a renewed sensibility in design and social sciences—and in our everyday lives.

Even beyond any professional practice, approaching design and the social imagination as human capacities is crucial to dealing with the realities of our vulnerable and precarious world today. This is because it shifts from abstract conceptualizations

---

[37] Bauman, page 36, notes that: "Humanity is the only known project of rising above the level of mere existence, transcending the realm of determinism, subordinating the *is* to the *ought*. Human culture, far from being the art of adaptation, is the most audacious of all attempts to scrap the fetters of adaptation as the paramount hindrance to the full unfolding of human creativity. Culture, which is synonymous with the specifically human existence, is a daring dash for freedom *from* necessity and freedom *to* create."

of politics and social change, toward our everyday experience that presents a multitude of opportunities for action. While social reality can be described with systematized explanations and research methods, or national and international analyses of society, if people are not able to connect such explanations to their daily life, then meaningful action or social change may be less likely.

A powerful example of this comes from efforts to name and address climate change as a human-made crisis. For a long time, narratives by scholars and advocates focused on things like greenhouse gas emissions, polar ice caps melting, and species extinctions. While it may be possible to act based on empathy for polar bears and their threatened habitats, such framing likely contributed to years of inaction and apathy. Framing environmental destruction as a problem of greenhouse gas emissions worked for people who had the resources to travel or read studies of far-off places, but it was much less successful at engaging people whose lives were directly impacted by environmental degradation and injustice every day.[38]

When design and action are rooted in social realities related to environmental problems, the response looks more like the Evergreen Cooperatives in Cleveland, Ohio. In the wake of the financial crisis of 2007–8, and growing poverty rates in "rust belt" cities that experienced a long industrial decline, a range of groups came together to imagine new futures. Nonprofits, community activists, foundations, city government, and large anchor institutions aimed to stabilize and revitalize neighborhoods through a green economy. This long-term design process involved building a robust network of cooperative enterprises that enable worker ownership and wealth building for low-income residents while also reducing the region's carbon footprint and producing more

[38] The environmental justice perspective critiques the mainstream environmental movement in the 1980s to 1990s as mostly white and affluent, arguing that more could be accomplished from the standpoint of the everyday impacts of environmental pollution on poor, urban, and communities of color. See, for example: Robert D. Bullard, *The Quest for Environmental Justice* (Sierra Club Books, 2005); Van Jones, *The Green Collar Economy* (HarperCollins, 2008).

food and energy locally. The result is what's been called a model for creating more equitable and sustainable communities.[39]

It is in this sense that designing ought to be conceived as social action. On the one hand, design can engage groups of people who are directly impacted by social realities in imagining other futures. At the same time, it might harness a wide range of expertise in moving from actually existing to possible worlds, which could be more attuned toward human and ecological flourishing. Such an approach to designing has certainly not been the norm, however, the *possibility* of designing as social action can be transformative. The question then remains: What has constrained people and professions from participating more fully in this possibility? Certainly, the impulse to combine the action-oriented potential of design with the analytic capacity of social sciences is not new, and many issues remain for a generative relationship to flourish between design and social thought.[40] Some of these issues, including possibilities for overcoming them, will be explored in Chapter 2.

[39] Ted Howard, "Community Wealth Building in Cleveland, Ohio," in Federal Reserve Bank of San Francisco (editor), *Investing in What Works for America's Communities: Essays on People, Place & Purpose* (Federal Reserve Bank of San Francisco & Low Income Investment Fund, 2012), pages 204–214; Gar Alperovitz, Thad Williamson and Ted Howard, "The Cleveland Model," *The Nation*, March 1, 2010, accessed at: https://www.thenation.com/article/archive/cleveland-model/+&cd=1&hl=en&ct=clnk&gl=us&client=safari.

[40] In 1982, Clive Dilnot commented on the lack of attention to the design-society relationship, and particularly the lack of reference to design in sociology (which is, after all, the study of society). But even by 2018, Deborah Lupton notes that productive overlaps between design and social thought were only just beginning to be explored in an emerging field of "design sociology," which still does not necessarily focus broadly on the design-society relationship: Clive Dilnot, "Design as a Socially Significant Activity: An Introduction," *Design Studies*, volume 3, issue 3, 1982, pages 139–146; Deborah Lupton, "Towards Design Sociology," *Sociology Compass*, volume 12, issue 1, 2018, pages 1–11.

2 The Enduring Gap between Reflection and Action

In 2019, the World Health Organization added *burn-out* to the *11th Revision of the International Classification of Diseases.* Although not a medical condition, the WHO explained that burn-out is a "syndrome" that results from "chronic workplace stress that has not been successfully managed." This around the same time that journalist Anne Helen Petersen published a BuzzFeed article on "How Millennials Became the Burnout Generation," that very quickly garnered more than 7 million views.

As Peterson explains, although specifically associated with work, burn-out is a pervasive cultural experience in an era when work can happen everywhere and anytime. She explains that "burn-out is when you hit a wall, but instead of collapsing, or taking a rest, you scale the wall, and just keep going."[1] This response arises because of the way the culture of capitalism conditions us to believe that working hard and producing more is the solution to any personal, social, or organizational problem. Burn-out is especially prominent in Western societies, where getting a good education and working hard was once seen as a pathway to a stable job and social mobility, but the rise of temporary labor in the gig economy can make this sort of pathway more unlikely or precarious.

[1] Anne Helen Petersen, *Can't Even: How Millennials Became the Burnout Generation* (Mariner Books, 2021), page vii.

Burn-out is ultimately a profound malaise of looming catastrophe that manifests on the personal, organizational, and societal level. Diana Renner and Steven D'Souza describe the root of the problem as a widespread organizational and societal emphasis on "obsessive doing." This is epitomized in corporate cultures that have a "bias for action," valuing speed of action above almost all else. Personally, burn-out is a kind of "joyless urgency" where we are driven to doing more in futile efforts to control situations that may be beyond control. We develop a transactional relationship with time, where we scramble to meet deadlines, rush around at the whim of a calendar, and face endless to-do lists.[2] Even for those who may believe that their organization or work is aligned with some social or environmental mission, there is an increasing sense of burn-out. In such mission-driven non-profit work, efforts of an individual can have a sense of importance that is driven by hopes for transformational social change, which it seems could be arrived at more quickly if only more people were working harder for the right causes.

On the other side of this obsessive doing is a new wave of *information overload*. While every recent era has arguably scrambled to adapt to new technology with more information, the proliferation of media and personal computing throughout every aspect of life today presents unique challenges of saturation and distraction.[3] With constant exposure to email and social media, our minds are literally saturated with visual inputs, everything ranging from non-stop news of world events to new tasks that need to be completed this week. Given that people and objects now produce data in the "internet of things," while computers and algorithms can process this information ever more rapidly, the amount of available information seems to increase exponentially.[4] In this context, thinking can get caught up in an inner-looking focus that shifts from one distraction, bit

[2] Diana Renner and Steven D'Souza, *Not Doing: The Art of Effortless Action* (LTD Publishing Limited, 2018).

[3] Laura van Dernoot Lipsky, *Age of Overwhelm: Strategies for the Long Haul* (Berrett-Koehler Publishers, 2018).

[4] Rob Van Kranenburg, *The Internet of Things: A Critique of Ambient Technology and the All-Seeing Network of RFID* (Institute of Network Cultures, 2008).

of information, or urgent task to the next, rather than purposeful or outward-looking reflection.

While not specifically about burn-out and information overload, this chapter explores what could be considered one of the roots of these phenomena, which is an enduring, and arguably intensifying, disconnection between reflection and action. On the one hand, burn-out could be seen as a result of incessant action that is removed from deliberate reflection. At the same time, ways of thinking today are often so disconnected from action that they can only help us to more clearly see, from the sidelines, what new tragic circumstance is unfolding. This might be experienced or overcome to some degree on an individual level, but it is ultimately a societal malaise that is deeply rooted in the ways of thinking and acting that we have inherited.

Addressing the enduring gap between reflection and action therefore means first looking to why exactly this gap has endured. It might be easy to say that this is an individual problem that one might solve by reorienting individual minds—with more rest, perhaps a vacation or retreat, a workshop on mindfulness and self-care, or, in more extreme cases of the anxiety and depression that accompany burn-out, a professional therapeutic intervention. As this chapter will argue, however, the gap has endured, at least in part, because of professional practices in design and social sciences that continue to reproduce it. The result is the contemporary condition where "at a time when we badly need better designs and strategies for the future ... the people with the deepest knowledge of fields are discouraged from systematic and creative exploration of the future, while those with the appetite and freedom to explore often lack the necessary knowledge."[5]

Fortunately, in recent decades many scholars and practitioners, as described on the coming pages, have begun to point to where this gap—between forms of action and reflection—persists and how it might be overcome. Of particular relevance is potential of reimagining the critical and analytical gaze of social thought itself,

[5] Geoff Mulgan, *The Case for Exploratory Social Sciences* (The New Institute, 2021), page 6.

such that it might be capable of theorizing about alternative forms of social organization or generating knowledge about possible futures.[6] In efforts related to this promise of combining design and the social imagination is clear that social thought exposes a number of challenges for a designing (as a mode of social action), and at the same time, a design- or action-oriented lens reveals many limitations of mainstream forms of social research.

This mutual reflection, which will be a focus of the next sections, can be a starting point to radically reframe the foundations of design and social thought today. By no means is what follows meant to be a comprehensive review of literature at the intersection of social sciences and design, or a description of the historical development of socially engaged design or action-oriented research. In sketching the reframing of the relations between social sciences and design, the following sections point toward the ways that thought and action have become separated from each other in today's professional practices. In writing from this gap, the intent here is to open up the possibility for a new language about social thought and action that belongs to neither design nor social sciences alone. Translating and inter-relating the insights of both social thinkers and designers that are relevant to the present, this approach shows the need for models, ideas, and strategies of reflective action. As the concluding section of the chapter will explore, it also demonstrates the radical potential of the human imagination for sparking new relations between designing and thinking today.

DESIGN FROM THE PERSPECTIVE OF SOCIAL THOUGHT

While it has become clear that design has wide-ranging social implications, there tends to be a lack of rigorous social dimension in understandings of what design actually is and does. Social

---

[6] See, for example: Matt Dawson, *Social Theory for Alternative Societies* (Bloomsbury, 2016); Diane Davis and Tali Hatuka, "Imagination as a Method for Generating Knowledge about Possible Urban Futures," in Elisabete A. Silva, Patsy Healey, Neil Harris, and Pieter Van den Broeck (editors), *The Routledge Handbook of Planning Research Methods* (Routledge, 2015), pages 225–234.

thinkers have long critiqued designers for "lacking a view of the larger structural issues and subordinating their talents and skills to the service of the rich and powerful," arguing that they should instead "demand a voice in decisions of structural consequence," and aim to shape objects and environments that enable human flourishing.[7] More generally in social thought, there has been a strong critique of design based on its relationship to the emergence of industrial capitalism, in two main directions.

First, critics have argued that design processes have historically failed to adequately engage with social realities. Around the beginning of the twentieth century, this involved the work of scholars who sought to make organizations and workplaces more efficient in the midst of new social and technological conditions, or later, those conducting research to make products and services more responsive to the needs of users.[8] It also included social thought and criticism about urban interventions that were responding to rapid urbanization, such as urban renewal plans and policies of the mid twentieth century.[9]

Secondly, thinkers have forcefully condemned design as a set of interconnected industries that actively create oppressive social realities. This critique explains how industrial design's relationship to mass production, and graphic design's role in advertising, creates passive citizens. It also notes ways in which

---

[7] This was an argument made by C. Wright Mills at the 1958 Eighth International Design Conference in Aspen, Colorado, as described in: A. Javier Treviño, "C. Wright Mills as Designer: Personal Practice and Two Public Talks," *The American Sociologist*, volume 43, 2014, pages 335–360.

[8] For example, in various efforts to redesign or modernize organizations in the wake of Frederick Taylor's "scientific management," or later Donald Norman's popularization of "user-centered design."

[9] This was evident, for example, in Herbert Gans' widely read sociological critique of urban interventions in the mid-twentieth century, which he argued were out of step with the social reality of poor immigrant neighborhoods: Herbert Gans, *The Urban Villagers: Group and Class in the Life of Italian-Americans* (The Free Press, 1962).

design professions cater to elites with elaborate luxury products that ultimately reproduce economic inequality.[10] More recently, designers and social theorists have argued that twentieth-century society became so saturated with designed media, spaces, and language that designing ceased having any reference social reality.[11]

As design practice and thinking moved beyond the design of objects—scholars and practitioners offered fresh critiques of design from the perspective of social thought. These build on some of the historical scholarship about design industries and professions, while also anticipating new issues, and promoting alternatives. Three key areas of critique and alternative approaches to designing are briefly explored below.

Lack of Engagement with Social Realities. Design professions have long focused on aesthetics, outcomes, and forms, at the expense of genuine social engagement. The lack of relationship between design and social reality has not gone unnoticed, as many have opened up design to much wider potential applications in recent decades. For example, John Chris Jones notes that at the close of the twentieth century it was becoming clear that design needed to be more than making objects. That is designing could be the process of devising systems or environments, the involvement of public in decision-making processes, an educational discipline that unites arts and sciences, and creativity more

---

[10] Thorstein Veblen popularized the term "conspicuous consumption" to explain how, under capitalism, wealthy families sought increasingly elaborate designs to display their status publicly. Later, critical theory of the Frankfurt School (e.g., Adorno and Horkheimer) would condemn the "culture industry," which, they explain, in part, uses the design of mass communications media to manipulate people into passivity. See, for example: Thorstein Veblen, *The Theory of the Leisure Class: An Economic Study of Institutions* (Macmillan, 1899); Max Horkheimer and Theodor W. Adorno, *Dialectic of Enlightenment: Philosophical Fragments* (Querido, 1947).

[11] Jan van Toorn, "Introduction" and "Communication Design: A Social Practice," in Jan van Toorn (editor), *Design beyond Design: Critical Reflection and the Practice of Visual Communication* (Jan van Eyck Akademie Editions, 1998), pages 8–13 and 152–167; Jean Baudrillard, *Simulacra and Simulation* (Semiotext(e), 1983).

generally. Indeed, many now consider the notion of "designing without a product" to be a necessity in the present age.[12]

In the twenty-first century, "design thinking" has expanded to all aspects of life and is increasingly applied in attempts to remake public institutions. This has led to a now sprawling field of social design, which in theory aspires to bring design and the social together, but in practice often ignores key insights from social thought. Especially when applied to organizations and businesses, social design loses its potency to reconfigure the social if it does not address the contexts and power relationships in which designers actually practice.[13] Even in cases of social design or design thinking that do engage with social realities, the work is still hampered by unequal power relationships among public institutions, the private sector, and communities.[14] This is to say that even attempts to apply design thinking to governance or social change do not always adequately engage with social reality. From the perspective of social thought, design thinking in itself cannot simply "solve" problems like poverty, income disparity, structural racism, environmental injustice, or unregulated market capitalism in one fell swoop. Such systemic problems require ongoing and intentional strategies for social engagement, which might enable community leadership in framing the problems to be addressed.

At the core of this critique is the notion that design does not pay attention to the majority of people's needs, and therefore is too often indifferent to social reality. Such a perspective is epitomized in the Cooper Hewitt exhibition, "Design for the Other 90%" with the implication being that design in the twentieth century only engages with the needs of about 10 percent of people. The emerging works of design represented in the exhibition call for shifts in design practice toward designing processes rather than outcomes, using propositional thinking with people on-the-ground

[12] John Chris Jones, *Designing Designing* (Radical Thinkers in Design/ Bloomsbury, 2021).

[13] Lucy Kimbell, "Rethinking Design Thinking: Part I," *Design and Culture*, volume 3, issue 3, 2011, pages 285–306.

[14] Maggie Gram, "On Design Thinking," *N+1 Magazine*, issue 3, 2019, accessed at: https://www.nplusonemag.com/issue-35/reviews/on-design-thinking/

to spark larger changes, creating more collaborative spaces, or addressing place-based problems.[15]

Scholars have also pointed out that design has largely untapped political and social capacities to unfold new social realities. That is, design is too-often seen a solution that is prescribed from outside of social reality, when from the perspective of social thought, it is better utilized as a catalyst of new possibilities within social reality.[16] Although architects and designers are often complacent with conditions of exclusionary growth, economic inequality, social marginalization, and political polarization, designing could be mobilized differently—to reimagine and face down the most pressing challenges of today.[17] For instance, design practice could deliberately pay more attention existing social processes that are shaping communities, and work to translate between on-the-ground social realities, top-down policies, and institutions.

Similarly, the lack of deep social engagement could also be attributed to the ways in which designing is understood, both by professions and outsiders. For instance, the emerging field of social design argues that designing is, on some level, fundamentally a collaborative and social activity. In this context, social designing could become a practice that happens beyond commercial contexts, addresses unmet human needs, and is positioned to enable social change.[18]

The critique overall suggests a need to widen our understanding of what counts as design—to see how activists, social justice advocates and movements, or marginalized communities have been imagining and creating community-based alternatives to global systems, even if their work is not formally acknowledged

[15] Cynthia Smith (editor), *Design for the Other 90%* (Cooper-Hewitt, Smithsonian Design Museum, 2007).

[16] Fernando Domínguez Rubio and Uriel Fogué, "Unfolding the Political Capacities of Design," *Diseña*, volume 11, 2017, pages 96–109.

[17] Teddy Cruz, "Where Is Our Civic Imagination?" in Miodrag Mitrasinovic (editor), *Concurrent Urbanities: Designing Infrastructures of Inclusion* (Routledge, 2016), pages 9–23.

[18] Cameron Tonkinwise, "Is Social Design a Thing?" in Elizabeth Resnick (editor), *The Social Design Reader* (Bloomsbury, 2019), pages 9–16.

by conventional design professions.[19] In other words, it's not necessarily a matter of making design more socially engaged, but in creating opportunities for design professions to learn from the ways that groups with deep commitments to social engagement are already designing.

Over-Emphasis on Short-Term Outcomes. It is also evident that economic constraints of contemporary design professions limit professional design practices, to a focus on short-term outcomes. This critique is rooted in the notion that designers need to keep their studios or projects financially sustainable, and therefore rely upon existing economic systems. A result of this situation, in terms of the broad relations between design and society, is that design professions have mainly worked to "support and sustain the political economy of urbanized capitalism."[20] This is to say that design practices miss opportunities to create long-term change when they over-focus on popular trends or the demands of present social, political, or economic systems.

The focus on short-term outcomes can especially be observed in the context of design and urban practice, where, although cities are constantly in flux, urban design and development often still conceptualizes the city as fixed three-dimensional object. Such an approach emphasizes techniques that aim to create a "stable framework for urban life" (that is essentially frozen in time) through design guidelines, form-based development regulations, signage controls, pattern books, and design review processes.[21] The short-term focus of contemporary design professions also over-emphasizes the intentions or ideas of designers, while neglecting the potential long-term social consequences of design projects.[22] A shift toward long-term possibilities of design would require designers be more open to participating proactively in social and political processes related to their local contexts.

There has also increasingly been scholarship on the relationship between ecology and contemporary design, which argues

[19] Arturo Escobar, *Designs for the Pluriverse: Radical Independence, Autonomy, and the Making of Worlds* (Duke University Press, 2018).
[20] Paul Knox, *Cities and Design* (Routledge, 2011), page 4.
[21] Aseem Inam, *Designing Urban Transformation* (Routledge, 2013), page 61.
[22] Inam, pages 112–113.

that conventional design practice has failed to see its long-term ecological consequences. Some note that the industrial revolution birthed a "cradle to grave" thinking in design, which led to lasting social and ecological problems of waste and pollution.[23] Others argue that this challenge has implications for the very philosophical and ethical foundations of design, beyond the way we make objects, systems, and products. For example, design practices have not traditionally considered their relationship the future. That is, design does not recognize how all sorts of human-initiated acts have reverberating implications, where "designed things go on designing."[24] This is especially true with how human interventions might have destructive long-term social and ecological impacts, from waste streams to carbon emissions. In a sense, thinking more ecologically, beyond the short-term immediate impacts of design processes, might mean seeing individual places, objects and people as part of a wider living context—which is both shaping and being shaped by human activity.

Emerging perspectives in social design similarly critique conventional design practices for their failure to situate problems in a wide enough spatial and temporal context. In particular, the field of transition design argues that designing ought to make better use a wide range of design methods, approaches, and tools, such as "future visioning," to bring stakeholders together toward long-term systems-level change.[25] Design for transitions has also been portrayed as a potential way to mobilize a political ecology of design, which could situate designing as part of larger visions for advancing ecological democracy and therefore begin to overcome design's conventional emphasis on short-term outcomes.[26]

---

[23] William McDonough and Michael Braungart, *Cradle to Cradle: Remaking the Way We Make Things* (North Point Press, 2002).

[24] Tony Fry, *Design Futuring: Sustainability, Ethics and New Practice* (Berg, 2009), page 3.

[25] Terry Irwin, "Transition Design: A Proposal for a New Area of Design Practice, Study, and Research," *Design and Culture*, volume 7, issue 2, 2015, pages 229–246.

[26] Damian F. White, "Ecological Democracy, Just Transitions, and a Political Ecology of Design," *Environmental Values*, volume 28, issue 1, 2019, pages 31–53.

Divide between the "Users" and Professional Designers. The twentieth century saw the ascendancy of new technologies along with the cultural view, in Western societies, that the advance of science and technology would solve social problems. This was especially prevalent in the politics and imagination of post-Second World War planning in the United States, which sought to remake (what planning and design professionals described as) disorderly slum neighborhoods with the design of massive urban renewal policies and plans. In theory, trained experts would designate areas for interventions to improve society through rationally remade space. This radical technological optimism at the center of much design in the mid-twentieth century—that sought technically designed and managed solutions to social problems—would be the subject of much social thought.[27]

Throughout the twentieth century, social critiques of design were evident more broadly in the emergence of design methodology as a field of inquiry. While initial work in the field was later seen as overly scientific, it did open up many forms of reflection on the social and technical processes of design.[28] This was especially true in the emergence of "user centered design," including related fields of human-computer design or interaction design, which focused on computing systems or devices, and service design that emphasized the design of people's experience with public and private services. These approaches argue, among other things, that when objects or services do not work well it is because they are poorly designed and have not considered how someone would actually use the object or service from within their social context.

Accordingly, user-centered design argues that design practice needs to focus on making the operations of an object or system

[27] For instance, Jane Jacobs became known for her popular accounts of city planning and design practices, which she argued involved expert interventions that did not consider the desires of people who would actually use urban spaces. Jane Jacobs, *The Death and Life and Great American Cities* (Vintage Books, 1961), page 13. On the symbolism of Jacobs as an alternative approach to design and planning, see: Anthony Flint, *Wrestling with Moses: How Jane Jacobs Took on New York's Master Builder and Transformed the American City* (Random House, 2009).

[28] Nigel Cross, "Forty Years of Design Research," *Design Studies*, volume 28, issue 1, 2007, pages 1–4.

visible to the user—by understanding how people might respond in the process of using a particular object.[29] Like user-centered design, human-centered approaches similarly give priority to what design can accomplish for people, but perhaps push further in urging reconsideration of the underlying theories and principles of design. They suggest a shift from applying new methods or techniques in design and toward a practice that is grounded values of human dignity and human rights.[30] In other words, "users" of products, systems, or services would be better viewed as co-creative participants, who contribute their own perspectives, ideas, and tactics to designing processes.

Similarly, the field of design for social innovation tends to advocate for something beyond the user-professional dichotomy all together. Perhaps most notably, is the notion of "diffuse design" where non-professionals are increasingly innovating and using their design-capacity to solve problems.[31] In this context, design no longer only about expert designers designing for a user, but rather it can be conceptualized as professionals and non-professionals reciprocally collaborating in co-design processes, to invent and enhance modes of being and ways of doing things. Overall this approach to designing calls for bridging the longstanding divide between the professional designers and people's everyday lives, in ways that are sensitive to emerging social realities.

Despite much pushback to the dominance of credentialed experts in mainstream designing, the legacy of expert knowledge and practice has ongoing global implications that are only beginning to be explored. This is especially prevalent in discussion of the divide between the Global North, which includes wealthier nations of Western Europe and North America, and the Global

---

[29] Donald Norman, *The Psychology of Everyday Things* (Basic Books, 1988).

[30] Richard Buchanan, "Human Dignity and Human Rights: Thoughts on the Principles of Human-Centered Design," *Design Issues*, volume 17, issue 3, 2001, pages 35–39. This impulse is also present in the critique of conventional architectural design that apparently does not "give a damn" about urgent humanitarian crises. See, for example: Architecture for Humanity (editors), *Design Like You Give a Damn: Architectural Responses to Humanitarian Crises* (Metropolis Books, 2006).

[31] Ezio Manzini, *Design, When Everybody Designs: An Introduction to Design for Social Innovation* (MIT Press, 2015), page 54.

South nations of Asia, Africa, and Latin America. At issue here is how the legacies of expert knowledge drive longstanding global power imbalances that privilege Euro-centric ideals, culture, and forms.[32] Overall, such perspectives point to a need to look beyond universal conceptions of design or development and toward an understanding of the diversity of local knowledges and practices that may already be making new worlds.

SOCIAL SCIENCE FROM THE STANDPOINT OF ACTION

Design is an intervention-oriented approach to the world, which can be viewed as fundamentally concerned with acting. Those whose work involves various forms of social action and design have long critiqued social thought, and social science research in particular. Activists and practitioners note frustration with social research for being too slow, irrelevant to on-the-ground realities, or difficult to apply in practice.[33] The image of "ivory tower" academia attests to a perceived disconnection between academic scholarship and the "real world."

In practice it is also evident that social sciences become distanced from action with an analytical gaze focused on the past and present, instead of the future. Such a focus resorts to descriptions and explanations of social conditions instead of creative explorations of possible futures. Despite some efforts to counter dominant trends, there remains "a remarkable lack of interest in how methods of creativity, art or design could be applied to the practice of social science," across a range of disciplines, organizations, and institutions.[34]

---

[32] Pablo Calderón Salazar and Alfredo Gutiérrez Borrero, "Letters South of (Nordic) Design," *NORDES 2017: Design and Power*, Number 7, ISSN 1604-9705.

[33] Ricardo Falla explains more broadly how research is often not relevant to social action, with a pervasive frustration among NGOs, governments, and researchers who all fail to adequately support each other's work. Ricardo Falla, "Research and Social Action," *Latin American Perspectives*, volume 27, issue 1, 2000, pages 45–55.

[34] Mulgan, page 9.

What is at stake here is the fundamental relationship between systematic reflection and action. Those who are making decisions each day related to their organizations and lives, facing deadlines for implementation, or trying to meet people's urgent needs, often do not feel they have the capacity to do serious reflection or scholarly research. In one sense, rigorous study and reflection are seen as a privilege that is not always useful to wider society. The designer, for example, typically needs to look for only that which is immediately useful to completing the project at hand. At the same time, it is also the case that thoughtful reflection and systematic study continue to be important to all types of social action—from local community organizing to policy and organizational decisions. So then, what stands in the way of social science becoming more useful for action? Here I explore three major challenges.

An Overly Narrow Methodological Imagination. The process of doing conventional social research often excludes the people and groups who are actually acting to address the social issues being studied. In large part, this is because the goal of systematically "understanding" an object of study (and testing or developing theory) is seen as separate from concerns of practice.

In theory, the focus of social science research and much social thought is qualitative or quantitative methods—that use accepted techniques within a specific subdiscipline to analyze some form of content, historical, interview, survey, geographic, or participant observation data. The goal is typically to answer a question in the existing academic literature, or a question formulated by the researcher. Social research gets its data by extracting information from people through interviews, observations, or surveys (or relying upon other large organizations, like the World Bank, to extract information). It then uses disciplinary methods to analyze data in the context of existing academic theory. Even in "applied" social sciences, researchers may cater their research topic or writing style to different audiences—for example, to describe the effects of a particular intervention—but they often use the same methodological approach.

Such a research process is arguably ineffective at illuminating social reality, and it actually works to constrain effective action. This perspective is seen most notably in participatory action research critiques of social science, which evaluate social research from the perspective of intervention and action.[35] These action-oriented critiques of social science emerged mainly in two, sometimes overlapping, contexts—organizations from North America to Europe, and activist movements of South America.

In one context, researchers like Kurt Lewin and colleagues developed the concept of action research to help non-professionals (such as entry-level workers) expand their capacities for reflective thought, collaboration, and decision-making. Lewin argued that typical research processes in much of Europe and North America were too narrowly conceived to be relevant to changing organizational and human needs. Overall, these early action researchers saw that social research methods could be applied beyond purely academic questions to serve an ongoing process of organizational reflection and intervention.[36]

In another context, action research developed from activist struggles across South America, as a way to inform systemic critiques of society. Scholars like Colombian Sociologist Orlando Fals-Borda argued that narrowly conceived research methodologies can be elitist impositions on communities that do not serve the people's needs or demands for action. In this view, social researchers ought to make their work relevant to possible alternative courses of action, by combining their skills with the knowledge of grassroots communities, which can become partners and co-researchers that are already engaged in acting on issues being considered.[37]

Overall, at the core of these critiques and alternatives to conventional social science is the notion that research methods

---

[35] Michelle Fine argues that Participatory Action Research can "widen the methodological imagination" of social research, making scholarship more connected and relevant to action: Michelle Fine, *Just Research in Contentious Times: Widening the Methodological Imagination* (Teachers College Press, 2018).

[36] Clem Adelman, "Kurt Lewin and the Origins of Action Research," *Educational Action Research*, volume 1, issue 1, 1993, pages 7–24.

[37] Orlando Fals-Borda, "Participatory (Action) Research in Social Theory: Origins and Challenges," in Hillary Bradbury and Peter Reason (editors), *Handbook of Action Research: Participative Inquiry and Practice* (SAGE Publications, 2001), pages 27–37.

need to be more participatory and collaborative, grounded in existing practices and lived reality rather than only academic literature.[38] They argue that there are many different ways of knowing, which are as valid as the knowledge that scientific academic research creates. A widening of the methodological imagination would involve, for example, embracing more creative forms of investigation or more collaborative research teams that have people with a diversity of roles and experiences outside of academia. These approaches, however, run counter to the individualistic and competitive modes of research that are the norm in graduate programs (where doctoral candidates write an individualized dissertation and a personal CV to compete for limited spots in the academic job market), and university departments more generally (that require publication in specific peer-reviewed journals, which are often not open to methodological innovation or creativity, for promotion and tenure).

Tendency toward Passive Observation. Perhaps the greatest challenge social science faces, from the perspective of action and intervention, is the tendency for the researcher or thinker to slide into the role of a passive observer. Social thought typically analyzes, documents, diagnoses, describes, or deconstructs. With each of these postures, the researcher is in danger of being more of an observer than an active participant. Some people and institutions may be contributing to inequality, or effectively implementing a new policy, but the researcher supposedly stands aside, using their academic expertise to develop theories that explain what has happened. In one sense, the attempt at value neutrality seems as if it would earn the researcher a sense of political legitimacy (with "just the facts"). At the same time, it is becoming increasingly clear that this attempted objectivity actually makes social science less relevant to social action today. Although many scholars would debate whether or not a truly

---

[38] There are also other critiques of the potentially harmful and narrow methodological imagination of social science from indigenous perspectives. See, for example: Linda Tuhiwai Smith, *Decolonizing Methodologies: Research and Indigenous Peoples* (Zed Books, 1999).

objective and value-neutral social science is even possible, the main point here is that such a stance is not particularly useful for acting in the world.[39] This is for two main reasons.

First, in an effort to appear legitimate so that it can influence social policy, social science relies on generating theories that are ultimately difficult to translate into specific contexts. The difficulty in translating from theory to practice arises because academic theory is meant to be a generalizable account of human activity. The core of the problem is that social science is often judged as if its main goal should be to produce cumulative body of knowledge as natural science disciplines do—through the development of explanatory (or even predictive) narratives and theories.

This goal has proven difficult to achieve in social sciences, and it can be a potential barrier to action. While social theory seeks to describe human activity in a way that can apply across different contexts, in practice people usually act based on the concrete details of a particular situation. Therefore, systematic reflection on the values of a society—that explores "the problems and risks we face and … how things may be done differently"—is more useful than purely academic social scientific theory.[40] This is not to abandon the rigorous collection and analysis of data, but rather to consider how such research might be relevant to different forms of action at all stages of a project.[41]

Secondly, traditional social science does not adequately explore possible courses of action that could improve society or address injustice, precisely because it assumes that values

[39] For more on critiques and debates about objectivity in forms of social research see, for example: Donna Haraway, "Situated Knowledges: The Science Question in Feminism and the Privilege of Partial Perspective," *Feminist Studies*, volume 4, issue 3, 1988, pages 575–599.

[40] Bent Flyvbjerg, *Making Social Science Matter: Why Social Inquiry Fails and How It Can Succeed Again* (Cambridge University Press, 2001), page 140.

[41] Some scholars argue for "public" versions of social science (like Burawoy's "public sociology") that would make research findings accessible to broader audiences, but for Flyvbjerg this may not go far enough if "public engagement" only comes at the end of a research process. Michael Burawoy, "For Public Sociology," *American Sociological Review*, volume 70, 2005, pages 4–27.

(about the way the society ought to, or could be) make social research less scientific. Many social science authors spend an entire article or book describing social inequalities or crises, with a few gestures toward relatively general policies or practices they might recommend tacked on at the end. Rarely is the process of imagining and implementing other possibilities the sole focus of a social science project.

The paradigm of "emancipatory social science" is one example that challenges this norm.[42] It argues that something more than the value-neutral mission of conventional social science is necessary for action today. This is because acting to confront twenty-first century challenges is not only a matter of getting better understanding of existing social realities, but it also requires explorations of possible social realities that do not yet exist. In this context, researchers can, and should, have a goal of creating conditions for human flourishing. With this objective in mind, they can investigate and develop alternatives to current social conditions. Social research that does this goes beyond objective accounts of existing social reality, and investigates the viability of different possible courses of action, exploring the possibilities and obstacles for transformation in different circumstances.

Above all, at a moment when we most need creative, thoughtful action in response to mounting social and ecological crises, the attempted neutral stance of much social science prevents people from participating in the creation of new social realities. Typical social science education and research norms actively encourage people (both professionals and the wider public) to spend more time being passive observers of the world, often in front of a computer screen looking at spreadsheets, academic literature, or documents. This stance is then rewarded in academic journals, university departments, and professional associations. Although some retain a commitment to different forms of activism, consulting, or action on the side, this is beyond what is expected within the typical boundaries of social science activity. From the perspective of action, if we assume that research (as a form of

[42] Erik Olin Wright, *Envisioning Real Utopias* (Verso Books, 2010).

systematic reflection) is meant to be passive and value-neutral, then we may ultimately fail to get the insights that we need to act differently.

Missing Dimensions of Human Creativity. Even in research or critical scholarship that seems most concerned with social change, there is sometimes a tendency to describe the world mainly in terms of systemic social constraints and oppressions. While it is certainly important to understand the extent to which systems marginalize, exclude, and harm people, the perspective of action pushes researchers to also do more. Knowledge that is useful for action articulates both constraints *and* possibilities of a particular situation with attention to people's emerging lived experiences, needs, and desires.

Much social research embraces a theory of change that documents harm or injury in order to achieve some kind of reparative intervention or social policy. While often well-intentioned (with a goal of calling attention to a specific problem or need), this approach portrays communities as fundamentally broken or damaged.[43] Effective action toward more systemic social change, however, requires a more nuanced understanding of social realities—that highlights the complexity and desires within communities. People do not respond to challenging or oppressive conditions in uniform ways. When given no other alternative, they may improvise and invent their way to new forms of survival—neither standing out nor becoming merely expendable.[44]

Other scholars have noted that social research, perhaps unintentionally, diminishes the role of human creativity when it fails to engage with actually existing practices. For example, in much conventional research, *the social* becomes a completed artifact to be understood or dissected rather than a web of relations that is constantly being assembled and reassembled. When social analysts use, "the words 'society,' 'power,' 'structure,' and 'context,' they often jump straight ahead to connect the vast arrays of life and history, to mobilize gigantic forces,

[43] Eve Tuck, "Suspending Damage: A Letter to Communities," *Harvard Educational Review*, volume 79, issue 3, 2009, pages 409–427.

[44] AbduMaliq Simone, *Improvised Lives* (Polity Press, 2019).

to detect dramatic patterns emerging out of confusing interactions ... to reveal behind the scenes some dark powers pulling the strings."[45]

In practice, people do not simply follow a script of pre-ordained social structures as if they are puppets being manipulated. They innovate and create based on their own theories and ideas about situations on-the-ground. The goal of a more actor- and practice-oriented social science (based on the relationships among different social "actors") would therefore strive "'To follow the actors themselves' ... that is try to catch up with their often wild innovations in order to learn from them what the collective existence has become in their hands, which methods they have elaborated to make it fit together, which accounts could best define the new associations that they have been forced to establish."[46] Surely people innovate from within particular social contexts, constraints, and moments in history, but the key critique here is that social science over-emphasizes the analysis and dissection of an already-made society (instead of engaging with emerging creative responses, interventions, and actions).

There is also a question of what worlds social researchers depict, or how social science writing imagines society itself. Early sociologist Max Weber has been widely referenced for his description of the modern social world as "disenchanted." This means, among other things, that capitalist industrial society traps people in an "iron cage" of rational bureaucracy, efficiency, and control—which is supposedly cold and calculating compared to more religious and communal premodern societies. In the disenchanted modern society, people are said to be profoundly alienated, and less able to act with genuine human creativity. Whether or not such a description is accurate, it could actually serve to discourage action and engagement.[47]

---

[45] Bruno Latour, *Reassembling the Social: An Introduction to Actor Network Theory* (Oxford University Press, 2005), page 22.

[46] Latour, page 12.

[47] Jane Bennett argues that the "disenchantment" narrative actually discourages people to care for and act in the world. Jane Bennett, *The Enchantment of Modern Life: Attachments, Crossings, Ethics* (Princeton University Press, 2001).

In other words, it seems that if people do experience frustration or alienation when they reflect on their world today, then it is, at least in part, because of the narratives created and worlds imagined by social science and thought—as it documents damage or mobilizes gigantic forces beyond human control. Overall, much scholarly reflection today, even the critical sort that has a concern for social justice and change, does not effectively contribute to new courses of action.[48] The core insight here (for how social sciences can be understood through the lens of design and action) is that while much research today closes down or ignores possibilities for action, it could (done differently) be a practice that seeks out and generates creative ideas for a better world.

DESIGN, THE SOCIAL, AND IMAGINATION

Taken together, the view of design from the perspective of social thought, and of social thought from the perspective of design (as a mode action), demonstrates the urgency of creating deeper relationships between reflection and action today. While traditional social sciences often see themselves as reflecting on social reality, it is evident that *reflection itself can be a potential intervention* from within social reality. Alternatively, design typically sees its practice as oriented toward intervention and action, whereas this book conceptualizes *acting as a significant subject-matter for reflection*. It is in this sense that designing can become a *process of reflection on what is possible*.

In the process of trying to make something happen, we learn more about what is possible within a certain time and place, even if these possibilities are always shifting—with new opportunities always presenting themselves and new limitations constantly emerging. From the perspective of social thought, it is clear that what we design or make is never innocent of its larger social

---

[48] Rosi Braidotti has explored how scholarship interested in social justice and social change often focuses on negative criticism, to the detriment of creative action. Rosi Braidotti, "Putting the Active Back in Activism," *New Formations*, issue 68, 2009, pages 42–57.

context. As much as we may see suffering, waste, and destruction in the world and wish to start fresh with a clean slate, or new canvas, page, or document, design today is called to do more.

Design must *contend with what we have made*, engaging deeply with the complex, contradictory, frustrating, and challenging realities of human life today.[49] There is no singular future that acts as an empty void, waiting to be filled by new products, spaces, systems, or services. Anything that is made today is constructed from within a social context that is already full of structures, objects, rubble, and wastelands.[50] As the broader critique of design from the perspective of social thought demonstrates, we must also contend with a wide range of inequalities that are woven into the social and physical worlds that are being made and remade today. The twenty-first century is a crucial moment to reckon with how our interventions are situated within social realities that are rife with uneven access to power. To design, or to act, in ways that are attuned to these complexities and contradictions of social realities is at the core of what it means to cultivate *both* a design capacity *and* a social imagination.

Although this book is, in some ways, about the combination of two ideas (design and social imagination), it is actually also about three dynamically interrelated concepts (design, the social, and imagination). That is, the book is not only about how design can improve social research, or how social thought can make design more socially conscious. Its fundamental concern is how thinking about social worlds, the practice of designing, and the human imagination can be brought together for action today.

Writing about imagination from within the culture of a United States university is a challenging task. This is because academic and public life does not typically take imagination seriously. Imagination is seen in the context of fantasy, childhood, and fairy tales. Children supposedly have rich imaginations because they

---

[49] Clive Dilnot, "History, Design, Futures: Contending with What We Have Made," in Tony Fry, Clive Dilnot, and Susan Stewart (editors), *Design and the Question of History* (Bloomsbury, 2015), pages 131–272.

[50] Tony Fry, *Defuturing: A New Design Philosophy* (Bloomsbury, 2020), page 238.

have not yet had to deal with the real world. This cultural notion is reinforced in the worldview of Western science. In particular, social scientific research focuses on what can be observed in the data, and those who have become adults are educated on how to comprehend reports of this data that they might read. In this context, to become an adult is to leave imaginary worlds behind, in favor of the best available information on how things actually are. Even when imagination is taken up seriously, it is often as a tool for advancing worlds that have little connection to social reality. This is especially evident in the "Imagineering" of Walt Disney Company, which is the ongoing design, construction, and management of profitable entertainment destinations.

In this context, expectations of what design is can also stifle our imaginations. Scholars are beginning to recognize how the Eurocentric and universal imagination that design has perpetuated, through and since colonization, fails to fully represent human experience, knowledge, and potential. This impacts the outcomes of design, what is considered design practice, and the contexts where designing processes unfold.[51] An ongoing "coloniality of design" constrains what may seem possible, as it shapes our perceptions and interpretations of the worlds we inhabit.[52] There is accordingly a need to decolonize our imaginations. This means, in part, seeing the social origins and implications of our own thinking, desiring, and imagining that we may have been conditioned to see as purely individual.

Truly awakening our social imaginations is therefore about reconsidering why we may be able to imagine some things more than others, and from what histories and relationships we are imagining. As Arturo Escobar demonstrates, part of this project is what design theorists describe as an ontological approach to design—that is, imagining designing as a way to initiate new ways of being. This involves thinking about "design's capacities

[51] Ahmed Ansari and Matthew Kiem, "What Is Needed for Change? Two Perspectives on Decolonization and the Academy," in Claudia Mareis and Nina Paim (editors), *Design Struggles: Intersecting Histories, Pedagogies, and Perspectives* (Swiss Design Network, Plural Series, 2021), pages 155–167.
[52] Madina Tlostanova, "On Decolonizing Design," *Design Philosophy Papers*, volume 15, issue 1, 2017, pages 51–61.

and potentiality through a wide spectrum of imaginations," which are emerging in both professional design practices and grassroots communities.[53] What needs to be reimagined then is not just material conditions, objects, or social systems, but the multiple possibilities of being human today.

Although design is deeply interwoven with what it means to be human beings, who are social creatures with profound capacities for imagination, it is not the case that every human activity is design. Designing is about making images, objects, spaces, organizations, books, buildings, services, systems, cities, communities, or processes. More fundamentally, design is social activity that makes new worlds, as it initiates courses of action that make imagined and desired futures possible. To design, then is to initiate deliberate courses of action that move from current conditions to preferred ones. Approaching designing as a primarily social and collaborative endeavor demands we develop our own unique set of skills, and at the same time, aspire to share what we know (or know how to do) with others.

Such an approach ultimately requires cultivating our imaginations for more than a tool in the creation of (or participation in) worlds of leisure, consumption, and fantasy. To be more fully awakened, our imaginations must therefore be oriented toward our ability to think, reckon with what we experience in our senses, and make new social realities. The imagination is a particular form of thought that we can cultivate—a mode of thinking where we not only direct our attention toward objects, words, images, and spaces that may appear in lived human experience but also see beyond the immediate present. This is why imagination is a potentially productive bridge between design and the social. Both require ways to think beyond our present circumstance in personal situations, pivotal organizational moments, or societal conditions.

As Cornelius Castoriadis reminds us, almost everything about our experience today, from social routines to policies, buildings and spaces, is a product of the human imagination. Indeed, even the Western Scientific Worldview that created so many present

---

[53] Escobar, page 19.

social realities was a product of imagining the world, including other plants, animals and ecologies, through the particular lens of Western science.[54] In this context, Castoriadis argues for a *radical imagination,* which is an "unbridled" and "defunctionalized" imagination that does not limit itself to what initially appears pragmatic or profitable.[55] This reinvigorated imagination is, therefore, not something to be achieved or a state of mind to master; rather, it is a potential toward which we can aspire.

What is so powerful about this sort of radical imagination is that it is ultimately *not fully determined* by present context or sensory experience. It has the potential to *mobilize thought* beyond existing circumstances. In this way, it runs counter to longstanding trends in design and social sciences which view designed forms or social forces as realities that govern, or even determine, human behavior.

The imagination has this unique characteristic of unification— to potentially bring together what is experienced and perceived here and now, with what does not (yet) actually exist. It is the imagination that connects reflective capacities to action in the world. As Castoriadis concludes: "it is impossible to talk of action without 'deliberation' concerning the future, and of 'deliberation' without imagination—that is without positing/presentation of several sets of composite or unified 'images' of what is not there."[56] The powerful implications, or necessity, of using the imagination to bring action and deliberation together today—combining social thinking, imagining, and designing—will be explored in the coming chapters.

Such an exploration is especially important now, when it seems that too many are failing to fully grasp current social

[54] Castoriadis resists the determinism that he sees in Western philosophy and science—which assumes that human senses perceive a singular, permanent, and objective reality, and that scientific observation is therefore somehow immune from the supposedly subjective effects of the human imagination. Cornelius Castoriadis, *World in Fragments: Writings on Politics, Society, Psychoanalysis, and the Imagination* (Stanford University Press, 1986), pages 227–228.

[55] Castoriadis, *World in Fragments,* page 247.

[56] Castoriadis, *World in Fragments,* pages 230–231.

realities and imagine possible alternatives at the very moment when these sorts of sensibilities are most needed. A fast-paced, connected global world has many advantages, but it also means that genuine, sustained relationship and understanding can be evasive as we hurdle across time and space on social media feeds with the swipe of a finger. As we see images and signs of a world in crisis, it may feel difficult enough to eke out enough individual financial stability day-to-day or month-to-month, and we may be afraid or apathetic by what we see around us, unable to imagine something different. We are bewildered by an ecological context that seems unstable at best, and at worst, headed for total collapse. Political polarization increasingly seems reconcilable only though the force of violence. An economic system that generates dazzling profits for a few churns on, while making so many more people poor, sick, and vulnerable. In the midst of these crises, our governments and institutions seem willfully corrupt, simply unable to rise to the challenge, or both. What, then, is to be done? How exactly do we cultivate capacities for social imagining and designing that are needed today? With the limitations of present forms of design and social thought, where might we find models and inspiration for action?

PART TWO
Three Key Thinkers: Their Lives, Contexts, and Projects

Hannah Arnedt believed that even in the darkest of times we can still find some illumination if we look in the right places. This is not an enlightenment that comes from academic theories or concepts, but more so from understanding the lives and works of individuals in their social contexts.[1] In the way that people live their lives—the projects they develop with others, the communities they join or catalyze, and the causes that animate their days—they demonstrate potential ways of being and doing. This is one reason why Part Two explores design and the social imagination from the perspective of three foundational scholars, activists, and practitioners who began their work in the late nineteenth century: Patrick Geddes, Jane Addams, and W.E.B. Du Bois. These are not biographies; they are future-oriented histories of their life, research, and practice. The work of Geddes, Addams, and DuBois is used as a way to explore the potential relationships between

---

[1] Richard Bernstein describes Hannah Arendt's notion of "dark times" this way in his book: Richard J. Bernstein, *Why Read Hannah Arendt Now* (Polity Press, 2018), pages 1–3.

design, imagination, and social thought today. Taken together, these three offer some possible foundations for reflective action.

They are people whose collaborative projects are models of social activism and thought, opening up a multitude of actions related to their theorizing and thinking process. While each of the three pursued different kinds of scholarship and action, it is important to note that they would not typically describe their work as design, and they would not always refer to their work as social science. Their limits as individuals can and perhaps should be critiqued, however, the goal here is to draw on the strengths of their communities of thought and practice. The emphasis is on how these scholar-practitioners show what it means to cultivate a design sensibility and a social imagination. As such, the book explores ways that they offer a foundation to draw upon for reflective action—in forms of thinking, imagining, and designing that are attuned to social realities today.

Overall, the focus on design and the social imagination here gives more emphasis to an affirmative politics fueled by the "creative potential of critical thought" than it does to "negative criticism and oppositional consciousness."[2] The reason for this approach is not to dismiss negative criticism, but rather to empower the future and world-making potentials of critical social thought. At a moment when it seems critique has "run out of steam," it just might be the case that design can contribute to new practices of critique that assemble people, materials, and ideas differently, offering spaces for people to gather, to more deeply care for and about social realities.[3]

Design offers imperfect but important ideals for the potential of critical thought, especially of the model of iterative and constructive critique that is often an aspiration in design education. Critical thought can juxtapose present realities with future possibilities, and a design sensibility can orient thought toward

[2] Braidotti distinguishes these two approaches to critique, noting that they are not necessarily mutually exclusive. Rosi Braidotti, "Putting the Active Back in Activism," *New Formations*, issue 68, 2009, pages 42–57.

[3] Bruno Latour, "Why Has Critique Run out of Steam? From Matters of Fact to Matters of Concern," *Critical Inquiry*, volume 30, issue 2, 2004, pages 225–228.

its creative potentials—imagining or initiating courses of action and trying to make things happen. Fusing creativity and critique in this way seems especially important in a moment when Western cultures are saturated with images ranging from ecological crisis to human catastrophe and extinction, which social thought often amplifies.

At the same time, there is a danger in pursuing only "practical solutions" or jumping on a bandwagon of the latest cultural trends, innovations, best practices, or technologies to address complex challenges. It is a main contention of this book that design, as a concept and a practice, can help to imagine the in-between or beyond these two dispositions—of unbridled scientific, cultural, and technological optimism, on the one hand, and a pessimism that collapses into despair and inaction on the other.[4] One way the book attempts to demonstrate this possibility of design and thought today is by exploring specific contexts, models, practices, and histories related to three key thinkers who were working on the margins of early design and social science professions, to reframe issues of the present anew.

Overall, on the pages that follow, the work of Geddes, Addams, and Du Bois is viewed through the lens of designing, as a process that included what could, today, be described as various forms of professional design practice. All three employed a variety of social and spatial design practices—from visual design of information and the design of collaborative networks (Du Bois), to co-design of public policy and services (Addams), or urban and environmental design (Geddes). In some sense, the examples focus on the urban contexts of their work, however, the models they offer for practice are relevant to designing more generally in the wake of industrial capitalist urbanization. Their practice also

[4] Damian White makes the point that bringing critical design and critical social sciences into conversation might help to expand and pluralize futures beyond these two dominant approaches. Damian White, "Critical Design, Hybrid Labor, and Just Transitions: Moving Beyond Technocratic Ecomodernisms and the It's-Too-Late-O-Cene," in Manuel Arias-Maldonado and Zev Trachtenberg (editors), *Rethinking the Environment for the Anthropocene: Political Theory and Socionatural Relations in the New Geological Epoch* (Taylor & Francis, 2019), pages 180–200.

draws out the connections between physical form or materials and social systems or services.

As social thinkers who also intentionally engaged in a series of life projects, Geddes, Addams, and Du Bois will be presented as designers or project makers in this book. This approach follows Ezio Manzini's definition of designing as project-making in every-day life, which involves "making a critical evaluation of the state of things, imagining how we would like them to be, and having the necessary relational system and tools at hand to transform them."[5] As Manzini notes, design scholars and practitioners have increasingly recognized that in global economies, with a prolif-eration of non-physical products, designing is increasingly about making of services, systems, and forms of social organization more broadly.

The related field of social design is especially relevant to the thought and action explored in the coming chapters. It underscores how designing can be crucial for mobilizing political possibilities or addressing urgent human needs that are not being met by the conventional large institutions of the public and private sectors. In this context, "social design is not merely a helpful partner to other social professions, but could, if it took itself seriously be a distinct new (trans)discipline, perhaps even be a replace-ment."[6] It is not necessarily that design professions must lead the way, but rather that those who are trained as professionals can accompany the cultural activists, grassroots organizations, and design activists who are experimenting with new forms of social organization to address urgent complex problems of today.[7] Geddes, Addams, and Du Bois can be helpful reference points and models for these emerging practices in social design and design for social innovation. They were all, in different ways, practicing forms of socio-spatial design that are relevant to emerging fields today, long before many of the current trends in thought and

[5] Ezio Manzini, *Politics of the Everyday* (Bloomsbury/Designing in Dark Times, 2019), page 34.

[6] Cameron Tonkinwise, "Is Social Design a Thing?" in E. Resnick (editor), *The Social Design Reader* (Bloomsbury, 2019), page 13.

[7] Ezio Manzini, *Design When Everybody Designs: An Introduction to Design for Social Innovation* (MIT Press, 2015).

practice. Perhaps what is most useful to learn from is the ways they designed within, and imagined beyond, their social historical contexts—acting toward what they and their collaborators imagined could be possible.

Geddes, Addams, and Du Bois all began working in Europe or the United States in the late nineteenth century within a rapidly changing world and academic context. The effects of industrialization and urbanization were beginning to be felt in tangible ways. People who were moving to cities for industrial work endured a poor quality of living, the global slave trade and colonization had set accelerating mass migration and displacement into motion, and pollution from rapid urbanization was noticeably impacting the air, land, and water. A new generation of social reformers sought to respond to urban inequalities through policy and practice. Scholars similarly began to develop theory and research, including the discipline of sociology, as they sought to better understand the implications of this industrializing society.

In retrospect, scholarship and action in this era were not always effective or empowering for the people most in need. Reforms were often unreflective or paternalistic, and academic knowledge could be disconnected from social realities.[8] Instead of getting deeper into social realities, much social science turned toward theoretical debates and efforts to distinguish disciplines from each other. Those that frequently crossed disciplinary boundaries became marginalized because they were less relevant to the professional advancement of disciplines, and discrimination against women and Black scholars made it easier to focus on a more singular white male debates over the advancement of the field. This is what makes Geddes, Addams, and Du Bois unique and important for their time, and ours. Although today they may be considered sociologists, they were often on the margins of the discipline, as they developed practices of action-oriented research that were rooted in on-the-ground conditions.

---

[8] See, for example: Willard Gaylin, Ira Glasser, Steven Marcus, and David Rothman, *Doing Good: The Limits of Benevolence* (Pantheon, 1978).

Their work was also emerging in the wake of an unprecedented historical break or rupture that occurred in Western societies. This era, which followed the enlightenment and industrial revolution, created the conditions for a way of being human to emerge that enabled self-reflection on society and its institutions. Geddes, Addams, and Du Bois were accordingly living in a contradictory moment in history. On the one hand, their era saw the advance of new and violent forms of capitalism, racism, environmental destruction, and empire. At the same time, they were also working in a historical moment where new forms of social thought had enabled increasing numbers of people to "call into question the very laws of existence," conditioning the possibility "of genuine political action, of action toward a new institution of society."[9]

In this context, Geddes, Addams, and Du Bois can be excellent models—of how to harness the transformative potentials of social thought for the dual project of *investigating the real* and *articulating the possible*. Their work is prescient for our times—at a moment when design and social thought are reckoning with the complicity of design professions in producing social exclusion and marginalization.[10] In many ways, their approaches to thinking and designing offer alternatives to the methods that came to dominate professional design and social science practices. That is, they offer possibilities for what acting and thinking can be today, beyond conventional disciplinary boundaries, as they offer new insights to emerging efforts to challenge dominant paradigms in design and social thought.[11]

[9] Castoriadis explains the contradictions in the wake of enlightenment thinking that persisted into the nineteenth and twentieth centuries. Cornelius Castoriadis, *World in Fragments: Writings on Politics, Society, Psychoanalysis, and the Imagination* (Stanford University Press, 1986), page 17.

[10] Claudia Mareis and Nina Paim, "Design Struggles: An Attempt to Imagine Design Otherwise," in C. Mareis and N. Paim (editors), *Design Struggles: Intersecting Histories, Pedagogies, and Perspectives* (Swiss Design Network, Plural Series, 2021), pages 11–22.

[11] In a sense their projects share some commonalities with decolonial challenges to Eurocentric perspectives in design from the Global South. At the same time, Geddes, Addams, and Du Bois show how the seeds for an effort to challenge dominant paradigms may also be found on the margins of their own societies.

It is also significant that the three scholar-practitioners explored here worked between organizations, institutions, and communities—gathering information, developing theories, proposing new ideas, and implementing interventions. In our current moment, when non-profit, policy, and governmental organizations are increasingly interested in design (e.g., through various approaches to social design, civic design, or co-design) the lives of Geddes, Addams, and Du Bois demonstrate the long and relevant history that connects a design sensibility with community action and the public sector more generally. Of particular importance in the story of these three scholar-practitioners presented here is how their *practice of research and theorizing* has implications beyond academia.

That is to say that they had a certain orientation to praxis, which aimed for both the *clarification and transformation* of social realities.[12] Their praxis did not envision a sharp divide between reflection and action; they pursued them concurrently, recognizing that reflection and action mutually support each other and overlap. Their ultimate goal was transformation of the society that had been born into—whether that was the given relationship between society and the environment, pervasiveness of racism and social marginalization, or the lack of adequate infrastructure and housing in the midst of increasing urbanization. All three implicitly and explicitly embraced a dynamic relationship between theory and practice. Social action and lived experience informed their theorizing, and their research investigations shaped how they acted, within and beyond an academic context. It is their positioning—between acting or trying to make things happen, and reflecting on the contexts where they live and work—that will be the focus of the coming chapters.

---

[12] This is in the sense that Castoriadis describes praxis, for example when he explains that "The clarification and transformation of reality progress together in praxis, each conditioning each other." Cornelius Castoriadis, *The Imaginary Institution of Society* (Polity Press, 1987), page 76. Although influenced by Karl Marx, the Castoriadis view of praxis is distinct in its attention to the autonomous possibilities of the creative imagination. See, for example: Castoriadis's critique of how both capitalist and anti-capitalist thought historically relied on a similar social imaginary in: Castoriadis, *World in Fragments*, pages 32–43.

Geddes, Addams, and Du Bois present significant differences from the conventional "cannon" of social thought that mainstream scholars identified in the twentieth century, challenging professional social research practices and pointing to different foundations for how designing and thinking can be harnessed for reflective action today. For the purposes of this book, a primary distinction is that they intentionally developed their social thought based on their evolving work with actually existing social conditions, and participation in a wide range of social and ecological interventions. Although it is certainly the case that other academics or thinkers of their time participated in projects outside of universities, Geddes, Addams, and DuBois typically began and ended beyond the academy, viewing formal knowledge production as a contribution to acting in the world, and action as a step in creating new knowledge.

This meant, in different ways, bringing their practice into everyday life—blending the personal, professional, and political in ways that seemed to work for themselves and their communities. For instance, Geddes theorized on how practices from across disciplinary boundaries could inform effective urban ecological action, from experiences in his own neighborhood; Addams helped to create an alternative hub for research and action at the Hull-House, where she also lived much of her life, even though she was not fully accepted as a woman in university departments; and DuBois theorized and practiced against racism, based in part, on his experience being discriminated against as a Black social researcher in the United States.

As will be explored in the coming chapters, the personal social location of Geddes, Addams and Du Bois is especially important. They were not simply observers of social realities unfolding around them. Part of their practice was an investigation of how their own lives were actively influenced by the social and historical contexts they sought to shape. It is both the constraints of their situations and their creativity that can contribute to models for the interrelationship between social thought and design, or more broadly, reflection and action. Although their work belongs to neither design nor the social sciences alone, together their lives, contexts, and projects offer models, ideas, and inspiration for action today.

Patrick Geddes, for example, was a biologist and founding voice in town planning and sociology. With inspiration from his relationship to living plant environments, he was primarily concerned with ecological issues, in a broad sense. His relational and ecological thinking, which moved fluidly across disciplines develop courses of action in specific places, differed from other dominant voices in early social theory. Like his more widely cited contemporaries, such as Karl Marx, Max Weber, or Emile Durkheim, Geddes was concerned with the rise of urban industrial societies, and the destructive impacts of industrialization on human community. His work went beyond only explaining society in abstract theories, to develop a mode of research practice that aspired to civic engagement. This ranged from urban gardening and environmental education initiatives, to organizing residents for the design of neighborhood spaces and curating an Outlook Tower that served as a civic center to inspire participation in planning processes. Overall, he worked with collaborators and neighborhood residents, to imagine the transition to a new, more ecologically attuned democracy at both the local and regional scale.

Jane Addams similarly began her own thinking with urgent issues of her day—of urban poverty, breakdown of community, and immigration. Although today many consider her a founding voice in social work and sociology, her intent was not necessarily to found a discipline or professional practice. Her main collaborative life project was the Hull-House. There she helped to build a community of solidarity over decades and brought wealthier or established residents together with new immigrants. Her social thought emerged out of the relationships and conversations that came from the experience of meeting the immediate needs of poor immigrants, and organizing for larger systemic changes. Although she did not receive appropriate credit for her scholarly work during her lifetime, the ideas that emerged from her practice would eventually be considered important for urban sociology and pragmatist philosophy. Even William James (who is considered a major social thinker of the twentieth century) acknowledged that he relied on insights that people like Jane

Addams developed in trying to make things happen, which a more distanced kind of social thinking may have never been able to produce.

W.E.B. Du Bois took up the project of understanding and countering racism through creative forms of organizing, representation, narrative, and imagination. As the first Black scholar to graduate with a PhD from Harvard University, he saw that race and racism were deeply woven into the culture and conventions of knowledge production. This recognition led him to insights about how racism and colonialism are deeply intertwined in the foundations of Western society, that scholars are only recently beginning to more widely acknowledge. In the course of his broader project to reckon with the dominant culture of white supremacy he initiated insurgent research networks, co-founded the NAACP (National Association for the Advancement of Colored People), created a forum for creative and artistic expression (*The Crisis* magazine), and supported a range of initiatives based on social and economic cooperation. For Du Bois, research and knowledge were more than documenting existing realities because they held the potential for the transformation of human consciousness. This is perhaps why throughout his many projects, he sought to forge a connection between the liberatory potential of the human imagination to envision new worlds and the cooperative action that might begin transforming existing conditions into other futures. These combinations of thought and action were essential to see beyond what had been preordained as *the future* of hierarchical human relations (with whiteness enshrined as the model of civilization) under the dominant colonialist worldview.

To an extent, Geddes, Addams, and Du Bois together offer some models for another way of thinking, acting, and being. They lived in a time when many in the social sciences were attempting to appear more objective through abstraction, transforming the lived subjective experience of being human into a series of objects to be studied. In contrast to this dominant trend, Geddes, Adams, and Du Bois began with direct experiences of the human and ecological crisis at hand. This was to start with people and places that were being decimated by the worlds made under urban industrial capitalism. In struggling against the abstraction of the world, they resisted the separation of subjective experience from objective knowledge. While they certainly developed focused areas of study, the systems, objects, and processes of their practice were never completely removed from the knowledge that comes from lived experience. This is why they offer alternative foundations for thought and action to move beyond the dualistic separation of subject and object that continues to constrain ways of thinking, acting, and being today.[13]

Even when other more mainstream voices of academic disciplines in their time did emphasize the importance of human experience or action in social thought, they tended to focus on theories *about* action, instead of trying their theories out *in* action or developing useful knowledge *for* possible courses of action. It is certainly the case that Geddes, Addams, and DuBois have some resonance with leaders in philosophical pragmatism, such as John Dewey and William James, who saw the importance of producing knowledge from experience and connecting theory to practice. They also share some overlap with some aspects of the transcendental movement, with writers like Ralph Waldo Emmerson who emphasized bringing ethical aspirations into everyday life.

Yet what set Geddes, Addams, and Du Bois apart (even if in quite different ways) is their marginalized professional status in their own time and in the development of the disciplines related to their practices. That is, because they could be considered outsiders due to their identities and/or their ideas (to different extents), their approaches often operated outside the formations of mainstream disciplinary and institutional practices during their lifetimes or in the years after. In many cases, their unique perspectives are directly a result of their struggles against dominant practices of their time, to create an approach of social study and practice otherwise. Indeed, it is only in recent decades that their work is being discovered

---

[13] See, for instance, what Arturo Escobar describes as "the limits of social theory" which—even today, as a result of the founding traditions of professional academic disciplines—remains trapped in many dualisms, including the separation of subject and object. Arturo Escobar, *Designs for the Pluriverse: Radical Interdependence, Autonomy, and the Making of Worlds* (Duke University Press, 2018), pages 97–100.

anew in a range of fields, such as sociology. Rather than focus primarily on their relationship to disciplines, however, the coming chapters look to how they can be seen as portraying a particular spirit, which placed great importance in attending to and creating forms of *the social*.

This unique emphasis on remaking the social is one major way in which the issue of design(ing) is relevant to the work of Geddes, Addams, and Du Bois. Part Two will argue that it is worthwhile—as a model for designing, social thinking, and analysis today—to view them as activists and scholar-practitioners who fused together a sensibility to designing or making and social imagination, as they co-created a variety of social and spatial interventions. In this context, they offer foundations for reflective action, toward the possibility of cultivating a social imagination fused with capacities to design and enact new institutions and initiatives. They also offer inspiration for reimagining designing today, especially in how they used design capacities to develop new social practices, spaces, and organizations that differed from the prevailing thinking of their time.

The three chapters in Part Two are accordingly structured to both (1) describe some of the context of their projects and thinking—in terms of how key social issues in the era of Geddes, Addams, and Du Bois are relevant to our own—and (2) explore key concepts, strategies, and approaches of their work, as they relate to possibilities for thought and action in the present. Each of the three chapters in this part of the book is organized to offer an opening vignette, introduce the social context of each thinker, and describe how this context is relevant for today. Then, they address the general approach of the thinker, and finally explore two or three key themes, with light linking back to thought and action in the present before returning in some way to the opening vignette. In this sense the chapters do not outline a purely chronological lineage, from the late 1800s to the twenty-first century, but rather they seek to uncover traces and potentials of Geddes, Addams, and Du Bois in contemporary moments. It is overall an attempt to put their work into relation with more recent theories and practices—toward what design and social thought are capable of becoming now.

3   Patrick Geddes: Thinking Ecologically

Vacant land has become a major characteristic of urban space today. Walking through the city, vacant land might be encountered as cracks in the order of things—a window into other forms of life beyond the steel and concrete of major population centers today. Sometimes vacant land is abandoned and strewn with trash, and other times it is fenced-off from the rest of the city to keep people out as a private property owner or municipality decides what to do with the space.

I first began to pay attention to vacant land walking through the Rockaways in New York City after Hurricane Sandy in 2012. As a low-lying area at the Southeast edge of the city that can take more than ninety minutes to reach by subway, the area named the Rockaways is far removed from the dense city blocks and towering skyscrapers of Manhattan. While it was once mostly a summer beach retreat from the city in the early days of New York, it later came to be series of neighborhoods along the peninsula—with a diverse mix of housing and people. The built environment is varied, including large city public housing complexes, smaller apartment buildings, and multi-million-dollar single-family homes.

Walking in various parts of the Rockaways in the year after the hurricane, one would encounter land that had been inundated with water and wind during the storm. This included public and private land—apartment buildings destroyed or boarded up, stretches of open space strewn with rubble. Vacant land was not only an issue because of a storm. The storm revealed a much larger condition of uneven urban development today, where places that are closer to wealth and power see faster recovery, stronger political representation, and more rapid economic investment in general. There had, indeed, been a larger social and political storm brewing for decades which led to vacant land and disinvestment scattered across the city.[1]

Just before Hurricane Sandy, in 2011, a New Yorker created a spreadsheet of vacant land based on city records and found that there were at least 596 acres of publicly owned vacant land in Brooklyn alone.[2] On further investigation, most this land had been vacant for years, or even decades. And it was not all vacant by accident. Much of the vacant land was acquired by the city throughout the twentieth century, for what were supposed to be large-scale Urban Renewal plans—grand visions of affordable housing, open space, community centers, and more. While funding was available to demolish existing structures—and subsequently displace poor, Black, working-class, or immigrant residents—the money to finance the construction phase never fully materialized. By the 1970s, financial crisis in New York City and nationally made it even less likely that development would happen. The population declined, and the city started fencing the land to prevent people from gathering, selling illegal drugs, or dumping trash. Municipal government slashed city services, using a strategy of "planned shrinkage" in some neighborhoods, where among other things, they shut down key infrastructure including, subways, fire houses,

---

[1] Krasny and Tidball explain how, although disasters do come in the form of weather-related events, they also take the form of social, political, and economic disinvestment and catastrophe: Marianne Krasny and Keith Tidball, *Civic Ecology: Adaptation and Transformation from the Ground Up* (MIT Press, 2015).

[2] Paula Z. Segal, "Room to Grow Something," in Ron Shiffman, Rick Bell, Lance Jay Brown, and Lynne Elizabeth (editors), *Beyond Zuccotti Park: Freedom of Assembly and the Occupation of Public Space* (New Village Press, 2012), pages 156–169.

and schools. This led to even more vacant land after structures burned to the ground.[3]

In early twenty-first-century New York, as the population was on the rise again and property values were surging, the public and private vacant land was now an asset and opportunity for profit. That is, it was no longer a sign of decay, but it was seen as a financial opportunity. Even still, pockets of vacancy persisted as local markets fluctuated. In other cities, vacant land continues to be a powerful symbol of deindustrialization that occurred in the United States in the end of the twentieth century. Most striking of course is the city of Detroit, where there were more than twenty-five acres of vacant land in 2011, which, when combined, is larger than the land area of the entire borough of Manhattan.

In one sense it is easy to pass vacant land by, especially if it is a fenced-off and taken-for-granted sight in everyday routines. In the context of a city like New York, whose growth was fueled by speculative real estate in the early twenty-first century, the land may seem out of reach. Alternatively, in the context of large-scale disinvestment and decline, evident in New York in the 1970s or Detroit in the early twenty-first century, it is part of the normal everyday experience of the city. But in both contexts, vacant land is also potentially a chance to encounter other species of living plant and animal life—no matter how "invasive" or weed-like these species may be. Vacant land is ultimately a connection to ecologies that might otherwise be paved over and inaccessible beneath massive human-made buildings and infrastructures. It is potentially a window into the land beneath the built environment, beyond the routines of everyday life, the grind of the subway, and the hardness of concrete.

---

[3] This history was explored in a project of 596 Acres in New York City, called Urban Reviewer, which created the first digital publicly accessible map of urban renewal plans in the city, in addition to a series of publications and exhibitions about Urban Renewal (archived at: www.urbanreviewer.org). Deborah and Rodrick Wallace tell the story of "planned shrinkage" across New York and nationally in their compelling history: Deborah Wallace and Rodrick Wallace, *Plague on All Your Houses: How New York Was Burned Down and National Health Crumbled* (Verso, 1998).

But what is *vacant* land in the first place? Land only becomes vacant after it has been considered part of municipal, state, or national boundaries. It is vacant because it is either not legally occupied, or has not been formally built upon, within the logic of municipal governance and capitalism. From a social-historical view it is clear that vacant land is not a blank slate, but a window into the past and present of a particular place. That is, localized or widespread vacant land points to the dynamic interactions between human settlement and the more-than-human ecologies that such settlements require. It also tells a story of a regional context and ecology that supports human life—traces of what existed before human settlement or colonization, and may continue to persist in spite of, or in some cases because of, human intervention.

By exposing the city as a process in-the-making, revealing that which has "not yet" been developed or that which is "returning to nature" before our eyes, vacant land can spark a new social imagination. While some claim this as an opportunity for financial profit, it is also an opportunity to grow something beyond economic value alone. Vacant land in this sense is potentially an opening within the taken-for-granted social-spatial reality we inhabit, where the legacies of human intervention can be traced, new alliances can be forged, and alternatives tried out. This sort of action also requires deliberation and reflection.

Seeing vacant land as a possibility for community and relationship (not just a blank slate for profit) requires a deeper sense of social imagination. But how might this imagination begin? How can deeper engagements with the surrounding unfinished or left-behind environments be catalysts for creating more human and ecological flourishing? How is it possible to see gaps, contradictions, openings in the social and spatial order of things as an opportunity to make new worlds?

In some ways these questions, about how urban society might be remade today, from within cracks and breaks within the prevailing order, require a social-historical outlook. The urban condition today did not appear overnight, but it is part of a story that began with the rise of industrial capitalism that was also being studied by early sociologists and social scientists. This is why the chapter looks to the life, projects, and context of early sociologist, planner, and ecologist, Patrick Geddes who began his work in the late 1800s.

Overall, Geddes' work offers both a historical context of the present urban-ecological condition and also a series of relevant designs, interventions, practices, and theories by which he tried to engage with the realities of his time. What is perhaps most significant is his praxis of thinking *and* designing—the process through which Geddes sought both *to clarify and to transform social reality*—as he formed a unique way of proceeding in the midst of a rapidly shifting and urbanizing society. After exploring the context in which Geddes practiced, his general approach, and the current relevance of these issues in the next section, the final three sections explore central strategies and ideas from his work, with connections to design and social thought today.

URBANIZATION AND THE ENVIRONMENT, THEN AND NOW

Patrick Geddes was born in 1854. He grew up in Perthshire, Scotland where he experienced a wide range of ecological terrains, from the River Tay basin to mountainous Southern Highlands and agricultural land. He would go on long walks in the Perthshire countryside with his father, collecting and studying plants. "I grew up in a garden," Geddes once said about his childhood.[4] Although he never liked exams, he loved learning and would go on to study under prominent biologist T.H. Huxley. In 1879, the British Association for the Advancement of Science assigned him to study botany in Mexico.

While in Mexico, Geddes went blind due to an illness. Although the blindness was only temporary, this experience was profound for Geddes. His work had been focused on scientific observation of the world, but in his illness, when he could no longer see through a microscope, he turned inward—reflecting on his relationships to the organisms he studies, their relationships to

[4] Patrick Geddes Centre, "Rediscovering Geddes," accessed at: https://www.patrickgeddescentre.org.uk/patrick-geddes/

each other, and the relationship between individuals, groups, and their wider environment. This time marked a transition from study of biological sciences toward more transdisciplinary thinking about organisms, environments, and human settlements. Geddes explained the key insight this way: "If a creature survives best in an environment most suited to it, then surely so do humans. And as humans have more of an ability to shape their own environment than most of the rest of nature, then shouldn't we be doing so to bring maximum stimuli to both body and mind?"[5] As he began to study and work across disciplines, he sought to make connections that would be useful for intervening in human environments, rather than only accumulating knowledge within a particular field. For this reason, in addition to his work in biology, Geddes is today considered an important founding voice in sociology, town planning, and educational philosophy.[6]

What makes his thinking and practice particularly important is that his work was in direct response to a central issue of his time—the challenge of unevenly advancing urbanization and industrialization, which was beginning to show very noticeable human and environmental impacts. He, like many others of his time, was inspired to understand and act in a context of industrial capitalism that was fundamentally reorganizing people's relationship to labor, the land, and each other. What exactly was Geddes witnessing? And how were these relationships being remade in the wake of industrialization?

In the mid-to-late 1800s, the territories near Geddes were becoming some of the most urbanized and industrialized areas in the world. Early social researchers and commentators began to explore the implications of this emerging society. In particular,

---

[5] Malcolm Tait, "A Man of All Reason," *Discover: A Magazine of the National Library of Scotland*, issue 11, Spring 2009, pages 22–24.

[6] For instance, Maggie Studholme retrospectively describes Geddes as a founder of environmental sociology. On Geddes' praxis, she further comments "All things biological and social, natural and cultural, scientific and artistic, theoretical and practical, were, for him, interlinked in basic and essential ways." Maggie Studholme, "Patrick Geddes: Founder of Environmental Sociology," *The Sociological Review*, volume 55, issue 3, 2007, page 453.

Friedrich Engels offered a number of reflections on the impacts of industrialization. He wrote a series of articles based on his observations that were published as an 1845 book, *The Condition of the Working Class in England*, where he described both the human and the environmental impacts of industrialization across England.

Engels primarily notices the stark unevenness of urbanization, where factory workers live in densely populated, inhumane, and poor-quality environments where people are dying of starvation and illness. The plight of workers was more or less out of sight from the wealthy factory owners who were living in increasingly large and lavish homes on the other side of town. In the slums of British cities Engels notes how "The streets are generally unpaved, rough, dirty, filled with vegetable and animal refuse, without sewers or gutters, but supplied with foul, stagnant pools instead. Moreover, ventilation is impeded by the bad, confused method of building of the whole quarter, and since many human beings here live crowded into a small space."[7] Dwellings in these slums were either potentially dangerous to live in, or so poorly maintained that they had been abandoned and were unfit for human dwelling. In London, there were increasing numbers of houseless people, and even the growing "refuges for the houseless" were becoming overcrowded. In Edinburgh, Engels notes the concern of the living conditions that leave a visitor alarmed at the "shocking stench, with filth and swarms of vermin."[8]

While industrialization created the conditions for precarious housing, the instability was directly related to of the impact of industrialization on the environment. In one section of *The Condition of the Working Class in England*, Engels details the relationship between workers, housing, and the environment along the River Irk in Manchester. Looking down from the Ducie Bridge, Engels describes looking upon "piles of debris, the refuse, filth, and offal from the courts on the steep left bank; here each house is packed close behind its neighbor and a piece of each

[7] Friedrich Engels, *The Condition of the Working Class in England* (Allen & Unwin, 1943 reprint), page 26.
[8] Engels, page 35.

is visible, all black, smoky, crumbling, ancient, with broken panes and window- frames. The background is furnished by old barrack-factory buildings."[9] The river itself had been extremely polluted:

> At the bottom flows, or rather stagnates, the Irk, a narrow, coal-black, foul-smelling stream, full of debris and refuse, which it deposits on the shallower right bank. In dry weather, a long string of the most disgusting, blackish-green, slime pools are left standing on this bank, from the depths of which bubbles of miasmatic gas constantly arise 40 or 50 feet above the surface of the stream.[10]

The contamination of the river, a combination of sewage and waste from industry, was part of the workers' everyday living environment.

For Engels, and others writing in this time, the human and environmental effects of industrialization were deeply concerning, and even shocking. This is because such environmental devastation and human suffering had advanced quickly and was increasingly widespread. In addition to observing the patterns of urban industrialization, Engels and others also analyzed how and why cities were evolving in this age.[11] Building on this analysis, it was becoming clear to some that this sort of neighborhood was not a symptom or external effect of capitalist industrialization; it was inherent to how the system functioned.

In in this context, Patrick Geddes saw his theory and practice to be a fundamental critique of the modern industrial order. He was especially skeptical of the emerging culture of individualism and emphasis on economic progress above all else. He wrote of industrialization as an "organized sacrifice of men to machinery," with a tendency of "dissipating the national store of energies

---

[9] Engels, page 50.

[10] Engels, pages 49–50.

[11] Steven Marcus, "Reading the Illegible," in H. J. Dyos and Michael Wolff (editors), *The Victorian City: Images and Realities*, volume 2 (Routledge & Kegan Paul, 1973), pages 257–276.

for individual gain."[12] In particular, Geddes hoped to awaken a consciousness about the interconnection of humans with plants and wider living ecologies:

> By leaves we live. Some people have strange ideas that they live by money. They think energy is generated by the circulation of coins. But the world is mainly a vast leaf-colony, growing on and forming a leafy soil, not a mere mineral mass: and we live not by the jingling of our coins, but by the fullness of our harvests.[13]

In this spirit, Geddes was less interested in negative critique than in trying to clarify emerging conditions in order to discern opportunities for interventions that might shape the evolution of society—toward new relations with the ecologies of the places where he worked.

While many political reformers of his day "looked back to the medieval period as a golden age that was to be reestablished," Geddes saw an opening in present conditions to bring about "an improvement in people's relation to nature and to temporal power though a revitalized sense of community."[14] Geddes thought that the industrial capitalist system had an over-focus on maximizing profit, which he believed was undermining community solidarity and leading to environmental degradation. He saw a need for designs and interventions that would remake the social—as part of a larger vision for societal "reconstruction, re-education, and renewal" that builds on a "new vitalism" where there could be "full development

---

[12] Patrick Geddes, "The Twofold Aspect of the Industrial Age: Paleotechnic and Neotechnic," *The Town Planning Review*, volume 3, issue 3, 1912, pages 176–187. For context on Geddes' critique of the industrial social order also see, for example: Peter Ryley, *Making Another World Possible: Anarchism, Anti-Capitalism, and Ecology in Late 19th and Early 20th Century Britain* (Bloomsbury, 2013).

[13] Patrick Geddes, *Cities in Evolution* (Williams & Norgate, 1949), pages 216–217.

[14] John Scott and Ray Bromley, *Envisioning Sociology: Victor Branford, Patrick Geddes and the Quest for Social Reconstruction* (State University of New York Press, 2013), page 91.

of the civic qualities of life, personality, citizenship, community and collective endeavor."[15] He positioned the work of sociology and social thought in this moment as means to build coalitions for action from within a fragmented society. For Geddes, the goal of social thought was therefore to "combine the intellectual role of understanding with the energizing role of statesman or educator, mobilizing human energies in the pursuit of social ideals."[16] Rather than explain social reality, his speculative diagrams and theories showed what could be or what ought to be through future action.

***

Today, the issues Geddes was working on have been magnified. The urban ecological crisis has deepened, combined with advancing social fragmentation and marginalization, and is beginning to undermine the very possibility of human society. Precarious urban housing is a global phenomenon. Uneven development leaves some areas vacant or abandoned, while others see unprecedented real estate speculation. Scholars of "planetary urbanization" suggest that there is no place on the Earth that has not been touched by the reach of urbanization.[17] Geologists and social theorists now explain that we live in the era of the Anthropocene, where human activities are the dominant influence on the Earth's atmosphere, air, land, and water. Remaking society, and especially its relationship to the environment, no longer seems like a choice. Rather, it is a moral imperative brought on by the threat of an impending, and already underway, global mass extinction.[18]

Indeed, the ecological devastation of industrializing Manchester is now global. It is often the poorest regions and countries, including those who have been historically subjugated under colonization or marginalized in global economic systems, that feel the worst impacts of climate disruptions and environmental

---

[15] Scott and Bromley, page 92.

[16] Scott and Bromley, page 92.

[17] See, for example: Neil Brenner, "Theses on Urbanization," *Public Culture*, volume 25, issue 1, 2013, pages 85–114.

[18] Elizabeth Kolbert, *The Sixth Extinction: An Unnatural History* (Henry Holt and Company, 2014).

degradation. Although disasters can bring international attention to the uneven impacts of this environmental suffering, action is constrained because the violence of environmental crises, from pollution of the air and water to flooding and drought, are often slower and more difficult to see.[19]

Overall, while different from the 1800s, the crisis in the twenty-first century has roots in the intertwined periods of colonization and industrialization, where a Western Scientific Worldview began to be exported around the world.[20] Settlers conquered the lands of indigenous peoples, in the name of expanding the frontiers of European economies and societies, relying on increasingly expansive global networks of resource extraction, labor exploitation, manufacturing, and distribution—often leaving unprecedented human and ecological destruction in their wake.[21] Indeed, central to the project of colonization was the replacement of native peoples and culture with a logic of extraction and exploitation to supply a global economy and accumulate wealth. Along with the genocide of indigenous peoples came a loss of a connections between humans and wider living ecologies. In contrast, being native involves a sense of reciprocity and care for the land that is not present in the settler colonial world view. As plant scientist and Indigenous author Robin Wall Kimmerer describes, "For all of us, becoming indigenous to a place means living as if your children's future mattered, to take care of the land as if our lives, both material and spiritual, depended on it … To be native to a place we must learn to speak its language."[22]

[19] Rob Nixon, *Slow Violence and the Environmentalism of the Poor* (Harvard University Press, 2013).

[20] Heather Davis and Zoe Todd, "On the Importance of a Date, or, Decolonizing the Anthropocene," *ACME: An International Journal for Critical Geographies*, volume 16, issue 4, 2017, 761–780.

[21] On the historical relationships between industrialization, colonization, and the environment up to the twenty-first century in his book, see, for example: John Bellamy Foster, *The Vulnerable Planet: A Short Economic History of the Environment* (Monthly Review Press, 1999).

[22] Robin Wall Kimmerer, *Braiding Sweetgrass: Indigenous Wisdom, Scientific Knowledge, and the Teachings of Plants* (Milkweed Editions, 2013), pages 9 and 48.

Now, more than ever, from within the widespread alienation of the contemporary city, it seems important to reimagine, or remember, what it means to belong to a place. How might people who have inherited the cultural legacy of colonization—especially individualism and disconnection from the surrounding environment—begin the work of reconnecting to the land, repairing harm, and ultimately remaking urban society? There are traces of this kind of project, and inspiration for action today, in the work of Patrick Geddes.

ACTING WHERE YOU ARE

The projects that Geddes initiated had a philosophy of *learning by doing*, which was central to most of his work. He became known for the phrases "by living we learn" and "by creating we think." These expressions underscore that Geddes saw his own interventions in the world to be a form of reflection. He saw that as we act within our particular social and ecological reality we develop more knowledge, even if this is not a formalized academic knowledge. Some twenty-first century observers explain that Geddes "saw learning not simply as an end in itself, but that through learning/education social transformation can and perhaps should occur." This was driven by a lifelong commitment in his projects that were "applying learning to action and learning from action," and it involved a disposition he cultivated "to embrace new knowledge and experiences, to learn from these, and then to inform and lead others through example and teaching."[23]

Even though Geddes witnessed the beginning of social science professions that aimed to codify knowledge into academic theory for specialized fields (which arguably is even more pervasive today), he countered this with an ongoing experiential approach to learning and practice. That is, experience in one project could inform how to approach the next project differently, and also potentially catalyze a reevaluation of established academic theo-

[23] Peter Higgins and Robbie Nicol, "Sir Patrick Geddes: 'Vivendo Discimus'—By Living We Learn," in Thomas E. Smith and Clifford E. Knapp (editors), *Sourcebook of Experiential Education: Key Thinkers and Their Contributions* (Taylor & Francis, 2010), page 35.

ries. This approach informed how he sought to engage other people in developing new sensibilities toward the problems of his day—not by collecting and analyzing data or refining a professional practice, but by acting in his local environment.

One especially powerful current that ran throughout the social thought and action of Geddes was the role of gardens and gardening, as a way of understanding how urbanization ought to happen. That is, people are part of a living ecology of life that they can care for, shape, and transform as a gardener would—even as the context transforms the garden and the gardener. In other words, the garden was not just a metaphor. While some social scientists in the early twentieth century were beginning to use ecology as a metaphor for urban space, the ecological thinking and sensibility of Geddes viewed ecology as a physical and inescapable reality of human settlements. The act of gardening—in *both* literal *and* figurative sense—was therefore a way of acting from where we are. It was a way of beginning to be acquainted with the living urban ecological context.

This was a philosophy that guided his writing and the actions he took throughout his personal and professional life. Early in his career, after getting a job at Edinburgh University, Geddes moved to the Old Town of Edinburgh. The area was increasingly considered a slum as more wealthy citizens moved out, leaving dilapidated housing and poor neighborhood sanitation. He organized neighbors to make gradual improvements to housing, and also develop public open spaces and gardens on previously vacant land.

In the midst of abandoned spaces in the Old Town, he imagined, with his new neighbors, the transformation of seventy-five plots into a network of gardens, maintained by voluntary associations of local residents and school children. These interventions involved coordination not only on the ground, but also on the level of municipal governance through an Open Spaces Committee. By the early twentieth century, nearly a dozen of these spaces had been created and were being actively managed.

What was significant about these gardens, for Geddes, was that they were a network of connective tissue that linked together streets and surrounding areas, and they were ultimately a window into wider regional ecologies. Garden design focused not only on exotic plants or aesthetic design, but rather on the range of species

FIGURE 3.1 King Wall Garden, Johnston Terrace (before).

Source: Centre for Research Collections, University of Edinburgh (Catalog Number: Coll-1167/B/27/10/9).

that were native to the area—so that people could reconnect with the regional ecologies. These were also meant to be open and welcoming spaces that people could stop by for a few moments

FIGURE 3.2 King Wall Garden, Johnston Terrace (after).

Source: Centre for Research Collections, University of Edinburgh (Catalog Number: Coll-1167/B/27/10/5).

or spend longer periods of time. Formal and informal programs in the garden spaces brought people together for various forms of art and education—from plant science observation to music, theatre, sculpture, pottery, and dance.[24] Historical photos of the garden, which were collected for a 1904 collaborative exhibition (Figures 3.1 and 3.2), show the transformation of a vacant plot into a community and ecological space in Edinburgh, as part of a larger vision for civic transformation.

The gardens were connected to a wider theory of social action and intervention. Geddes believed that that participating in this sort of project was both a practical skill and a way for people to familiarize themselves with the regional history, culture, and biology,

---

[24] Sofia Leonard, "Patrick Geddes and the Network of Gardens in the Old Town of Edinburgh," Talk Presented at the Edinburgh International Festival, 2007, accessed at Patrick Geddes Trust, accessed at: http://www.patrickgeddestrust.co.uk/articlespapers.htm

including possibilities for social action. The goal of the garden designs was to create opportunities for *sympathetic contact with life* and develop communities of people who would encourage each other to participate in their local political and ecological context.[25]

For Geddes, social change was not only a matter of material or technological transformations, it was also profoundly spiritual and cultural. It was not so much that the individual, cultural, or community level was opposed to larger systemic economic and policy changes. Rather he saw that spiritual and cultural renewal in specific interventions could be seen as working in-tandem with more macro-level systemic changes—as both a catalyst and process for bringing about wider transformations in society.[26] The trick was in learning to see beyond the constraining paradigms of industrialism—noticing how everyday actions can reverberate within and across larger global systems.

In this sense, the garden was also a way in which people could break out of the isolation, individualism, or alienation of industrial capitalist society. The exercise of body and mind through community participation was both an end in itself and a means through which people realized their potential for acting. This is why interventions had to involve some form of education and mutual learning. Intellectual, academic, or technical expertise about neighborhood revitalization needed to be brought into conversation with experiential knowledge from people's lives.

The garden was an ideal place for this mingling of knowledges because it brought people's lived experience and desires together with both scientific observation and creativity. It was a place that was meant to be accessible to all, to develop new

[25] Catherine Ward Thompson notes this philosophy in his contributions to designs for the zoological park in Edinburgh, where he saw the layout and physical design as way to create opportunities for active learning and engagement, not just passive observation. Catherine Ward Thompson, "Patrick Geddes and the Edinburgh Zoological Garden," *Landscape Journal*, volume 25, issue 1, 2006, pages 80–93.

[26] Volker Welter explores the kind of vitalism that underlined Geddes' inventive combination living ecologies and social and political organization of society. That is, for Geddes, intentional transformations of society require working with a living social-ecological context. Volker Welter, *Biopolis: Patrick Geddes and the City of Life* (MIT Press, 2002).

sensibilities and ways of relating to the world, regardless of a person's ability, age, or prior knowledge. This is why Geddes would come to define the iterative process of reflection and social action as cultivation—an evolving process that involves working with the life force of communities and places. At the core of such a process was advancing an ethos of action and reciprocity that could be nourished into a new civic awakening.[27]

Overall, the role of thinking and learning is not necessarily in dissecting social realities, mastering a particular approach, or mobilizing some institutional intervention on a large scale. Instead, Geddes emphasizes the possibility of generating useful or transformative knowledge from local actions. This may mean, for instance, learning from the implicit knowledges of communities that are already doing something to make alternatives to existing conditions, even if it is not understood by conventional systems of knowledge. In other words, rather than ceding reflective capacities to formalized schooling system or professional disciplines, reflection ought to be embedded within process of acting in the world—as a way of living.[28] As some of the projects Geddes initiated indicate, rooting thinking in local places can also be a means to begin investigating the relationship of a specific site to larger regional and global forces. How this sort of approach might come about is the subject of the next section.

DEVELOPING AN ECOLOGICAL OUTLOOK

Studying the generation of planners and designers in his time, Geddes noticed a narrow focus. Their end goal was always

[27] He describes his cultural and systems-oriented approach to personal and social change, drawing a connection between culture and the verb "to cultivate" in a lecture published in an updated (1949) edition of *Cities in Evolution*. Patrick Geddes, "Geddes' Final Dundee Lecture: A Botanist Looks at the World," in *Cities in Evolution* (Williams & Norgate, 1949), pages 214–230.

[28] A perhaps more radical parallel to this project today be seen more recent efforts that have emerged in the Global South. See, for example: Madhu Suri Prakash and Gustavo Esteva, *Escaping Education: Living as Learning Within Grassroots Cultures* (Peter Lang, 1998).

immediately practical: the creation of new forms, buildings, streets, or neighborhoods. Geddes foresaw that the social reality of advancing urbanization—in which cities were increasingly interconnected to each other and to their wider regions—would make this kind of narrow technical focus ineffective. He coined the term *conurbation* to describe this condition of extended urban areas. Although he saw that city-regions were growing larger and more interconnected, Geddes also thought that this expanding urbanization had the effect of making people's outlook on life smaller—as they might come to feel unable to influence increasingly large social forces that seem to take on a momentum of their own. This was because although the emerging technological expertise of urban industrialization created many spaces and forms at a rapid pace, it neglected complexities and possibilities of interconnected social and ecological life on Earth. A society as disconnected from wider living ecologies, and the flow of life itself, came to seem as if it was natural in the urban industrial order.[29]

What was to be done about the human and ecological crisis facing these expanding urban regions in the wake of the industrial revolution? While early social reformers and town planners were beginning to refine their profession, Geddes believed planning itself was the problem. That is, this condition does not simply require better professional design and planning, but rather a broader "constructive effort" and "civic awakening."[30] Interventions are therefore are not only successful because of technical knowledge, expertise, or communication. Those seeking to intervene ought to, "above all things, seek to enter into the spirit of our city, its historic essence and continuous life," such that "design will thus express, stimulate, and develop its highest possibility, and so deal all the more effectively with its material and fundamental needs."[31]

For Geddes, dealing with the material and fundamental needs of the urban crisis requires that those interested in redesigning or

---

[29] Pierre Chabard, "Patrick Geddes and *Cities in Evolution*: The Writing and the Readings of an Intempestive Classic," in Christian Hermansen Cordua (editor), *Manifestos and Transformations in the Early Modernist City* (Routledge, 2016), page 175.

[30] Patrick Geddes, *Cities in Evolution* (Williams & Norgate, 1915), page v.

[31] Geddes, *Cities in Evolution*, page vi.

intervening must participate in the "collective soul" of a place, to promote the renewal of civic energies from within. It's not about bringing an imagination to a community from the outside, but of inspiring and fueling the social imagination of people from within communities, as a neighbor, in ways that move toward the creation of a better city and society. That is, design ought to be both grounded in social realities and also oriented toward ideals that might be realized. This better, more ideal city, or what Geddes refers to as Eutopia in his book *Cities in Evolution*, "lies in the city around us; and it must be planned and realized, here or nowhere, but us as its citizens—each a citizen of both the actual and ideal city seen increasingly as one."[32]

In the face of human suffering and environmental catastrophe, governments and specialists tend to treat isolated symptoms, but the larger question for Geddes is always how to step back from the immediate problem and design conditions that facilitate human and ecological flourishing. This requires a more holistic or integrated conception of the problem. While it may be tempting to view social "thought" as separate from larger flows of life on Earth, Geddes suggests that the process of thinking is, in fact, part of an ecology of life. The writings and visuals he produced did not only present analysis or description, but also a "call to action" to get to know life beyond its human-centric industrial forms.[33] Seeing "thought" as a relational intervention in this way changes the way we ought to approach thinking.[34]

Early design and social science professions had a reluctance to engage with actually existing on-the-ground conditions in this way. On the one hand, some thought themselves to be

[32] Geddes, *Cities in Evolution*, page vii.

[33] For example, in his "notion of life" diagram which suggested theories and approaches oriented toward "the improvement of the human condition." Welter, pages 31–32.

[34] In some ways, this resonates with the argument Kohn has made more recently, about how human thought participates in the significations made by other forms of life: Eduardo Kohn, *How Forests Think: Toward an Anthropology beyond the Human* (University of California Press, 2013).

"practical," and therefore were not in need of too much deliberate reflection. On the other hand, those who were theorizing were increasingly abstracting thought outside from the flows of human and ecological world. For example, Geddes argued that sociologists and designers could come together in an effort to explore, with residents, what they are thinking about their daily existence and challenges. In other words, the way that most people live can be quite different from what either practical-minded design or conventional academic theory portrays. As such, dialogue and exchange outside of academia is of critical importance.[35]

Accordingly, Geddes did not so much want to advance a professional theory of town planning, but rather to *popularize* planning and design. For him, this involves increasing partici-pation and engagement with wider publics and ecologies. The larger outlook and potential of planning—to describe a place in diagrams, images, and representations that connect the everyday to wider social ecological contexts—is a kind of imagination that should be accessible to the people who already live in the place that is being planned. How can this sort of wider outlook be encouraged? For Geddes it is partly by curating different ways of seeing of the city—in diverse images, locations, activi-ties and processes—that encourage people to engage with each other and their environment anew. One project that sought to symbolically embody and promote this ecological thinking, and a renewed social imagination, was the Outlook Tower in Edin-burgh, Scotland.

The Outlook Tower building (shown in Figure 3.3) was origi-nally built in the 1830s. Patrick Geddes bought it in the 1890s with plans to turn the tower into a public space to advance urban study and action. He intentionally redesigned the Outlook Tower interior with an immersive participant experience in mind. The curation of materials on each floor (shown in Figures 3.4 and 3.5) was intended to bring visitors from the global to the local so

---

[35] A line of thought Geddes pursues, especially on pages 90–92 in: Geddes, *Cities in Evolution.*

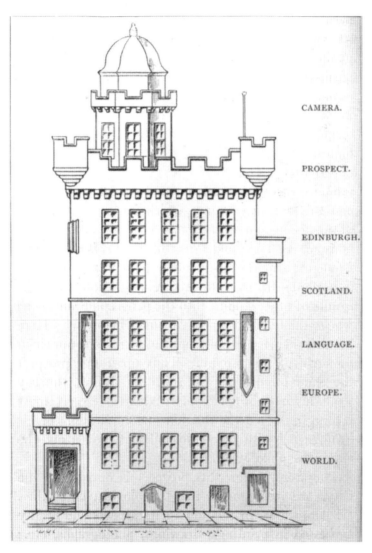

FIGURE 3.3 Outlook Tower plan.

Source: Patrick Geddes, *Cities in Evolution* (Williams & Norgate, 1915).

FIGURE 3.4 The Outlook Tower Interior—Edinburgh Room, Southwest Corner.

Source: Centre for Research Collections, University of Edinburgh (Catalog Number: Coll-1167/B/27/24/1).

FIGURE 3.5 The Outlook Tower Interior—Edinburgh Room, Mural.

Source: Centre for Research Collections, University of Edinburgh (Catalog Number: Coll-1167/B/23/13).

that they could visualize how built settlements are intertwined with regional ecologies, and to explore the past, present, and possible futures of their own local communities.

For its physical design, the Outlook Tower was a series of levels that begin on the ground floor with global events, and became increasingly local. From the ground floor up, the floors deal respectively with world, Europe, language, Scotland, and Edinburgh. Thus, while the lower floors told a story of world history and how Edinburgh resonated with this global history, the more local floors featured practical issues being faced by the city in the present. These exhibitions—with images, artifacts, and documents—were meant to be accessible to a wide audience, but also contain more detail for those with some prior background. There were also meeting rooms formal programs and informal conversation.[36]

The location of the Outlook Tower was important because on the top floor promontory overlooked the city and the location of the built environment within the wider region. Overall, the Outlook Tower did not attempt to present a finished history; rather, it integrated multiple disciplines and speculative designs with the clear intent to spark people's imagination. It sought to position people in the historical context of their particular place, where "Past and present were also shown presenting the problem of the city's opening future."[37]

Geddes explains that the Outlook Tower was conceived as a "Civic Observatory and Laboratory together—the type of institution needed … in every city, with its effort towards *correlation of thought and action, science and practice, sociology and*

---

[36] Geddes, *Cities in Evolution*, page 324.

[37] Geddes, *Cities in Evolution*, page 256. This objective of positioning also resonates with the potential for non-experts to identity larger patterns in their surroundings and address complex design problems: Christopher Alexander, Sara Ishikawa, Murray Silverstein, Max Jacobson, Ingrid Fiksdahl-King, and Shlomo Angel, *A Pattern Language: Towns, Buildings, Construction* (Oxford University Press, 1977).

morals."[38] In everyday life, people can have a narrow outlook, ceasing to see the features of local environments, but by immersing in curated events, programs and spaces, it is possible to learn to observe the social and ecological context of dwelling in a new way.[39] Accordingly, the professionalization of observation in the sciences only makes the problems of industrial society worse because it further alienates people from this basic process of relating to actually existing living ecologies.

The kind of observation Geddes promoted was oriented toward action, encouraging people to understand the urban ecological context within which interventions could or should be made. In seeking to build a synthesis among individual lived experience, shared spaces, and the larger regional whole, the Outlook Tower goes beyond the professionalization of design or the taken-for-granted elements of everyday life: "For there is a larger view of Nature and Life, a rebuilding of analyses into Synthesis, an integration of many solitary experiences into a larger experience, an exchange of the narrow window of the individual outlook for the open tower which overlooks the college and city."[40]

Overall, the whole point of the Outlook Tower was to demonstrate the *need to design social interventions that are deeply rooted in social and ecological realities.* That is, it points toward social thinking, designing, and imagining that is informed by concrete knowledge of conditions on the ground. Such a model

[38] Geddes, *Cities in Evolution*, page 287, emphasis added. On the same page he follows up with the questions: "Can we review the civic activities of the past, the needs of the present, the possibilities of the future, towards worthy Civic Activities of our own? May social feeling and reasoned design find expression in some great re-orchestration of all the industries and arts ...? How, in short, is Civic Aspiration to be developed, guided, applied to the needed Art of City-making, which has ever been implied in Citizenship?"

[39] This resonates with Heidegger's critique of non-places in modernity that do not facilitate a meaningful orientation to a wider world, a tendency that has only accelerated in the wake of post- or super-modernity: Martin Heidegger, "Building Dwelling Thinking," in Albert Hofstadter (translator), *Poetry, Language, Thought* (HarperCollins, 1971), pages 143–159.

[40] Patrick Geddes, "The Sociology of Autumn," *The Evergreen: A Northern Seasonal*, volume 2, 1895, pages 27–38.

conceives of interventions into the social fabric as part of a process of developing wider public capacities for thought and action—rather than forcing plans on to the public.

As more recent scholars explain, summarizing the relevance of the Outlook Tower, "With the Outlook Tower, Geddes facilitated a view of the city of Edinburgh surveyed within its historical and geographic context, so that visitors could comprehend it as a synthesis of interrelated systems. It provided the construct through which to reacquaint the visitor with her/his role as a citizen and to advocate for social wellbeing and city betterment."[41] The Outlook Tower was also connected to the core of Geddes' approach—where thinking and reflection are essential to an unfolding process of action. That is, reflection itself is a form of intervention, which then informs other actions.

A central insight of the Outlook Tower was the need to catalyze new forms of reflection on the social, historical, and regional context of places and communities. This is of crucial importance today. The reality of uneven urbanization that neglects or disadvantages certain neighborhoods over others persists. Moreover, the regional and ecological histories of a place continue to be relevant to social action today. For example, in her long-term practice in Philadelphia, Anne Whiston Spirn explores the regional and ecological context that characterized the Mill Creek neighborhood in the beginning of the twenty-first century. Mill Creek was one of the poorest neighborhoods of Philadelphia that had nearly as much vacant land as buildings, with both ecological and social problems: "standing water after rain; slumping streets and sidewalks; vacant house lots, rubble-strewn; whole square blocks of abandoned land; men standing around street corners on a workday afternoon, jobless."[42] This was not due to lack of outside intervention, but rather *because of* and as a direct result of misguided interventions. Prior interventions did not adequately

[41] Joshua F. Cerra, Brook Weld Muller, and Robert F Young, "A Transformative Outlook on the Twenty-First Century City: Patrick Geddes' Outlook Tower Revisited," *Landscape and Urban Planning*, volume 166, 2017, page 91.

[42] Anne Whiston Spirn, "Restoring Mill Creek: Landscape Literacy, Environmental Justice, and City Planning and Design," *Landscape Research*, volume 30, issue 3, 2005, page 403.

consider the ecological context, and they did not fully engage the community in understanding or acting to make a change. As Spirn notes, while designers and social scientists continually drew up static maps and plans to describe the neighborhood, they failed to recognize that effective action requires an understanding of place and community across time—"an understanding of how it came to be, how the built landscape evolved, through what processes and actions, when, and which of its features have had a sustained impact on their surroundings over time."[43]

In her words, with framing that echoes Geddes, there is a need for a renewed "landscape literacy" among community members and professionals. That is, in order for action to be effective, the community needs a way of reflecting on its local social and ecological conditions. To develop this sort of landscape literacy, Spirn looks beyond conventional professional design activity (e.g., by bringing university students together with students form a local middle school) to learn about the ecological context of the neighborhood. While such a combination may seem unconventional, the ages and qualifications of participants were not of primary importance. The main tools were, "their own eyes and imagination, the place itself, and historical documents such as maps, photographs, newspaper articles, census tables and redevelopment plans."[44] Also important was that landscape literacy is a long-term process that evolved over years of engagement with different groups of students and stakeholders including city development authorities.

The tradition within which Spirn is working, of landscape and ecological urbanism, was, in part, related to the approach to thinking regionally about social-ecological problems that Geddes had employed in Scotland. Geddes inspired the field of professional practice known as "landscape urbanism," which would, at times, be a counter-narrative to mainstream design throughout the twentieth century. Landscape urbanism advocated for including ecological contexts in the post-Second World War era, which was characterized by developments that led to massive expansions of built environment at the expense of living ecologies. Ecology

[43] Spirn, pages 396–397.
[44] Spirn, page 403.

was not conceived as something "out there," but rather regional context was seen as intimately connected to even the most urbanized places. The key is in bringing regional ecological thinking to human systems. As a site of intervention, the landscape can be a way of bringing people together across different professions, and even beyond the professional context altogether.[45]

This approach is especially relevant today in the era of the so-called Anthropocene, where humans have unprecedented influence on planetary ecologies and climate disruptions unevenly impact different regions of the world. With increasing storms floods, droughts, and other weather events, ecological instability is already impacting communities. A key question of our times is: how to respond to this shifting ecological terrain? Particularly relevant is the need to work with local communities to clarify and imagine possible futures on a local level as part of adaptations to local disruptions caused by a changing global climate.[46]

This is to say that in the present era, urban ecological infrastructures are increasingly vulnerable on a planet that is undergoing unprecedented transformations. These infrastructural vulnerabilities are especially evident in the aftermath of disasters, but they point to the ongoing need to engage new social and political imaginations. As Bill Morrish suggests, the major task for today is not to grow or expand economies more, but rather to re-evaluate and redeploy existing resources with new forms of civic participation and imagination to rebuild infrastructure "as a cultural repository of memories and future hopes."[47] Much like the theorizing of Geddes, which saw a need for society to transition to a new form of social organization, many today are also engaging

[45] Ian McHarg, *Design with Nature, 25th Anniversary Edition* (John Wiley & Sons, 1992). See also, Anne Whiston Spirn's review of Ian McHarg's ideas and methods: Anne Whiston Spirn, "Ian McHarg, Landscape Architecture, and Environmentalism: Ideas and Methods in Context," in Michel Conan (editor), *Environmentalism in Landscape Architecture* (Dumberton Oaks, 2000), pages 97–114. For more on Geddes' relationship to the origins of landscape urbanism, see Shanti Fjord Levy, "Grounding Landscape Urbanism," *Scenario Journal*, issue 1, 2011, pages 13–25 https://scenariojournal.com/article/grounding-landscape-urbanism/

[46] Cerra, Muller, and Young, pages 90–96.

[47] William Morrish, "After the Storm: Rebuilding Cities upon Reflexive Infrastructure," *Social Research*, volume 75, issue 3, 2008, pages 993–1014.

with various approaches to "just transitions" and "design for transitions" in the present context of the climate crisis.[48]

Overall, regional and ecological thinking, from Geddes to the present, points to a need for designing that does not just tinker with the edges of what has already been made, but seeks to create fundamental transformation the systems that shape our everyday interactions to the local environment. In areas impacted by ecological instability today, acting is not just about having the most complete data or analysis of the problem. As Geddes and those who work in a similar tradition recognized, multiple perspectives on social ecological realities (across disciplines and communities) are needed to arrive at useful and transformational knowledge.

Adapting to changing ecological conditions therefore requires the sort of deep, ongoing engagement in local environments that Geddes employed. Geddes shows how the process of cultivating an intentional relationship to ecological, social, and political histories can inspire new ways of thinking and acting. And this is not just work landscape architects or professional designers, but it requires all to be involved across conventional professional identities from activists, organizers, academics, and scientists to farmers, designers, engineers, and artists.[49]

THE POTENTIAL OF CIVICS AS REFLECTIVE ACTION

In light of Geddes' advocacy to create networks of civic spaces through gardening and promote participation in design processes

---

[48] Damian White, "Just Transitions/Design for Transitions: Preliminary Notes on a Design Politics for a Green New Deal," *Capitalism Nature Socialism*, volume 31, issue 1, 2019, pages 20–39.

[49] Steiner, Weller, M'Closkey, and Flemming explain the relevance of McHarg's landscape urbanism to the twenty-first century in terms that resonate here. As they note in their introduction, the idea of synthesizing knowledge across professions in order to better relate with place (which was also a main focus for Geddes) is an ongoing project: "For McHarg, Western culture's greatest promise was a synthesis of the sciences and the arts that had yet to be applied to how we dwell on the land." Frederick Steiner, Richard Weller, Karen M'Closkey, and Billy Fleming, *Design with Nature Now* (Lincoln Institute of Land Policy, 2019), page 2.

at the Outlook Tower, it is worth returning to the story about vacant land that opened this chapter—including what such vacancies tell us about current social realities and possibilities. Part of this story is the actual experience of vacant land and the people who live near it, including how communities are mobilizing to participate in designing the future of their neighborhoods and cities (with and without professional designers). These experiences draw out some potential interrelationships among thinking, designing, civic engagement, and reflective action today.

In 2014, a global network of "community land access advocates"—activists, scholars, and practitioners who saw vacant land as an opportunity to meet social and environmental goals—gathered in New York to share their experiences and impressions on transforming vacant urban land into community resources. They told stories about small changes that positively improved people's everyday lives, but they also described how their tactical interventions within a system sometimes spiraled into much larger transformations for neighborhoods, cities, and even entire regions.[50]

Vacant land was not seen as an opportunity for grand urban renewal plans to be imposed on communities, but rather it was presented as a site of tactical intervention within an urban ecological context that marginalizes and alienates people along lines of race and class. The primary goal was to build upon the strengths of already existing residents of a neighborhood. Rather than viewing land as a blank slate, participants in the conference conceived it as part of social-political histories and ecological contexts. Designs and interventions for vacant land were therefore seen as a catalyst for civic engagement—a way to participate in the local environment and develop processes to steward it for the long term.[51]

---

[50] This meeting, and its broader significance, was documented in a special issue of the journal *Cities and the Environment*: Peleg Kremer and Zoé Hamstead, "Transformation of Urban Vacant Lots for the Common Good," *Cities and the Environment*, volume 8, issue 2, 2015, article 1.

[51] I have written more about the lessons from these practices elsewhere, especially for their relationship to emerging conceptions of civics and citizenship: Matthew DelSesto, "Cities, Gardening and Urban Citizenship: Transforming Vacant Acres into Community Resources," *Cities and the Environment*, volume 8, issue 2, 2015, article 3.

These present-day urban interventions have much in common with the work of Patrick Geddes, and the advocates who, both implicitly and explicitly, work in a similar tradition. Much like many land-access advocates today, the networks of gardens in Edinburgh were part of a larger urban development philosophy, which opposed the kind of large-scale demolitions and urban renewal (e.g., that continued to take place in cities like New York throughout the twentieth century). Geddes called his approach "conservative surgery," and it relied on the role of small tactical interventions instead of sweeping clearances. As is evident in the Outlook Tower and garden projects, this demonstrates one way of thinking and designing from within the contradictions of urban space today. That is, the importance of opening up taken-for-granted logics about how things should be, through propositional design rooted in social reality, experiential learning, and curation of civic spaces that are open to all.

Central to this sort of social imagining and designing is Geddes' conception of civics which he saw as a process of both understanding and transforming social reality.[52] Of particular importance for Geddes is the *role of scale* in design and social interventions, which is of critical importance today. While the planetary scale of social problems may seem to call for global mobilizations and large organizations to intervene with massive plans, the model of Geddes helps us to remember that scale does not always work in linear ways.

More, bigger, or technically advanced designs and interventions are not always better, and the most important impacts are not only what can be quantified in numbers. A single small intervention (one building, or one garden) that is well-attuned to social-ecological reality can cause cascading effects or ripples, which do not work on linear scale across space and

[52] Geddes elaborated on his view of civics, especially the relationship between civics and social research, in a series of presentations for the 1904 Sociological Society Meeting at the University of London, titled: "Civics: as Applied Sociology."

time.[53] In his approach to civics, design, and ecology, Geddes urges us to take an integrated and systems-view of our present context in any process of designing or acting—as opposed to the materialistic and technocratic view he saw in capitalism and state bureaucracy.

This is especially evident in his emphasis on the role of a Civic Survey, which he developed alongside the Outlook Tower. For Geddes, the survey is one way for a group or person, who wants to make an intervention, to begin. An initial goal of a survey is to "become at home" in a region and clarify areas for regional development or interventions. The survey is open to speculative possibilities beyond purely scientific interest. It ultimately culminates in civic and political actions for community empowerment. A survey does not just examine material conditions in the present but analyzes the implications of various actors (human and nonhuman) through history, focusing on how and why space has been produced the way it has. Finally, a civic survey traces how actors and conditions "unravel the explanation of the individuality, the uniqueness, of each of the towns and the cities."[54]

The civic survey is central to the process of acting toward the creation or fulfillment of any plan, because, for Geddes, we must first "know our ground," which requires a "deciphering of social origins" and "unraveling of contemporary factors."[55] Proper understanding of social realities through a survey requires civic hubs or centers—such as the Outlook Tower—which is a place where people can come together over a shared interest, place, or activity. Geddes explained that a civic center is generally a "clearing house of social science and social action, a vital intersection of

[53] A 2014 exhibition at the Museum of Modern Art in New York powerfully articulated the potential of these sorts of tactical interventions today. As Pedro Gadanho argues in an essay on the exhibition, "the anticipation of impending, plausible urban visions may prompt a critical understanding of present problems—thus contributing to fuel the public debate on the same issues." Pedro Gadanho, "Mirroring Uneven Growth: A Speculation on Tomorrow's Cities Today," in Pedro Gadanho (editor), *Uneven Growth: Tactical Urbanisms for Expanding Megacities* (The Museum of Modern Art, 2014), page 23.

[54] Geddes, *Cities in Evolution*, page xxvi.

[55] Geddes, *Cities in Evolution*, pages 94–95.

thought and deed."[56] This is a conception of civics that calls for us today to focus on spaces where theory and practice intersect, and to purposefully generate new opportunities for civic awakenings, in thought and deed.

Some major issues remain for community-led civic designs and interventions today. On the one hand, there is lack of public awareness about the process of changing the local environment. At the same time, there is a lack of visibility of the community members who have historically invested their time and energy in civic projects.[57] That is, there remains a disconnect between activists who have been designing their own local contexts and top-down municipal governance. As Geddes suggests, the most important space for design may be in the middle space of civics— which can be a connective tissue between individual residents, non-governmental organizations, and the private or public sector. Especially today, there is a need to radically reshape the relations between people and public institutions. There is growing potential for forms of design, technology, and social innovation to be implemented in ways that catalyze new collaborations and practices.[58]

One contemporary example of this work today is the organizing of 596 Acres in New York. As a small non-profit organization, initially founded by Paula Z. Segal, the organization formed in 2011 and sought to increase awareness of the potential that seemingly open spaces hold among community members. The goal was to "teach others to see" these spaces "as sites of opportunity, both for potential green spaces in neighborhoods that lack them, and as focal points for community organizing and civic engagement."[59] While the results can be seen physically in the form of dozens of new community spaces, equally important is that the

---

[56] Geddes, *Cities in Evolution*, page 287.

[57] Amy Laura Cahn and Paula Z. Segal, "You Can't Common What You Can't See: Towards a Restorative Polycentrism in the Governance of Our Cities," *Fordham Urban Law Journal*, volume 43, issue 2, 2016, pages 195–245.

[58] Ezio Manzini and Eduardo Stazowski (editors), *Public and Collaborative: Exploring the Intersection of Design, Social Innovation and Public Policy* (DESIS Network, 2013).

[59] Paula Z. Segal, "From Open Data to Open Space: Translating Public Information into Collective Action," *Cities and the Environment*, volume 8, issue 2, 2015, page 6.

interventions "built a constituency that is ready to engage with the mechanisms that shape the city and decide the fate of our shared assets."[60] Overall, 596 Acres identified critical gaps in urban communities—between space that had been unused or underutilized for years, people's knowledge, community capacity to act, and governmental processes.

The intervention of 596 Acres was an evolving project that learned from its practice.[61] It initially involved converting spreadsheets of government data into a clear publicly accessible map that identified city-owned vacant parcels of land. Then, organizers would make physical signs to label plots of land that are in this database. These signs would point people to the public website and map where they could learn more about the site and share information about ideas for organizing or historical and current events related to the site.

What began as an individual encounter with a space, or a virtual encounter online, would often lead to in-person meetings. Once people were organizing around a site, staff or volunteers from 596 Acres would help describe the legal process involved with getting access to the land—including what governmental offices or contacts might be most useful for a specific site. This process ultimately aimed to put "governance tactics into the hands of the communities of people," making law and policy more approachable for people who may have seen "government" as a distant or unapproachable entity.[62]

---

[60] Segal, "From Open Data to Open Space," page 7.

[61] Part of this evolution involved both scaling efforts up from all volunteers to full-time paid staff, and scaling down when deemed necessary. The process offered lessons on the challenges of developing a non-profit organization that strives to be based on anti-oppression principles and equitable inclusion but nevertheless still exists the context of socialized power and privilege that manifests in the workplace and legal/funding structures that are catered toward more hierarchical organizations. Paula Z. Segal, "Radical Transparency," *596 Acres News*, August 2018, accessed at: https://596acres. org/radical-transparency/

[62] Paula Z. Segal, "Room to Grow Something," in Ron Shiffman, Rick Bell, Lance Jay Brown, and Lynne Elizabeth (editors), *Beyond Zuccotti Park: Freedom of Assembly and the Occupation of Public Space* (New Village Press, 2012), page 159.

Overall, the practice of attempting to transform vacant land into community resources is relevant more generally to social thought and design today. It demonstrates how thinking can be a resource when everyday people, grassroots organizations, and activist designers come up against systemic constraints, but attempt to push on anyway. For instance, people may initially imagine collectively accessing and using land for a specific purpose, but this might come to seem impossible when rules and procedures are discovered that were hidden within layers of municipal bureaucracy. Future groups in other contexts can then learn from these efforts to secure land access—through *both* digital platforms that aggregate prior attempts *and* ongoing community organizing. Thinking ecologically in this practice is about being able to create a specific technical tool, like a website, that is situated in physical community and ecological relationships. It also involves seeing how there are many points of entry, or ways of engaging a specific site or situation, with multiple iterations to develop the sorts of nimble and useful knowledge to nudge conditions toward desired futures.

It is in this sense that social design can be much more than making governments and organizations more effective. This is to say that designing has the potential to be a process of enabling or inspiring new constituencies to push the limits of what seems possible through iterative reflection within an evolving social-ecological context.[63] By trying to make an intervention, the people working on a project can gain valuable clarity and insight about social realities. They learn about the communities, institutions, and ecologies that are related to a place. Professionals and non-professionals who are engaging in social design activities may not always need to conduct research as an academic social scientist

---

[63] Tunstall critiques the ways that some social design has focused on improving organizational and institutional outcomes, and instead models a "respectful design" that better attunes to the needs, creativity, culture, and aspirations of local people and their environments. Elizabeth (Dori) Tunstall, "Decolonizing Design Innovation: Design Anthropology, Critical Anthropology, and Indigenous Knowledge," in Wendy Gunn, Ton Otto, and Rachel Charlotte Smith (editors), *Design Anthropology: Theory and Practice* (Bloomsbury, 2013), pages 232–250.

would, but their studies are no less rigorous. They are talking to each other, making new connections to people with information relevant to their particular focus—learning by living through their experience.

Examples explored here, from the time that Patrick Geddes was practicing to the present, demonstrate that the goal of design need not necessarily be to apply innovation to existing organizations and institutions. Rather it can be in pursuing a practice of *designing and thinking as reflective action*, which centers people's everyday potential to remake the social. Accordingly, for Geddes, civics involves active, thoughtful, or reciprocal engagement with ecologies or communities, not simply activities in alignment with the status quo of a particular nation's government.

In this model, imagined futures are never completely untethered from the dynamic imaginations of those who are most involved in these futures, which is a constituency that is morphing or growing over time through ongoing action. On the one hand, such an approach urges us to cultivate new ways of thinking—the kind of ecological view that always situates thought and action in living social-ecological contexts.[64] On the other hand, it also may sometimes be necessary to *act ourselves into a new way of thinking*. That is, when we act where we are, we have new encounters with people and environments that allow us to see ourselves differently. Maybe we see that more is possible than we had anticipated, we put a face to a large bureaucracy, learn the struggles of a particular community, or we are surprised by how the history of the land offers up its own teachings about who we are and where we are going. Perhaps, in new conversations and debate with neighbors, we are able to imagine new possibilities for the places that we call home.

[64] Resonance can be seen, for example, in new modes of thought and action to address the climate crisis today: Hannah Knox, *Thinking Like a Climate: Governing a City in Times of Environmental Change* (Duke University Press, 2020).

4   Jane Addams: Theories in, of, and for Practice

Global migration and displacement have become defining issues of the twenty-first century. The current crisis lurched into public consciousness with media portrayals of people on the road or at sea—in images of migrants huddled together on boats crossing the Mediterranean to Southern Europe or groups making the difficult journey from Central America to the United States. Yet debates about immigration and the social change spurred by changing populations are not new. Social realities of immigration go much deeper than simplistic media spectacles of the incoming "huddled masses" that are stereotyped as a danger to the social order, good for economic development, or in need of charity.

Central to immigration is the issue of how people, communities, and nations treat newcomers, which is a conversation that often revolves around citizenship. Although some notion of citizenship has existed at least since ancient Greece, the modern conception of the citizen in Western cultures was born in the French and the American Revolutions, alongside the rise of the nation state. If individuals were to be equal before the law in a democratic republic, rather than subject to the will of a monarch, it seemed necessary to determine of who should be counted as part of the nation, and where boundaries should be drawn.

For example, the 1790 Naturalization Act in the United States was an early law in the newly established nation to regulate citizenship. It described the exclusive process through which property-owning white men "of good character" who had lived in the country for more than a year could obtain legal citizenship. Over the coming 150 years there would be much debate and struggle over the shifting definition of citizenship along lines of race, class, and gender. The formalization of boundaries of citizenship became especially important in the United States as increasing numbers of newcomers arrived in the late 1800s.[1] What would be the status of these groups? How, if at all, would they be able to integrate into society? Would these groups have the same rights and opportunities that the founders of the republic had given to white, property-owning men?

With these questions it is essential to foreground the broader social origins of global human migrations. That is, rather than seeing the mass migration of people as a social problem in the present, it is perhaps more relevant to see global migrations and displacements as *a symptom of more generalized community breakdown*, catalyzed by militarized intervention, political polarization, ecological crisis, and economic inequality on a global scale. In this sense, immigration is directly related to the forces of colonization and industrialization that initiated massive environmental and societal transformations.

At first glance, it may seem that nations of the Global North with power and wealth today are suddenly dealing with the "problem" of an influx of immigrants. Yet with a deeper social and historical imagination, it is clear that global migrations are a result of the systems that allowed these nations to accumulate wealth in the first place. The accumulation of wealth and power relied on the increasing globalization of trade, aggregation of manufacturing in growing cities with low-wage jobs, transformation of the environment to extract raw materials, and global warfare required for colonization (or later to secure an economically stable

[1] On the historical context of exclusionary US immigration policies, see, for example: Daniel Denvir, *All-American Nativism: How the Bipartisan War on Immigrants Explains Politics as We Know It* (Verso, 2020).

global "world order").[2] The political economic transformations of industrial capitalism that began in the 1800s are therefore deeply intertwined with the displacement of people from their homes, along with the ongoing transformation of environments, economies, and social realities.

This is the social-historical context that Jane Addams would be born into in 1860, just outside of Chicago. The realities of the American Revolution and industrial capitalism created an unprecedented scale of both opportunities and inequalities. The achievement of the revolution—to assert that people ought to be autonomous creators of their own social laws and government—was at odds with the social realities of continuing racism, Native American genocide, the exclusion of women, and the effective exclusion of most lower-class immigrants.

Millions of immigrants arriving in the late 1800s posed new and particular challenges to democracy, as they faced prevalence of disease and poverty. It was not only that the living conditions were challenging, but these immigrants also faced a profound condition of social marginalization and political disinvestment, which might create new classes of people to be locked out of the promise of democracy. What exactly was the context in which Addams was working? How might an understanding of this era be useful for thought and action today? To explore these central questions the chapter first explores the historical context of the Hull-House as it compares to the present. Then, it looks at the general approach of Jane Addams and her colleagues, and concludes with three sections that begin to relate the model of the Hull-House to theories and practices of the present.

GLOBAL MIGRATION AND SOCIAL CHANGE, THEN AND NOW

Jane Addams has more recently been acknowledged as a founding voice in sociology, social work, and public administration, but her path to scholarship and practice emerged out years of

[2] Douglas Massey summarizes much more detail on these and other "causes" of immigration throughout history in: Douglas S. Massey, "Why Does Immigration Occur? A Theoretical Synthesis," in Charles Hirschman, Philip Kasinitz, and Joshua DeWind (editors), *Handbook of International Migration* (Russel Sage Foundation, 1999), pages 34–52.

grappling with central issues of her time. Addams spent most of her childhood during the 1860s and 1870s in the suburbs of Chicago. She was born into a wealthy family, and contracted tuberculosis at the age of four. Her illness left her with a limp making it difficult to fit in with other children and ultimately gave her life-long health problems. Perhaps because of this, she became an avid reader, and while reading Charles Dickens' depictions of poverty and disease in England she was inspired to pursue formal education with a dream of becoming a doctor. After attending Rockford Female Seminary in Illinois, she followed her family to Philadelphia, where she began studying at the Women's Medical College of Philadelphia. Unfortunately, surgery for a back condition pulled her out of school and made her unable to return.

Addams, at this point, was at a crossroads. She had abandoned the typical path of wealthy women, which would have likely been to find a husband and spend life at home, but now her larger dream of working in medicine had also collapsed.[3] During a visit to England she had witnessed the contrast between people in destitute poverty and wealthy industrialists who were benefiting from unprecedented social and technological change. This disparity, combined with her own status of being unable and unwilling to conform to the ideal of a privileged maternal homemaker, left her in a "state of nervous exhaustion."[4] In the midst of her existential and spiritual crisis, she wondered what people like her, with access to education, wealth, and political power, could do. Charity did not seem like enough, and there were few models for social action to address the emerging chasm she saw growing at home—between citizens who benefited from the structure of United States society, and new immigrants who neither knew nor experienced the freedom and opportunities that were promised in the ideal of "America."

[3] There are now several biographies of Addams that go into much more detail, such as Louise Knight's very comprehensive book: Louise W. Knight, *Citizen: Jane Addams and the Struggle for Democracy* (University of Chicago Press, 2005).

[4] Jane Addams, *Twenty Years at Hull-House* (Signet Classics, 1961 [1910]), pages 42–46.

In the forty years after 1880, more than twenty million immigrants would arrive to the United States. By 1920, foreign-born residents made up 14 percent of the US population.[5] They were mostly from Southern and Eastern Europe—fleeing religious persecution, the desperation of economic collapse and lack of political representation, or just seeking a new life in the United States. Many of these immigrants came to the United States looking for freedom, but instead found themselves packed into dense urban neighborhoods, working long hours in dangerous positions with little pay and lack of access to basic necessities for life.

Journalists, governmental officials, researchers, philanthropists, and the general public were beginning to pay attention. A generation of "muckraking" journalists exposed brutal working and living conditions. Jacob Riis had shocked the nation with photo journalism of the New York City tenements (in *How the Other Half Lives*, 1890), and Upton Sinclair described the struggle and suffering of working-class immigrants in Chicago's meat-packing industry (in *The Jungle*, 1906).

On the one hand, some people saw immigrants as responsible for bringing poverty, crime, and disease. The majority of these immigrants did not speak English and they were often Catholic or Jewish, while the white establishment was Protestant. At the same time, some of the wealthier established residents were sympathetic to the immigrant experience. This sentiment led to a new generation of social reformers, within communities and in the government, who sought to address the conditions in the so-called urban slums. In Chicago, however, like many cities, there was a widespread "spirit of generalization and lack of organization" in these sorts of "charitable efforts."[6] That is, public and private sectors did not adequately consider the social realities they were trying to address. They were also poorly organized in their attempts to intervene.

[5] See, for example: Elijah Alperin and Jeanne Batalova, "European Immigrants in the United States," *Migration Policy Institute*, 2018, accessed at: https://www.migrationpolicy.org/article/european-immigrants-united-states–2016.

[6] Addams, page 107.

The 1890s were also a period of social unrest more broadly. The 1893 Chicago World's Fair celebrated industrial progress and made Chicago a center of national and international attention. An immaculate exposition and fair grounds were constructed while poor neighborhoods sank deeper into crisis. The Financial Panic of 1893 led to deep depression and job loss. Active anarchist, socialist, and populist movements were on the rise. A lack of social integration and opportunity for immigrant youth prompted many to organize outside of formal institutions. In 1901, the twenty-fifth President of the United States William McKinley was assassinated by a self-identified anarchist who had lost his job in the depression after 1893. A sense of social and political polarization ran deep as the country struggled to come to terms with the rapid social changes in the wake of industrialization.

For Jane Addams the root causes of social and industrial problems were not merely located in specific immigrant neighborhoods, nor were they simply immigrant problems. Rather, she saw issues like sporadic access to good jobs and education, unsanitary living conditions, lack of assimilation of immigrants, to be symptoms of a wider social crisis of polarization under industrial capitalism that involved "overaccumulation at one end of society, and the destitution at the other."[7] Yet her vision goes well beyond debates over public versus private approaches to addressing social problems—for example, in debates from Addams' time and the present over ideals of free-market capitalism versus government intervention. Instead, she embraced an approach to theorizing in, of, and for practice, through widening webs of solidarity and hospitality. In this she saw that the growing concentration of wealth under capitalist industrialization, combined with white cultural fears of the "foreign other," required an approach that was different from the conventional modes of thought and action in her time.

Her multi-dimensional and evolving response to this condition was the Hull-House, which she co-founded in 1889 and helped to lead until her death in 1935. As a social settlement that aimed to support newly arriving immigrants and advance social change

[7] Addams, page 83.

efforts, Hull-House was a series of projects that involved many forms of research and practice. At its core, the Hull-House was grounded in a process of designing spaces and opportunities for intentional engagement with community. This meant understanding the social context and possibilities of immigrant neighborhoods, beyond the professionalization and individual isolation that was coming to characterize industrial capitalist society. Inspired by the settlement movement in England, Hull-House was a response to the larger social contexts of global migration.[8] It was a means to both understand and transform the emerging social realities of the late nineteenth and early twentieth century.

***

Although much has changed since the time of Hull-House, many of the challenges that Addams and her generation faced have intensified. Like the end of the nineteenth century, the end of the twentieth century saw rapid social change brought on by the spread of new technologies. This has involved an advance of computing in corporate and personal life alongside increasing global access to the internet with on-demand communications, entertainment, and information. In the United States, the spread of automation in a context of global markets led to a wave of social change and deindustrialization of cities and towns. Areas with no industries to replace manufacturing were slowly (or in some cases, suddenly) left behind. The economic gap between the wealthiest and poorest in the United States continued to grow.

At the same time, the legacy of colonialism and international policies of the United States—including the instigation of wars across Latin America and around the world—has created the conditions for unprecedented global migrations to the United States and beyond.[9] Alongside many other moments, 2014 made immigration

[8] Addams, page 83.

[9] Juan Gonzalez calls this relationship between the United States and Latin America—where US military interventions across Latin America triggered widespread instability and subsequent migrations to the United States—the "harvest of empire." Juan Gonzalez, *Harvest of Empire: A History of Latinos in America* (Penguin Books, 2000).

the center of a national debate as nearly 70,000 "unaccompanied minors" came to the United States from Central America. In some ways, reactions to this crisis were emblematic of the larger condition of global migration and displacement—where record numbers of migrants and refugees were on the move around the world. According to the United Nations, by 2019 nearly eighty million people around the world were forcibly displaced from their homes—due to climate-related disruptions, economic instability, war, or conflict. Among them are nearly thirty million refugees, over half of whom are under the age of eighteen. By 2018, the population of immigrants in the United States was nearly 45 million.[10]

Globally there has also been a rise in more punitive, exclusionary, and nationalist rhetoric and policies toward immigrants. From 1997 to 2012, the United States removed 19.7 million immigrants, who were returned to their country of origin. The expanding immigration enforcement systems that facilitate arrests, detentions, removals, and returns inflict lasting damage on immigrant communities and society more broadly.[11] Today the migration crisis epitomizes the inability of institutions to adequately reimagine their practices in the midst of fluidity that characterizes today's world of accelerating global flows of information, communications, capital, and people.

With these shifting social, political, and historical forces—where people everywhere (most especially the poor and marginalized) are constantly under threat of being uprooted by war,

[10] United Nations High Commissioner for Refugees, "Global Trends: Forced Displacement," 2019, accessed at: https://www.unhcr.org/en-us/figures-at-a-glance.html; Pew Research Center, "Modern Immigration Wave Brings 59 Million to U.S., Driving Population Growth and Change Through 2065: Views of Immigration's Impact on U.S. Society Mixed," Washington, DC, 2015, accessed at: https://www.pewresearch.org/hispanic/2015/09/28/chapter-5-u-s-foreign-born-population-trends; Allison O'Connor, Jeanne Batalova, and Jessica Bolter, "Central American Immigrants in the United States," *Migration Policy Institute*, 2019, accessed at: https://www.migrationpolicy.org/article/central-american-immigrants-united-states–2017.

[11] See, for example: perspectives on early twenty-first century immigration policies in: Danial Kanstrom and Brinton Lykes (editors), *The New Deportations Delirium* (NYU Press, 2015).

state-sanctioned violence, famine, ecological degradation, land grabs of multi-national corporations, climate disasters, and forced removals—what is being lost is the human relationship to place and community. There is an urgency to this moment, where it seems that human beings may be in danger of forgetting of how to orient toward participation in society, from the local to the global. Overall, the challenges of today are worth viewing in light of the experience of Hull-House. How can conditions of the present be engaged? What sorts of thinking and acting might adequately respond to the roots of the problems being faced? And what is the relevance of Jane Addams and the nineteenth century for social thought, design, and action today?

PRODUCING NEW KNOWLEDGE THROUGH SOLIDARITY AND HOSPITALITY

Overall, the Hull-House designed spaces and services to meet the needs of immigrant communities, while also pursuing activism in the public and private sectors. The approach began with rather simple acts of hospitality. Jane Addams leveraged her connections with more wealthy and established residents to initially meet basic needs of people in poor immigrant neighborhoods—offering food for the hungry, care for the sick, providing spaces to play for children. Within a few years of its opening, 2000 people entered into Hull-House every day, which grew to become like a community center for the entire city of Chicago with more than a dozen buildings (one of which is sketched in Figure 4.1 by Hull-House resident Norah Hamilton). It eventually functioned as a boy's club, art museum, theater, music school, gymnasium, refuge for houseless, a place for those looking for work. Art and creativity were both part of the programming (Figure 4.2), and also woven into all of the initiatives. The Hull-House was not just a space to provide services to passive service recipients. It intentionally evolved into a neighborhood hub for everything ranging from singing and celebration to research, activism, and advocacy efforts.

FIGURE 4.1 Sketch of Hull-House building.

Source: Jane Addams, *Twenty Years at Hull-House* (MacMillan Company, 1910).

FIGURE 4.2 Sketch of child drawing.

Source: Jane Addams, *Twenty Years at Hull-House* (MacMillan Company, 1910).

FIGURE 4.3 Jane Addams reading to a group of children.

Source: Special Collections and University Archives, University of Illinois at Chicago.

A major force of Hull-House was its residents, who were meant to be immersed in a process formal and informal learning—namely through acts of hospitality. Although consistently led by women, residents from neighborhoods around the city were recruited to move into the Hull-House, which was surrounded by immigrant communities, and welcome all who entered. Residents of Hull-House came from many professions and backgrounds and were usually "people who worked in other parts of the city, who wanted to live and share their talents ... They were doctors, lawyers, college professors, school teachers, social workers, students, musicians, actors, writers, poets, artists, politicians."[12] While they may have had professional skills, the goal was not to try to save or fix the immigrant communities, rather, Addams insisted that the residents "must be content to live quietly side by side with their neighbors, until they grow into a sense of relationship and mutual interests."[13] The Hull-House residents were also meant to live simply and completely immerse themselves in the needs and relationships of the community. Especially in the early years, days were "blurred with fatigue" as residents had to become accustomed to the "unending activity and to the confusion of a house constantly filling and refilling with groups of people."[14] Central to the hospitality of Hull-House was that residents must always be available to act, in whatever capacity the surrounding communities needed in the moment. Jane Addams was a resident for most of her life, actively involved in everything from research to educational programs and everyday activities of the house.

Of particular importance for Hull-House was an ongoing exploration of the origins and implications of the "industrial condition" as it related to the immigrant experience. For Addams and the Hull-House, research and knowledge on the industrial condition were part of a process of forming relationships with a community. Recognizing that poverty and inequality have *social*

---

[12] Wallace Kirkland, quoted in: Clifford Terry, "The Many Faces of Hull-House," *Chicago Tribune*, October 8, 1989.

[13] Addams, page 85.

[14] Addams, page 98.

causes (not just individual or situational ones) required a different approach to addressing social problems—one that was highly participatory and collaborative. Addams also believed that it was too easy to see industrialization as some kind of impersonal mechanistic series of forces, when, in fact, every aspect of the new industrialization had been imagined and created by human beings. She observed a tendency for both the rich and poor to see complex machines or gigantic factories and assume that such forces were hopelessly beyond human influence.

Accordingly, one particular research product led to the creation of series of educational exhibitions and projects—to spark a social imagination by engaging immigrants and longstanding residents of the city with the social-historical context that led to industrialization. It sought to demonstrate how the development of complex machinery of industrialization had "evolved from simple tools."[15] These workshops, exhibitions, and discussions were a sort of collective investigation of the history of industrialization, with particular attention to how it was influencing people's lives. The purpose of this knowledge about the local and global contexts of industrialization was ultimately to demonstrate the needs and opportunities for action.[16]

More generally, a key dimension of any workshops, lectures, or discussions was to give poor immigrants, who lived in communities around the Hull-House, leadership roles in researching and developing the content. They would then ultimately facilitate workshops for others. According to Addams, this approach is important because it "puts the immigrants in the position of teachers," where visitors come to learn from immigrants, for example, about how the design history of different textiles or machines was impacting industrial conditions of the present.[17] Perhaps for the first time, established and well-off city residents were hearing from new immigrants as authorities or experts on industrialization—thereby enabling a different sort of social imagination about the potential of newcomers.

[15] Addams, page 156.
[16] Addams, page 158.
[17] Addams, pages 158–159.

Workshops, discussions, and events at the Hull-House were also generally meant to be building bridges between groups with widely differing experiences and positions in society. The implications of this approach implications are profound. For Addams, knowledge about industrialization could not be adequately produced without the participation of those who were most directly impacted by its destructive consequences. Activities at Hull-House were set up on the principle that people closest to the problems are closest to the solutions. As Addams put it, she wanted to prioritize the knowledge and concepts that come from experience because, people who are socio-economically at the bottom of society have been "most directly in contact with those failures and suffered the most."[18] This was the birthplace of a new solidarity that could be the foundation for (not yet conceived) courses of action.

The notion that learning, research, and knowledge required a diversity of voices—including both those who benefit and those who are negatively impacted by industrialization—would carry though all of the work at Hull-House. In particular, the principles of reciprocity and solidarity had been alive as part of Hull-House's founding spirit: "Hull-House was soberly opened on the theory that the dependence of classes on each other is reciprocal; and that as the social relation is essentially a reciprocal relation."[19] The exploitation of poor immigrants was neither an object of analysis nor charity case for elite researchers and wealthy philanthropists who were part of the existing power structures of society. Instead, Addams saw that the knowledge necessary for social change would come from a *process of forging long-term relations across differences*. In this, she pointed to urgency of hospitality, for those with social or economic privileges to genuinely welcome strangers into their lives with a willingness to learn.

Addams emphasized that the purpose of either formal research or informal learning was not to define social reality of these industrial neighborhoods *for* immigrant communities, but rather to complement and work *with* existing groups. Addams was well aware that such acts of solidarity are never a perfectly equal

[18] Addams, pages 121–122.
[19] Addams, page 59.

playing field—in that a gap was likely to persist between privileged residents of Hull-House and the poor immigrant working class community members.

Lectures, writing, and research at the Hull-House accordingly emphasized "the way power distorts relationships," even as it "showed how to recognize and undo the harmful effects of privilege and disempowerment."[20] What was important, therefore, was to include consciousness and recognition of privilege within the process of knowledge production, and build in opportunities for different power relations to emerge. The idea was that reflecting on power differences or social inequalities in the process of acting could build new power relationships into future aspirations and projects of the neighborhood.[21]

Learning and research were accordingly about forging relations of solidarity, whereby Hull-House residents sought to learn from community members. They would then document what they were learning in and through the relationships they were building over the course of years. Emerging out of interactions with neighborhood residents at the Hull-House, which ranged from serious study to celebration and singing (pictured in Figure 4.4), Jane Addams and colleagues set out to understand the neighborhood conditions. While formal city institutions often neglected poor immigrant neighborhoods, the Hull-House research affirmed the emerging presence of people from different nationalities and documented economic conditions. Among some of the more widely known products of this research process, the Hull-House produced a series of maps and papers, which portrayed the demographic information and living conditions of the neighborhood, such as

[20] Charlene Haddock Seigfried, "Introduction to the Illinois Edition," in Jane Addams, *Democracy and Social Ethics* (University of Illinois Press, 2002 [1902]), page xxi.

[21] Addams writes "Could we ... make their individual efforts more effective through organization and possibly complement them by small efforts of our own?" in *Twenty Years at Hull-House*, page 89. Wynne Walker Moskop notes that this sort of orientation, to begin to bridge seemingly irreconcilable differences, requires a true sense of "political friendship" that involves "reciprocal contributions" to a mutual purpose. Wynne Walker Moskop, *Jane Addams on Inequality and Political Friendship* (Routledge, 2020), pages xxvii–xxxv.

FIGURE 4.4 Hull-House Friendly Club gathering.

Source: Special Collections and University Archives, University of Illinois at Chicago.

household wages (represented in Figure 4.5). Yet the process of research and investigation was only the beginning of their work.

While the practice of Addams and the Hull-House had a sense of urgency about engaging with the "job at hand," through mutual learning and practical acts of hospitality, it also saw that what they were collectively learning ought to be oriented to action. This involved organizing and advocating in all levels of the public and private sectors for long-term systemic change. Such advocacy would be done in a spirit of solidarity with and leadership by those who are most impacted by the problems. Central to Addams' approach is that advocacy must be connected to actually exiting experiences of people who are already trying to solve problems as individuals, groups, or organizations. While she would often be invited to speak from various philanthropic or governmental groups, she preferred to speak about the neighborhood with community members or neighborhood activists who could discuss the realities they faced from the perspective of their lived experience.

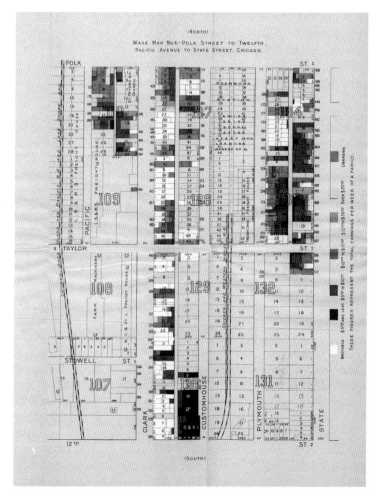

FIGURE 4.5 Neighborhood map.

Source: Residents of Hull-House, *Hull-House Maps and Papers* (Thomas Crowell, 1895).

For example, Hull-House was quite involved with creating new social policies to end child labor. Addams saw that deeper engagement than new policy and law was needed. The point was to both clarify and transform this social reality. To get broad public support for ending child labor, Addams saw that it would be necessary to clarify the scope and impact of child labor and, in this process, to transform identified injustices. The clarification of social reality involved documenting industrial conditions, and residents of Hull-House effectively persuaded the Illinois State Bureau of Labor to investigate labor conditions. Yet at the same time, in the process of calling attention to this issue, was the imperative to bring families and children who had experience with child labor into conversations with the wider public, including those of the private sector. Accordingly, part of the work that Hull-House catalyzed also involved creating spaces for the local community to organize trade-unions, where workers of different sectors met to clarify their shared social realities and then to advocate for what they needed with business owners.[22]

In retrospect it is clear that while Hull-House took on individual issues, the ability to address any one issue was only possible by putting it in a wider social-historical context. That is, investigations into labor conditions led to issues of waste disposal, which led to questions about housing safety, availability of playgrounds and open space, health, roads, and infrastructure. While these might be different specializations or government agencies today, the evolving theory and practice at Hull-House showed how the most effective interventions came about through a more integrated approach to thinking and acting. Such an integrated view was attained through long-term engagement with communities that was oriented toward solidarity and hospitality.

Overall, it could be said that Addams and Hull-House approached their work as a process of social thinking, imagining, and designing—conceiving of a needed intervention based on existing social realities and identifying future courses of action. Yet, in this case, designing was also the act of bringing different groups together—for example, poor immigrant workers and activists, business owners, and the public sector—to generate new policies, procedures, and practices. In each stage of the process, the end goal was not to pass the right law or implement the perfect

[22] For example, Addams recounts Hull House's involvement with changing child labor laws in: Addams, pages 132–152.

program, but rather to always broaden the circle of solidarity through expanding networks of solidarity and hospitality—both within and beyond formal institutions.

Addams and her colleagues insisted that ideals like community or democracy are not only instrumental concepts about a preferred set of technical dimensions in political systems, but they are about the sometimes-invisible *life-giving bonds between people that "data" can never fully capture.* Much like her contemporary Patrick Geddes, Addams saw how true civics and democracy were more about building the capacities of imagination, trust, and cooperation to make things happen with others, than they were about a set of legal rights or procedures for technical management.[23] This is to say that designing or intervening effectively in the given state of affairs is not merely the result of having the right professional techniques or data. It requires evolving participatory processes that invite people into expanding networks of solidarity through thinking and acting.

Such a conception points away from a vertical approach to knowledge whereby researchers or universities gather data from communities that is then applied to policy, and instead points to the need for horizontal or collaborative modes of engagement. As Addams noted, real inclusion and integration is more than charity for the foreign "other." It is a mutual process of learning with others, which is especially needed in contexts of profound social division, from the era of Jane Addams to our own.[24] Of particular relevance is the ongoing need to bring forms of theory and practice together, which is a focus of the next section.

[23] Victoria Bissel Brown explains how, although Addams was not always religious, she increasingly embraced an ethical and spiritual orientation to her practice as a form of reflection. Victoria Bissell Brown, "The Sermon of the Deed: Jane Addams' Spiritual Evolution," in Marilyn Fischer, Carol Nackenoff, and Wendy Chmielewski (editors), *Jane Addams and the Practice of Democracy* (University of Illinois Press, 2009), pages 21–39.

[24] For instance, today, Cruz and Forman explore the relationship between hospitality and knowledge production in their work on the US/Mexico border: Teddy Cruz and Fonna Forman, "Critical Proximities: Notes on the Redistribution of Knowledges across Walls," in Farhana Ferdous and Bryan Bell (editors), *All-Inclusive Engagement in Architecture: Towards the Future of Social Change* (Routledge, 2021), pages xxvi–xxxv.

THEORIZING PRACTICE, PRACTICING THEORY

Addams and colleagues hoped to make connections between the particular experience of Hull-House and more general theories or strategies for systemic change. For Addams, the most accurate and useful theories emerged in practice, where people were struggling to solve concrete problems. Theory did not require some kind of professional intervention, but it could be found in people's everyday lives and practices—the concepts and ideas they used to make sense of their worlds. The reflective work of theory could also be employed to catalyze new imagination, possibilities, or courses of action. In this way, there was a potential to develop theory in, of, and for practice.

In other words, for Addams and colleagues, *the process of inquiry itself could be an intervention*—a form of acting in the world that aimed to understand the emerging social realities of industrial capitalism. Knowledge therefore is not only objective data about the world because the process of coming to know or understand a particular social reality creates relationship and interconnection. It is in this way that research can be an end, in and of itself, as a practice that inspires new ways of defining the context and imagining ways forward.

An example of a space that sought to combine theory with everyday life was the "Working People's Social Science Club" at the Hull-House. The club involved weekly moments for reflection on the evolving practice of Hull-House, including social and economic conditions facing the community. It emphasized guest speakers, democratic decision making, and wide participation. At each meeting a different community member was in charge of facilitating discussion, and scholars from universities around the country would sometimes visit.

At the center of her mode of theorizing practice and practicing theory was a commitment to "developing an applied philosophy immersed in social action"[25] that she would refer to as *intelligent*

---

[25] Maurice Hamington, "Jane Addams," in Edward N. Zalta (editor), *The Stanford Encyclopedia of Philosophy* (Summer 2019 Edition), accessed at: https://plato.stanford.edu/archives/sum2019/entries/addams-jane/.

or coordinated action.[26] While she had a lifelong interest in theory and philosophy, "Addams did not intend to engage in philosophical narratives removed from social improvement, but neither did she intend to pursue social activism without theorizing about the wider implications of her work."[27] In practice, intelligent action meant beginning with the immediate urgent needs of residents in precarious poverty, and using the experiences of this practice to inform future action.

Her view on theory and practice was especially shaped by the wider social context. In particular, Addams and her female colleagues at Hull-House were also struggling against institutionalized sexism in political and academic life—especially at the newly formed University of Chicago.[28] As the sociology department there developed, it evolved to be a separate male-dominated department that had a contradictory and troubling relationship to Jane Addams' work. In retrospect, it is evident that many male sociologists who saw themselves as developing the specialized discipline of sociology, like Robert Park and Ernest Burgess, appropriated the theories and ideas coming out of the Hull-House—even as they neglected to cite scholar activists at Hull-House or deliberately attempted to shape the ideas to be more abstract and less applied. Over time, the practice and legacy of Addams was overshadowed because of pervasive "hostility toward women as intellectuals" at universities and the perception that she was too involved in social critique and reform.[29] This stance toward engaged scholarship ultimately began to contribute the narrowing of the social science imagination—based on the (arguably misguided) notion that community-based work and practical application were at odds with the pursuit of objectivity.

Rather than looking to those who focused on academic contributions, Addams found inspiration in the theories of non-violent direct action and social change that were emerging from Leo Tolstoy and others in the early twentieth century (the same

[26] For example, in *Twenty Years at Hull-House.*

[27] Hamington, "Jane Addams."

[28] Mary Jo Deegan, *Jane Addams and the Men of the Chicago School, 1892–1918* (Routledge, 1988).

[29] Deegan, page 162.

sort of social thought that would influence the work of Mahatma Gandhi and Martin Luther King Jr.). Addams was particularly inspired by the spiritual and moral imperative Tolstoy issued in his 1886 book, *What to Do?* (or later translated as *What, Then, Shall Be Done?*). At a time when many had ideas about radical social change, Addams saw in Tolstoy someone who had developed the capacity to "lift his life to the level of conscience, to translate theories into action."[30] That is, Tolstoy had taken many of his ideas and tried to put them into practice, including his work to found more than a dozen schools with Russian peasants. For Addams, equally important in Tolstoy's vision was the spiritual and moral dimension, where she saw Tolstoy as someone who embodied the "sermon of the deed" (which is that theories or ideas are best demonstrated by showing others what they look like in practice).

Addams especially resisted emerging tendencies in social sciences to describe the world in terms of abstract theories, and saw the need to connect speculation to concrete on-the-ground realities of people who were implementing different courses of action.[31] In her experience with engaging actually existing social realties on-the-ground, she notes that "life cannot be administered by definite rules and regulations," because wisdom to deal with social difficulties comes only from knowledge of the "life and habits" of people "as a whole."[32] In this sense, intelligent action is *a distinct kind of social thought that emerges from the process of acting.* Knowledge is therefore not a resolved conclusion or social fact gleaned from a narrow methodological study, but rather it is created in and through experience.

The Hull-House embraced this *method of experience*, where insights from practice led to the adaptation or creation of new theories, and theorizing could be the basis for beginning possible courses of action. For Addams, theory and practice are at their best when they evolve together. The practice of theorizing can inspire people to act, and acting can be done intentionally to

[30] Addams, page 173.
[31] Addams, page 128.
[32] Addams, page 108.

stimulate further discussion and reflection.[33] The implications here are profound in that, if attempts are not made to apply or contextualize data or knowledge, then knowledge is in danger of becoming less truthful and removed from actually existing social realities.

Descriptions of social realities that only look backwards—that analyze data to say something definitive about what is—encourage those concerned with social issues to passively observe the world. Addams lamented that if this ideal of knowledge spread, it may come to seem that societies are best understood only in quiet moments of withdrawal. This sort of passive observation, according Addams, was only possible for those with economic and social privilege, and it led too many smart and talented people to be forever caught up in the "snare of preparation"—as they sought to increasingly understand aspects of social reality, but never actually tried to make things happen.[34]

Today there remains a chasm between theory and practice (in that professional practices are often considered separate from academic theory). Research is often seen as a means to an end; that is, a research practice can be considered successful in so far as it achieves new knowledge, through narrow theoretical or methodological framing, which might be reviewed and accepted by other specialized experts.

Addams' perspective, however, demonstrates that social theory is actually only possible because of people who are acting to remake social realities. Conversely, effective action requires some sort of orientation toward what could or ought to be accomplished. That is, although theory might be seen as if it is "about" social reality, it is actually potentially developed in the making of social realities. New generations of people shape the realities of their time through what they do, even if they are not starting with a clean slate. Accordingly, the most generative and actionable

[33] Looking back on twenty years of Hull-House Addams describes the dynamic between theory and practice this way: "I am inclined to think that perhaps all this general discussion was inevitable in connection with the early Settlements, as they in turn were inevitable result of theories of social reform." Addams, pages 129–130.

[34] Addams, pages 42–58.

theories emerge where the real (how things are experienced in the present) confronts the possible (what could be otherwise).

Addams explained her overall approach to practicing theories of democracy as a form of *translation and interpretation*—within and across conventionally top-down and bottom-up processes.[35] If institutions and organizations tended to think in broad generalizations, an on-the-ground view of people's experience revealed particular stories, cases, and problems. While it was often true that many people living in the poor immigrant neighborhoods were learning to speak English, Addams thought of interpretation in broader terms—that these communities also had little or no connection to city, state, or national institutions.

This inaccessibility of institutions had practical implications, in that some newcomers quite literally had very little idea about legal rights the US constitution afforded, or the civic ideals of the country. When people were dissatisfied, suffering, or in despair about the conditions of their lives, they did not often have formal public spaces or outlets for political expression.[36] Addams knew, however, that wealthier and more established residents had many pathways to representation in government. In wealthy neighborhoods, governmental agencies seemed to directly respond to the people—for example, complaints about garbage collection and public safety would have a swift response—but in poorer immigrant neighborhoods, city services were more sporadic. It is in this context that the task of translation or interpretation was meant to open up pathways of knowledge exchange between communities and larger organizations or institutions. What was at stake here was the very possibility of democracy in a time of growing inequality and polarization.

[35] Addams writes that there was a need to "interpret American institutions to those who are bewildered concerning them either because of their personal experience, or because of preconceived theories." This is not just about the formalities of citizenship, but all of the opportunities and possibilities of civic participation. Addams, pages 268–271.

[36] Addams theorized that this is one reason there was a rise in violent anarchism in the 1890s. Of course, she argued, people will want to violently takedown a system if it is either ignoring them or actively harming them, and they do not see any pathways to have their voice be heard.

Today, in an increasingly pluralistic society, with a fragmentation of both communities and knowledge, the need to translate
across theory, everyday life, policy, and practice is perhaps more
relevant than ever. For instance, Christine Gaspar describes the
practice of the Center for Urban Pedagogy in New York City,
which aims to explore "how the city works" with those impacted
by specific policies or systems. Based on expressed needs from
activist and community-based organizations, the center collab-
orates with designers to break down complex urban systems
into visual formats that are easy to share and understand. They
assemble groups, with those from marginalized communities,
to translate institutional policies and protocols into workshops
and visual representations that invite people to collaborate in
understanding and acting in their neighborhoods.[37]

In a different context, Jeanne van Heeswijk's Freehouse
worked in-between theory and practice in the Afrikaanderwijk
neighborhood of Rotterdam, the Netherlands, where 85 percent
of residents (in 2014) were of non-Dutch origin and 29 percent
lived below the poverty index. To some extent, Freehouse was
a means to practice theories about what the city could become.
The project begins with a research question: How to revitalize the
Afrikaanderwijk neighborhood in such a way that local inhabitants will not be displaced? But, like Addams, the investigation of
this question is not only through researching or theorizing *about*
the community. Instead, through 450 small-scale interventions
and 5 communal workshops, the project overall conceives ways
to bring diverse groups together: "putting forth counter forms of
urban and economic developments that thrive on social encounter,
collaboration and exchange."[38] Local inhabitants, shop-keepers, and
young people exchange knowledge, experience, and ideas across
social boundaries to develop interventions including food courts, a
neighborhood workshop for fashion production, gathering points,

[37] Christine Gaspar, "Images of the City: The Work of the Center for Urban
   Pedagogy," in Miodrag Mitrasinovic (editor), *Concurrent Urbanities:
   Designing Infrastructures of Inclusion* (Routledge, 2016), pages 76–86.
[38] Jeanne van Heeswijk, "Freehouse: Radicalizing the Local," in Nick Aikens,
   Thomas Lange, Jorinde Seijdel, and Steven ten Thije (Editors), *What's the Use?
   Constellations of Art, History and Knowledge* (Valiz, 2016), pages 298–311.

and a cooperative store. Although rooted in an understanding of social, historical, and political contexts, the actions associated with Freehouse show the imperative of thought to participate in creating new realities today. They demonstrate that now, and certainly in light of the model of the Hull-House, processes of creating can aspire toward a new ethic of knowing, making, and being.

CARING AND CREATING

While Jane Addams is increasingly described today as one of the founders of public administration, social work, and state welfare, the heart of her work went well beyond the institutionalization of a social safety net.[39] Although she lived within a time of increasingly bureaucratic responses to human needs that administered charity or services to the poor, the theories and practices initiated by Addams attempted to "take relations of care out of this kind of charity model."[40] That is, even if policies or services were to be created on a systemic level, she saw that sustaining a democracy would always require the ongoing design and practice of everyday maintenance and care-work. This was done as an evolving process of establishing and maintaining relationships—from the social connections among people to the built environment.

Practice at the Hull-House also recognized that as capitalism fragments and specializes societies it creates an intensifying necessity for services and systems to connect people and places that have been separated. Even today this is relevant, at a time when services continue to be commodified and/or bureaucratized in a way that fragments society further. Caring in this context

---

[39] Patricia Shields notes that Addams' approach to public administration looks different than current mainstream practices: Patricia M. Shields, "Democracy and the Social Feminist Ethics of Jane Addams: A Vision for Public Administration," *Administrative Theory & Praxis*, volume 28, issue 3, 2006, pages 418–443.

[40] Shannon Jackson, "Toward a Queer Social Welfare Studies: Unsettling Jane Addams," in Marilyn Fischer, Carol Nackenoff, and Wendy Chmielewski (editors), *Jane Addams and the Practice of Democracy* (University of Illinois Press, 2009), page 150.

may be thought of as a good disposition to have or something that involves specific techniques in professions of healthcare and human services, which "administer" care. Addams, however, reminds us that neither the individual nor the benevolent institution should be centered in designs for social innovation and transformation. Rather it is the human needs, and the responses to these needs in everyday life that ought to be of primary concern.[41]

One particularly notable example of ongoing care and maintenance is in Addams' work in city garbage removal and sanitation. Community members had raised the issue of unsanitary streets outside their homes, and the Hull-House subsequently set out to document sanitation issues, violations of the law, and neglect of the city government to maintain adequate waste removal services. When they submitted their report to the city, and it did not generate an immediate response, Addams applied to be an inspector of garbage removal within the city sanitation department. This position involved monitoring government contractors and getting directly involved with maintaining infrastructures for garbage removal (from procuring adequate receptacles for apartment buildings to participating in the disposal process).[42]

With this move into city sanitation services and systems, Addams demonstrated that while ideals or aspirations about what might be possible can help foster a new sense of social imagination, design ultimately must also include the everyday care and maintenance that actually makes daily life possible in the first place. Rather than waiting for an outside agency, institution, or organization to step in, Addams and colleagues at the Hull-House got to work themselves, nudging, even if in small ways, institutions that had failed to care toward new relationships and responsibilities. This approach is especially relevant today, in Western cultures that often idolize the production of flashy new objects and ideas over maintenance, at a moment when society

[41] For more on the role/relation of caring in design see, for example: Craig Bremner, Giovanni Innella, and Ian Coxon (editors), *Does Design Care? An International Workshop of Design Thought and Action*, Imagination Lancaster, Lancaster University, 2017. See also: Paul Rodgers and others, "The Lancaster Care Charter," *Design Issues*, volume 35, issue 1, 2019, pages 73–77.

[42] Addams, pages 187–190.

and space are saturated with dense networks of already-produced objects, infrastructures, buildings, and information.[43]

Public acts of caring (for people and communities), or maintaining systems and spaces (like getting directly involved in neighborhood waste removal), also challenged conventional ideals of care and gender. In particular, Addams and colleagues moved notions of kinship and care beyond what many of their contemporaries considered to be natural "maternal instincts" of the *private* heterosexual mother in her family, and into *public* spaces. The Hull-House, therefore, did not merely export a fixed gendered ideal of "care," but it also revealed new social possibilities in and through its expanding practices of caring.[44] Such care-work was especially powerful at Hull-House because it was focused in and with immigrant communities, who were physically part of the same city even as they remained socially distant strangers to the more established residents.

It could be said that the concepts and practices connected to the Hull-House, which have lived on in different communities to the present, point to the potential model of *thinking and designing as caring.* If *to care* is to pay attention and respond to the complexity and detail of the worlds around us, then genuine caring requires the sort of hospitality that Addams and the Hull-House demonstrated—to invite new ideas, people, and experiences into our lives and work. This is not only to allow others to "participate" in a project, nor is it merely to get "input" into the design of a system, service, or research study. Instead, Addams demonstrates how a primary commitment to establishing and maintaining relationships ultimately creates

[43] In reflecting on Mierle Laderman Ukeles' "Manifesto for Maintenance Art 1969!" Christine Wertheim emphasizes the need to uplift the role of maintenance in contemporary economic systems that idolize productivity: Christine Wertheim, "After the Revolution, Who's Going to Pick up the Garbage?" *X-TRA*, volume 12, issue 2, winter 2009, accessed at: https://www.x-traonline.org/article/after-the-revolution

[44] Jackson, pages 152–153. See also: Dolores Hayden, *Redesigning the American Dream: The Future of Housing, Work and Family Life* (W. W. Norton and Company, 1984); Judy Whipps, "Jane Addams's Social Thought as a Model for a Pragmatist-Feminist Communitarianism," *Hypatia*, volume 19, issue 3, 2004, pages 118–133.

knowledges and designs that are better attuned to people's needs and aspirations. From a caring disposition and acts of solidarity or hospitality, we can then begin to design and imagine with, not for, people who are most directly impacted by the challenges facing society today.[45]

The notion of thinking and designing as caring has implications for today well beyond what is considered the field of social or human services. For instance, Shannon Mattern notes "If we apply 'care' as a framework of analysis and imagination for the practitioners who design our material world, the policymakers who regulate it, and the citizens who participate in its democratic platforms, we might succeed in building more equitable and responsible systems."[46] Caring in this sense is not only an ephemeral or an individual gesture. It can be a foundation for creating new worlds. The task before us is accordingly not to rush toward an end point of a specific intervention, but first, to care for systems, relationships, and places that may already exist. From this caring, the work of creation, of bringing something into existence in and through community, can begin.

Overall, to center caring in processes of creating or making affirms that social thought and design ought to be pursued as a means of *establishing concrete relations* with others.[47] Addams models how thinking can relate distant people and concepts— bringing those with different life experiences together in the same room to explore possible courses of action that could be tried. At the same time, the practices of the Hull-House show how

---

[45] For a new generation of service design today, forms of active and empathetic listening are considered a core capability. See, for example: Laura Penin, *Introduction to Service Design: Designing the Invisible* (Bloomsbury, 2018).

[46] Shannon Mattern, "Maintenance and Care," *Places Journal*, November 2018, accessed at: https://doi.org/10.22269/181120

[47] In some ways Addams' practice provides a further elaboration of how design professions can learn from everyday acts of "gift giving," where one's effort in thinking or making is undertaken from a basis of trying to understand (perhaps even collaboratively) the genuine needs of people and communities. Clive Dilnot, "The Gift," *Design Issues*, volume 9, issue 2, 1993, page 55.

designing can be a way to begin transforming worlds that are indifferent to some people's fate into worlds that acknowledge, and even celebrate, human sentience, relationship, and potential.[48] This is especially evident in efforts that were initiated to design systems, services, and spaces with new immigrants. Such work also required, in part, that Addams and her colleagues move beyond purely professional thinking/making into everyday acts of care and hospitality.

In this sense, Jane Addams and Hull-House challenge us today—to imagine, theorize, and design for interventions that emerge from acts of solidarity and hospitality with others in our daily lives. Another implication of this model is that it is no longer enough to only make interesting analyses, objects, policies, spaces, or solutions. We must also deeply care for and about social realities, in an iterative process of trying to more meaningfully understand, act, and create as part of larger communities. While such a sensibility surely cannot be forced, the communities of practice related to Jane Addams show us that it is, indeed, possible to cultivate an ethic of care in the process of creating. Addams offers us useful place to begin (again) to care, even in moments when widening social divides and harsh social realities make relations with others seem strained, distant, or impossible.

ACTING TOWARD HUMAN COMMUNITY AND LIBERATION

The emphasis on care in Addams' practice, and in design today, brings us back to the media spectacle of mass global migration that opened this chapter. Although it is certainly important to attend to the needs of immigrants and dismantle exclusionary policies, it is also necessary to do more to confront deeper roots of the migrant crisis, which are embedded in ways of thinking, knowing, and acting. This is a larger societal crisis that design and social science professions perpetuate—for instance in divorcing theory from practice, or devising interventions *for* an imagined foreign other rather in solidarity *with* diverse groups.

[48] Dilnot, pages 55–56.

The broader issue of the present moment is related to what Hannah Arendt referred to as the perilous turn toward "inner emigration," where "in the face of an unendurable reality" people withdraw from the world into an "interior realm."[49] Today, the possibilities of public life and civic participation are further diminished in a culture of media-driven fear of the foreigner—with the threat of authoritarian leaders, further militarized borders, and increasing hostility toward migrants. Especially for those who are newcomers or struggling to survive in-between places and identities, the world can be hostile and precarious.

It is in this sense that Gloria Anzaldúa explains how those who are marginalized in a world of exclusionary political borders may struggle to recover a sense of home: "we shiver in separate cells in enclosed cities, shoulders hunched, barely keeping panic below the surface of the skin, daily drinking shock along with our morning coffee … we do not engage fully."[50] The implications of this marginalization reverberate well beyond excluded groups. As people retreat further by choice or necessity—into polarized identities, neighborhoods, and experiences—the technical and managerial capacities of the public and private sectors are further strained.

People lose trust in large institutions, and even in the possibility of civil society. As Anzaldúa explains, borders are not only physical constructions at international boundaries. They are also internal walls—differences in thinking, making, and being that put neighbors worlds apart. No data can bridge this chasm, and no policy can cure the profound sense of alienation. So then, how do we begin to see beyond the literal and figurative walls that separate us today? What sort of imagination and practice will enable us to engage more fully with new sorts of personal and civic possibilities?

The social thought and action of Jane Addams—as it relates to addressing political polarization and community breakdown—is

---

[49] Quoted in: Søren Rosenbak, "Alienation," in Eduardo Staszowski and Virginia Tassinari (editors), *Designing in Dark Times: An Arendtian Lexicon* (Bloomsbury, 2021), pages 37–41.

[50] Gloria Anzaldúa, *Borderlands/La Frontera: The New Mestiza* (Aunt Lute Books, 1987), pages 42–43.

especially relevant today. It is useful to see present conditions in light of some lineages related to the practice of Addams on theorizing in, of, and for practice. In particular, the legacies of Addams' work can be traced through efforts to shelter Jewish refugees during the Second World War, and later to the sanctuary movement to protect refugees in the 1980s United States. Although not always directly connected, the concepts and practices of sanctuary and hospitality might be seen as related to a broader tradition that Jane Addams and her colleagues helped to develop.[51] For example, in the 1980s, some Christian and Quaker communities began to respond to growing numbers of Central American refugees, based on philosophical and religious ideals of hospitality. They created safe spaces for refugees along the Mexican-US border and also contributed to building community in war-torn countries such as El Salvador.[52] In some ways, the very notion of sanctuary rejects the fear and fatalism of recent times. Rather than accepting the world as it is, a practice of sanctuary involves taking action that is inspired by theories of community and democracy. Practices of sanctuary ultimately see direct action as a means to *both* understand migrant experiences *and* act to make society more welcoming.[53]

For instance, in the case of El Salvador in the 1980s, many people that had been forcibly displaced from their homes would

[51] Mary Watkins, for instance, traces the praxis of hospitality from Hull-House to "mutual accompaniment" in the present: Mary Watkins, "From Hospitality to Mutual Accompaniment: Addressing Soul Loss in the Citizen-Neighbor," in Tomaž Grušovnik, Eduardo Mendieta, and Lenart Škof (editors), *Borders and Debordering: Topologies, Praxes, Hospitableness* (Lexington Books, 2018). Also see Hondagneu-Sotelo's connection between Addams and contemporary morally or religiously inspired movements for immigrant social justice: Pierrette Hondagneu-Sotelo, "Religion and a Standpoint Theory of Immigrant Social Justice," in Pierrette Hondagneu-Sotelo (editor), *Religion and Social Justice for Immigrants* (Rutgers University Press, 2007), pages 3–15.

[52] Linda Rabben, *Sanctuary and Asylum: A Social and Political History* (University of Washington Press, 2016).

[53] It's not so much what kind of religious and spiritual reflection people engaged, but rather that through the kind of reflection such traditions promote, people and communities came to place their trust in working for better worlds they could not yet fully see or know. Much like the work of Jane Addams, these activists sought a "sermon of the deed," to bring mobilize their theories and ideals about the world, in and for practice.

collaborate with local radical religious leaders and social activists to respond to the widespread forced displacements across the country. The Salvadoran Civil War (where the United States was sending up to 1–2 million dollars to El Salvador per day, to fund a repressive military regime) led to 80,000 deaths and thousands more disappeared after more than a decade of fighting from 1980 to 1992. By the end of the war, more than a million people had been displaced from their homes.[54] When militias, that the United States trained and funded, descended on rural towns, people often fled El Salvador to neighboring Honduras or Guatemala, where they stayed temporarily in refugee camps. About a half million people resettled permanently in other countries, like the United States, where an emergent Sanctuary Movement was challenging exclusionary attitudes and policies, but others began a process of resettlement in different parts of El Salvador.

In some cases, theories about the potentials of human community contributed to resettlement practices, which emerged from Salvadoran social movements and "Christian Base Communities." Those who were resettling in El Salvador often got to work on the literal and figurative construction of a community—through informal acts of town planning, neighborhood reconstruction, and design that led to the creation of everything from physical spaces, community centers, and roads, to cooperative agriculture, business, and governance processes. The goal was not only to make political and economic change, but it was also to engage in forms of cultural activism that might reweave people's relationship to each other and the land. This often revolved around community reflection, spiritual, and religious symbols, or narratives that instilled a sense of collective hope through perilous times or oppressive contexts.[55]

[54] The United States relationship to the Salvadoran Civil War is chronicled in: Mark Danner, *The Massacre at El Mozote* (Vintage, 1994).

[55] For more on the context of resettlement and El Salvador that has informed this analysis, see: Matthew DelSesto and Megan Donovan, "Roots of Resistance and Resilience: Agroecology Tactics for Resettlement," *Journal of Agriculture, Food Systems and Community Development*, volume 9, issue 1, 2019, pages 101–117.

Such work was inspired by the praxis-oriented social imagination of liberation theology. Rather than embracing an abstract theory about human community from the perspective of an afterlife, which prioritizes following established rules and accepting the way things are, liberation theologies embrace *the potential of liberating humanity from suffering and oppression through acting.* That is, they embrace a form of action based on moral and ethical ideals about the way the world could, or ought to, be. The shift that liberation theologies make in conceptualizing human beings differently is not simply of theological importance.

The imperative of these theories of liberation is to work to build a world that allows for the greatest expression of engagement, joy, justice, and human potential. In this approach to acting, ideals are not other-worldly dreams or fantasies of a perfect heavenly paradise. Rather, theologies and ideals of liberation are only fully expressed here and now—in the bodies, spaces, stories, and actions of people.

In this paradigm, *liberating action* is therefore ultimately about an orientation toward imagination and creativity—not a sense of inward focused imagining, but of a social imagination where people see themselves as part of a web or relations. This is a social imagination that opens up to questioning what is, imagining what is possible, and building a different world together.[56] Making plans for collaboration with organizations or raising demands from large institutions or organizations may still be necessary, but the notion of liberating action, especially in the context of global migrations and displacements, highlights the urgency of actually getting to work, to imagine and make new worlds. When liberatory theories of a preferred or better world are advanced from within a profound connection to social realities, the result can be the design of new public spaces,

---

[56] For example, Clodovis Boff and Leonardo Boff describe "liberating action" as a transformative, creative, or imaginative process of collectively reflecting on social realities and acting. Clodovis Boff and Leonardo Boff, *Introducing Liberation Theology* (Burns & Oates, 1987).

services, and systems.[57] The approach might also involve acting as a form of "pragmatic solidarity," to engage in concrete acts of support for grassroots community leaders, sharing resources and strategies across the many walls that divide us today.[58]

Overall, insights related to the legacy of Jane Addams and Hull-House point toward what it could mean to imaginatively practice the sensibilities of designing and the social imagination. Interventions in the context of global migrations and displacements, from the nineteenth century to the present, show the urgent need for reweaving connections between theory and practice—to connect aspirations of what *could be* with a spirit of hospitality, solidarity, and care. The work described here also models how it is possible to produce new knowledge in the process of addressing the root causes of social suffering and exclusion. Ultimately this legacy invites us to imagine ways of practicing theory and theorizing practice that might unleash and liberate human potential.[59]

[57] Public health leader Paul Farmer explains, in dialog with liberation theologian Gustavo Guttiérrez, how liberation theologies have oriented his work to create new public health spaces, services, and systems in communities facing dire poverty, and how his practice itself might lead to new theoretical insights about poverty and liberation. Michael Griffin and Jennie Weiss Block (editors), *In the Company of the Poor: Conversations with Dr. Paul Farmer and Fr. Gustavo Gutiérrez* (Orbis Books, 2013).

[58] M. Brinton Lykes and Erin Sibley, "Liberation Psychology and Pragmatic Solidarity: North-South Collaborations through the Ignacio Marín-Baró Fund," *Peace and Conflict: Journal of Peace Psychology*, volume 20, issue 3, 2014, pages 209–226.

[59] Tony Fry suggests some additional considerations for what could be considered a liberatory design praxis. The implications are, in part, that acting itself must be liberated from professional practices and norms that constrain possibilities in the present. Tony Fry, "Design, a Philosophy of Liberation and Ten Considerations," *Strategic Design Journal*, volume 11, issue 2, 2018, pages 174–176.

5 W.E.B. Du Bois: From Consciousness to Cooperation

In the twenty-first century, the world prison population has grown at a faster rate than the general population.[1] The United States had led the way in this global prison boom over the last four decades—with less than 5 percent of the world's population but more than 20 percent of the world's prisoners. This is not necessarily due to rising crime rates, but is rather a shift in how societies around the world, including those from the United States, are responding to crime.[2] How could it be that that a country like the United States, which is known to embrace the ideals of freedom and democracy, takes away people's freedom at the highest rates of any nation in the world?

While much research has been done to understand the causes of crime, or the potentially damaging effects prison has on people,

---

[1] While this is certainly not a uniform trend, and indeed some countries have seen decline in their prison populations during this time, the fact remains that incarceration has been increasingly seen as a solution to social problems around the world. See, for example: Olivia Rope and Frances Sheahan, *Global Prison Trends* (Penal Reform International and Thailand Institute of Justice, 2018), accessed at: https://www.penalreform.org/resource/global-prison-trends-2018/.

[2] Marc Mauer explains how there is not consensus among researchers that more incarceration actually leads to lower crime rates. Marc Mauer, *Race to Incarcerate* (The New Press, 2006).

it is equally significant to consider what prisons can tell us about this moment in history. Educator Lori Pompa suggests that "prison is a prism" to understand wider issues in society.[3] More than a single building or institution, the prison can be seen as containing or reflecting a wide spectrum of issues facing society today.

Perhaps more than any other challenge today, prisons reveal the persistent culture of intense competition, individualism, and punishment, where traditional communities have given way to an increasingly global, fluid, and individualistic economy. They shed light on the social marginalization and lack of economic opportunity that impedes people's ability to participate in society, while hindering our mental and physical capacities to act. As social institutions, prisons ultimately highlight the problems of political instability from generations of colonization and racism, which gave rise to formal and informal networks of violence, organized crime, and terrorism.

These problems have been further fueled by the continuing globalization of markets, interventionist policies of nations with accumulated resources and power, and growing pervasiveness of personal computing and the internet. In this context, prison is a stop-gap measure to force a sense of control onto an increasingly instable and uncertain world. That is, prisons are ultimately reactionary responses to crime—as an intervention *after* a defined criminal activity has occurred. In many cases, the focus on the individual criminal act, as a way to create social order, obscures the root causes of crime that are often connected to larger social contexts. Ultimately, today's prisons *exclude* those whose behavior is deemed inappropriate or dangerous (which is always a partially subjective assessment), but they also, more fundamentally, attempt to *manage* a deepening crisis of social, political, and economic instability.[4]

---

[3] Lori Pompa, "Breaking Down the Walls: Inside-Out Learning and the Pedagogy of Transformation," in Stephen John Hartnett (editor), *Challenging the Prison-Industrial Complex: Activism, Arts, and Educational Alternatives* (University of Illinois Press, 2011), pages 252–272.

[4] Carolyn Côté-Lussier, David Moffette, and Justin Piché (editors), *Contemporary Criminological Issues: Moving Beyond Insecurity and Exclusion* (University of Ottawa Press, 2020).

In the United States, it has become clear that the prison building boom, which took place from the 1970s into the early twenty-first century, has alienated entire communities from society. Incarceration is not applied universally for all crimes, but rather it disproportionately focuses on those who are poor, Black, indigenous, or people of color.[5] In recent decades, scholars have used the term "prison industrial complex" to describe how prisons, as social institutions, have gathered a momentum of their own. The prison industrial complex explains the alignment of public and private sectors around building and maintaining a vast network of prison infrastructures—now a 180-billion-dollar industry in the United States alone. The prison industrial complex becomes embedded in society through a spiraling combination of prison labor, promises of public safety, claims about economic development for communities near prisons, and a network of private vendors that build prisons, create and sell surveillance technology, or supply the wide range materials and products that prisons need.[6]

It is in this context that public trust in law enforcement—like many other institutions of democracy—continues to erode under current systems of policing, criminal justice, and social control. Scholars and much of the wider public have come to understand that the promises of democracy have not actually been fulfilled for the entire population. Indeed, as some have noted, the United States today is often experienced as a *punishing democracy*, where "daily mechanisms of governance, the everyday habits of citizenship, our embodied modes of consumption and sense-making, the very fabric of our national life, have become enmeshed in the technologies and rituals of punishment."[7] This is not just a problem

---

[5] Todd Clear, *Incarcerating Communities: How Mass Incarceration Makes Disadvantaged Neighborhoods Worse* (Oxford University Press, 2007).

[6] James Kilgore, *Understanding Mass Incarceration: A People's Guide to the Key Civil Rights Struggle of Our Time* (The New Press, 2015); Peter Wagner and Bernadette Rabuy, "Following the Money of Mass Incarceration," *Prison Policy Initiative*, 2017, accessed at: https://www.prisonpolicy.org/reports/money.html.

[7] Stephen John Hartnett, "Empowerment or Incarceration: Reclaiming Hope and Justice from a Punishing Democracy," in Stephen John Hartnett (editor), *Challenging the Prison-Industrial Complex: Activism, Arts, and Educational Alternatives* (University of Illinois Press, 2011), pages 1–12.

for the imprisoned or socially marginalized. The entire society is constrained by a lack of imagination and capacity to address the fundamental social crisis we face collectively today—especially its roots in histories of colonization and racism around the world.

The current era of "mass incarceration" in the United States is often seen as a major sign of the continuing legacies of slavery and impacts of racism today, with many using Michelle Alexander's language of the "New Jim Crow" describe the evolving relationship between criminal justice policies and racism. In recent decades, social movements and civil society groups have organized around issues related to criminal justice reform as a beginning to wider social transformation, with many describing mass incarceration as a major civil rights issue of our time.[8] If Jim Crow refers to state and local laws that enforced racial segregation after slavery in the United States, *New* Jim Crow implies that the forms of race and racism today can be, in part, understood by looking at the social-historical development of race and racism. This means that, although racism and social marginalization look very different today, there is also a need to understand present situations in a social-historical context.

William Edward Burghardt Du Bois is one of the notable early voices that sought to both understand and transform racism in his time. Born in 1868 in Great Barrington, Massachusetts, W.E.B. Du Bois grew up in a time when slavery had been formally abolished, but racist laws and ideas flourished. Like his contemporaries, such as Patrick Geddes and Jane Addams, Du Bois's research and practice was interested the problems of industrial society, but through a different lens. Du Bois came to focus his work on trying to understand the ways that racism was connected to the formation of modern industrial society, and discern what could be done to eradicate racism. His approach offers strategies and inspiration for engaging, understanding, and transforming social reality today.

Similar to Geddes and Addams in previous chapters, Du Bois's life and work is conceived here an evolving practice of designing. While he did not describe his work this way, bringing a design

---

[8] Michele Alexander, *The New Jim Crow: Mass Incarceration in the Age of Colorblindness* (The New Press, 2010).

lens to his projects shows how Du Bois clarified the issues he wanted to address, and initiated courses of thought and action to move toward the desired transformations. In particular, he hoped his thought and action would contribute to clarifying and challenging the causes of racial oppression—toward a project of overcoming the effects of racial injustice while building a new society. The community of thought and practice that emerged around Du Bois is relevant for the twenty-first century, when design scholars and practitioners have begun to grapple with the implications of colonization and Eurocentrism in design theories and practices. Du Bois was confronting these issues long before they were more widely discussed, and the remaining sections of this chapter will begin to explore some of the foundations he offers for thinking and designing today.

It is also notable that Du Bois's scholarship and practice was rooted in *the possible*. That is, his work was grounded in a social imagination that would be centered on human freedom, especially for those whose freedom had been denied.[9] This was not an individual vision of utopia. The courses of thought and action that Du Bois initiated were part of a social process of ongoing personal and collective reflection—from within the social and historical forces that were shaping the world around him—with a growing community of activists, artists, scholars, and visionary leaders. The next section looks at the context the Du Bois was facing, and how it remains relevant for today. After this general orientation, the remaining three sections explore three major themes in Du Bois's work, in the light of their implications of the social theory and social action in the present.

RACE AND RACISM, THEN AND NOW

Born in 1868, W.E.B. Du Bois would come to know and understand racism first hand. Although he grew up in a small town in Massachusetts that was somewhat more tolerant, he attended

---

[9] Scholars, including as Aldon Morris, describe Du Bois's vision as an "emancipatory sociology."

college at Fisk University in Tennessee before being the first African American to graduate with a PhD from Harvard University. He also spent time studying at Berlin University, where he gained a renewed perspective on race and racism in the United States, and globally.

Early in his life, it became very clear to him that although slavery had formally ended in the United States, the ideas and effects of racism were persisting into the twentieth century. Educational access and attainment among Black citizens remained low. Most continued to work for meager wages in a hostile environment, often under constant threats of racist violence or imprisonment for minor violations. Many laws and policing practices were explicitly designed to target Blacks, so that they could be more easily sent to prison. Once in prison, they did not have to be paid for their labor (the Thirteenth Amendment to the US Constitution had outlawed slavery, "except as punishment for a crime"), and prisoners were essentially re-enslaved as they were put to work in chains or under watch of law enforcement, farming, or maintaining highways. Moreover, Jim Crow laws were enacted to mandate racial segregation, restrict voting access, and limit economic opportunities of former slaves and those who white society could not identify as white. These laws would be actively enforced for nearly 100 years after the end of slavery, until the 1960s.

There were also dramatic changes happening in US society. Most social thinkers on the topic of race were white, and their theories were shaped by white reactions to the arrival of Black migrants in northern cities (as they fled racial terror in the South) and the arrival of new, more racially ambiguous immigrants. In this context, Du Bois dedicated his life to trying to understand the continuing effects of racism and exploring possibilities to end it. He did not, however, initially anticipate just how deep race and racism was in the United States' culture. From the beginning of his studies at Harvard he met scholars and well-read elites actively writing and arguing for the inherent inferiority of so-called non-white races.

Many scholars at, what some believed to be, the best universities claimed they were advancing new social theories and sciences that justified the racial inferiority of people of African descent. This was significant because racist theorizing was coming from those who were considered the more respected and intelligent members of white society. In this context, white academic institutions intentionally ignored and marginalized Du Bois's scholarship on racism.[10]

From Du Bois's wide range of experience with people of different races and classes in the United States and abroad, it had become obvious that someone's racial identity did not define their other human characteristics or potential. He understood that racism was not just a matter of behavior or policies, but rather racism stemmed from *ideas about race that had been socially constructed, spatially arranged, and institutionalized*—because they were convenient for European colonists, slave owners in the United States, and the expansion of empires more broadly.[11] Du Bois realized that by inventing scientific explanations about why Blacks, indigenous peoples, or other people of color were inferior to white Europeans and colonizers, the white establishment could justify their violence as part of an unquestionable natural order.

***

At first glance, the context of the twenty-first century may seem much different from this era. Many today recognize the evils of racism, and most people do not believe in the inferiority of races as a scientific fact (or if they do, they are less willing to say these beliefs out loud in academic circles). Moreover, the twentieth century saw substantial policy changes in the wake of civil rights movements, and the dawn of the twenty-first century

[10] Aldon D. Morris, *The Scholar Denied: W.E.B. Du Bois and the Birth of Modern Sociology* (University of California Press, 2015).

[11] Scholars today observe that the notion of "racialized modernity"—which sees the development of race and racism as central to the project of colonialism, empire, and capitalism—was at the center of much of Du Bois's research practice. José Itzigsohn and Karida L. Brown, *The Sociology of W.E.B. Du Bois: Racialized Modernity and the Global Color Line* (New York University Press, 2020).

saw the election of the first African American president in the United States.

Despite the fact that some see this as evidence of a "color-blind" society, racial disparities persist in almost every aspect of life—from wealth and health to education and incarceration—with deadly consequences. In one sense, the current moment could be considered an era of "racism without racists," where the forms of racism persisting today do not necessarily involve individual racist thoughts and behaviors.[12] Even though people may no longer explicitly use racial categories to designate some groups biologically inferior, it is clear that racialized stereotypes and images have actually implicitly strengthened to some extent. For example, there is strong evidence that employers use cultural judgements and stereotypes to evaluate the work ethic, likelihood of success, and choices of Black US job-seekers in a way that makes racial differences appear as if they are natural.[13] In other words, racist speech today may be constrained in some spheres, but racist thought, systems, and outcomes have proliferated in new ways.

The twenty-first century has also seen the emergence of Black Lives Matter as an unprecedented movement for racial justice that has brought global consciousness to race and racism.[14] A central impetus for such efforts has been police violence that disproportionally impacts those who are Black, indigenous, and people of color—which activists often portrayed as part of a history of a larger social historical condition of marginalization and violence. In this context, the unfinished work of civil rights today can be understood not only in an abstract legal or policy analysis, but also from how violence is concentrated in marginalized communities. For instance, people's everyday experiences

---

[12] Eduardo Bonilla-Silva, *Racism Without Racists: Color-Blind Racism and the Persistence of Racial Inequality in America* (Roman & Littlefield, 2003).

[13] Moon-Kie Jung, *Beneath the Surface of White Supremacy: Denaturalizing U.S. Racisms Past and Present* (Stanford University Press, 2015).

[14] Larry Buchanan, Quoctrung Bui, and Jugal K. Patel, "Black Lives Matter May Be the Largest Movement in U.S. History," *The New York Times*, July 3, 2020.

with basic human needs such as safety, friendship, and dreams are "part of a bundle of rights and privileges that constitute full membership in the American community," and yet governments fail to protect these basic social entitlements in high-poverty African American communities.[15]

Race has also continued to be relevant for social thought and action more generally on a global scale up to the present. In the twentieth and twenty-first centuries, racial and ethnic categories fuel wars, genocide, and exclusionary policies. By the end of the twentieth century, some were predicting that racial and cultural conflicts were an inevitable "clash of civilizations" between Western European cultures and other cultures of the world that could, at best, only be managed. Even if many today disagree with this assumption, it symbolizes a deeper sense of cultural cynicism—where there is a doubt that social thought and action can adequately reckon with the deep, systemic legacies of racism and colonialism.[16]

Considering the endurance of race and racism, and the need for creative strategies to remake the socio-spatial conditions that allow racism to persist, it is accordingly ever more urgent today for those interested in social change to look to people's creative voice and capacity. This is not only as it might come through institutional laws, social programs, and policies, but in terms of how people innovate, and invent their way to survival in daily circumstances. Of particular relevance is how these everyday experiences might be connected to a larger potential of social thinking, to explore social possibilities and

[15] Monica Bell, "Safety, Friendship, and Dreams," *Harvard Civil Rights-Civil Liberties Law Review*, volume 54, 2019, page 706.

[16] On the one hand, mainstream social theory has considered critiques of colonialism and empire irrelevant, and, on the other hand, more critical or postcolonial thinkers have, at times, dismissed the entire project of social science and theory as inherently racist. This results in a sort of nihilism that can impede thought and action, while it fails to reckon with the realities that social theories were born in the age of empire, and even critical postcolonial scholarship relies on conceptual work of social theorizing. This dynamic is described with much more detail in: Julian Go, *Postcolonial Thought and Social Theory* (Oxford University Press, 2016).

reimagine institutions.[17] It is here, perhaps, that viewing Du Bosian traditions of social thought through the lens of design theory and practice is particularly important, in situating ongoing struggles to face down racism and make new forms of social organization possible.

In this context, it is worth returning to W.E.B. Du Bois's work on understanding and transforming society. The forms of race and racism that are present today have their roots in the urban industrial societies that were exploding in growth throughout the nineteenth century and into the early twentieth century. Du Bois and his colleagues were therefore uniquely positioned to understand how racism was developing as a form of social exclusion, marginalization, and violence, and how it could be faced. To what extent is it possible to intervene and act in ongoing logics of exclusion that are so deeply rooted in the institutions of society? What approaches and courses of action might begin to address longstanding forms of social marginalization? The life and work of Du Bois offer a starting point, to begin facing the social realities related to challenge.

CATALYZING NEW CONSCIOUSNESS AND CREATIVITY

Du Bois believed that new forms of consciousness or understandings of social reality are essential for social transformation. On the one hand, he saw a need to raise consciousness among whites, about the continuing effects of racism—to challenge white complacency and convince white people to address racial injustice. At the same time, he recognized that overcoming the violence of oppression may require a new consciousness in marginalized communities.

Today it may be easy to underestimate just how dominant "scientific racism" was in academic culture and wider society at the start of the twentieth century. Early in his career, Du Bois came to realize that emerging social sciences were both directly and

---

[17] Bell, pages 738–739. See also: Roberto Mangabeira Unger, *What Should Legal Analysis Become?* (Verso, 1996).

indirectly working to advance empire, racism, and colonialism—both at home and abroad. In attempting to explain the forms of inequality between people with different skin tones, theories of scientific racism maintained that Black inferiority and white superiority were natural. The leading proponents of this view were elite universities and established scholars. Moreover, wealthy white philanthropists who were funding the new social sciences and university departments embraced scientific racism, and they would typically support scholarship that advanced these views, which were considered an established social fact.[18] In this context, it is not difficult to see why Du Bois remained marginalized in academic sociology, as he tried to raise consciousness about the continuing effects of racism, and develop alternative theories, throughout his life. The critique Du Bois had of the emerging social sciences, however, went much deeper than theoretical disagreements.

In his work, Du Bois developed a profound critique of the role of social thought in society. He had a distinct vision about what should count as knowledge and what methods should be used to develop new knowledge. The central concern for Du Bois was a dangerous tendency he observed, which was gaining momentum in social sciences: reflection and theory that, in a quest for further understanding, could become too abstract to be relevant for human life and action.

The issue for Du Bois was that, in attempts to mimic the natural sciences, emerging social sciences sought to develop abstract universal laws about social reality. This led to a certain sense of *determinism* at the center of social science theorizing—a form of thinking that emphasized identifying social laws that determine the organization of society. In this view, different social outcomes based on race could be justified with abstract theorizing about racial groups. Du Bois saw that, while the tendency toward passive observation (or what Du Bois referred to as "car window sociology") was done in the name of objectivity and truth, abstract theorizing at a distance

---

[18] Morris, pages 183–186.

from the social worlds that theories claimed to explain could actually distort truth.[19]

This was especially evident in theories of scientific racism, whose proponents argued they were getting closer to the truths of racial difference, even though their claims relied on hearsay, speculation, and abstract arguments. Early in his writing and research, Du Bois pursued an alternative way of creating knowledge. He combined reflection and action—as he sought to understand how modern industrial society was being made. Rather than establishing or justifying a natural social order, this meant challenging taken-for-granted ideas. For instance, Du Bois's theorizing about race showed how ideas and effects of racism were socially created, and it challenged longstanding social scientific theories that sought to naturalize race.

To develop his theories, Du Bois did not only use abstract arguments made after withdrawing from the world; he iteratively theorized in and through engagement with social realities. Through neighborhood and regional surveys, interviews, observations of what people actually did in their everyday lives Du Bois showed how, with close inspection of actually existing social realities, it was obvious that, even after the end of formal slavery, Black communities continued to be systemically marginalized and denied equal participation in society. The data that he collected not only directly challenged scientific racism, even more importantly it meticulously documented and theorized *the ways that racism had been designed* into social structures and physical spaces.[20]

[19] Du Bois critiqued "car window sociology" of his time, which he considered "quick and superficial generalizations about complex social phenomena like the impressions one might gather by glancing at scenes through the window of a fast-moving automobile." Morris, page 25.

[20] For instance, in his seminal work *The Philadelphia Negro* (University of Pennsylvania Press, 1899), W.E.B. Du Bois documents how racism was designed. Aldon Morris describes how "Through his extensive use of maps, Du Bois captured how spatial configurations of Philadelphia were shaped by racist practices generated by the color line … Unlike the urban analysts of the Chicago School three decades later, Du Bois documented racial configurations within city spaces as planned phenomena rather than as outgrowths of natural ecological processes." Morris, page 49.

In other words, Du Bois understood human society, including race and racism, as an ongoing project of configuring worlds—including, in the United States of his time, effectively different "worlds" for those who were considered white and Black. Rather than trying to describe how social reality had been determined or was evolving in accordance with social laws as other social scientists did, Du Bois argued for the "presence of meaningful alternative courses of action" in the present; people's lives may be shaped by history, but histories of racism and colonialism did not entirely determine possibilities for action.[21] In sum, for Du Bois, "human agency had to be studied as a creative force capable of generating new directions and possibilities."[22] Du Bois accordingly pursued a form of social research and action under the premise that if realities of the present had been deliberately designed, *they could therefore be redesigned or designed differently through collective reflection and action.*

In the beginning of his career Du Bois believed that increased scientific rigor was the key to defeating racism. He thought that, if only the right facts could be accumulated, white people would be able to develop a new consciousness about racism, and they would then work to end it. But he soon realized that facts alone were not enough. This is because he came to see how racism did not operate on only the level of rational calculation, it was deeply woven into spaces, materials, systems, and cultures.

A central part of Du Bois's work to understand the effects of racism was the notion of *double consciousness*, which he describes as "this sense of always looking at one's self through the eyes of others."[23] For Du Bois, double consciousness is the kind of internal conflict that oppressed peoples experience, specifically those born Black in the United States, when white society teaches them to see themselves through the eyes of a world that looks back in "amused contempt and pity."[24] He saw that being Black in the United States meant experiencing tremendous harm—both direct violence in the form of lynching, and also the

[21] Itzigsohn and Brown, page 18.
[22] Morris, page 25.
[23] W.E.B. Du Bois, *The Souls of Black Folk* (A.C. McClurg, 1903), page 3.
[24] Du Bois, *The Souls of Black Folk*, page 3.

indirect violence of never being recognized as a full human being in the dominant culture and society.

Du Bois described how blackness meant living behind a "veil," with aspirations, struggles, and lives that were hidden from view of white society. In this context, Du Bois initially saw his work, in part, to be oriented toward the goal of raising consciousness among white society, of what social realities those face who live behind the veil.[25] Double consciousness was therefore a curse, as it was a result of systemic exclusion and violence, but it was also a potential gift because those with double consciousness had a unique capacity for understanding both white and Black social worlds.

For Du Bois, therefore, consciousness is not only about perception or knowledge, it is intimately connected to human "strivings" and "ideals." Du Bois explains how the endurance of racism that separates white and Black worlds produces a "peculiar wrenching of the soul, a peculiar sense of doubt and bewilderment ... Such a double life, with double thoughts, double duties, and double social classes, must give rise to double words and double ideals, and tempt the mind to pretense or revolt, to hypocrisy or radicalism."[26] From this perspective, consciousness is potentially future oriented precisely because of the way that it reveals the gap between existing social realities and what could be possible. Consciousness therefore is not just a quality that people possess or the increase of knowledge about fixed social facts. It is a way of seeing, and those who have experienced some form of marginalization or oppression have a particular view that Du Bois called "second sight." In this sense his work sought to raise consciousness on both sides of the veil—from privileged white society to marginalized Black communities.

But Du Bois did not just describe objective social realities of the Black experience in the United States; he also wove information gleaned from his research into compelling narratives that

[25] In his forward to *The Souls of Black Folk*, Du Bois explains to his readers (page viii): "I have stepped within the Veil, raising it that you may view faintly its deeper recesses—the meaning of its religion, the passion of its human sorrow, and the struggle of its greater souls."

[26] Du Bois, *The Souls of Black Folk*, page 202.

highlighted the subjective experience of race and racism. This is because Du Bois recognized early on that in order to reach wider publics it could be useful to place the real harms of racism in their subjective social context—to allow readers to understand the lived experience of others. He also saw that because of his own double consciousness or second sight he had had a better understanding of the realities of white society than most people who identified as white. Such a lens, of viewing white people from the perspective of Black experience, made it clear to him that white imagination was also constrained by white supremacist ideologies, but in different ways.[27]

A goal then, for Du Bois, was to develop strategies to portray the social realities of Black life for wider audiences who had been exposed to Eurocentric or white supremacist ideology. One example of this is evident in the exhibit he developed for the 1900 Paris Exposition. Du Bois collaborated with Daniel Murray and Thomas Calloway to create the interactive exhibit. The "Exhibit of American Negros" (Figure 5.1) included dozens of handmade graphs and charts, hundreds of photographs, and a series of books of research for viewers to browse. The display depicted the humanity and progress of the Black community in the United States, but also invited viewers to explore the unfinished work of racial justice. For instance, one chart (Figure 5.2) showed data portraying the percentage of Black population that was enslaved, in a way that gives a sense of how the reality of slavery cast a shadow over the reconstruction efforts after the US Civil War. Another image (Figure 5.3) portrays how Black property ownership was directly impacted by changing social and political conditions, including the Ku Klux Klan, which that initiated a campaign of racial terrorism, lynching, and "Jim Crow" disenfranchisement laws.

At a moment when his work was being silenced or ignored by US scholars, the exposition spoke to a wider international

---

[27] See especially the chapter on "The Souls of White Folk," in W.E.B. Du Bois, *Darkwater: Voices from Within the Veil* (Dover Thrift, 1999 [1920]), pages 17–29.

EXHIBIT OF AMERICAN NEGROES AT THE PARIS EXPOSITION.

FIGURE 5.1 Exhibit at the 1900 World's Fair.

Source: United States Library of Congress.

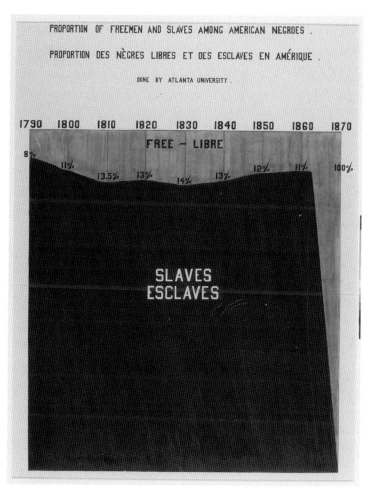

FIGURE 5.2 Proportion of freemen and slaves.
Source: United States Library of Congress.

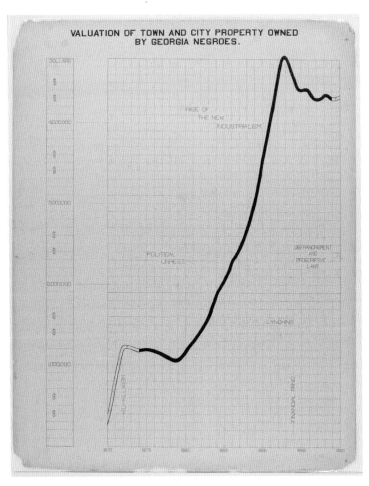

FIGURE 5.3 Valuation of town and city property.
Source: United States Library of Congress.

audience where "Du Bois and his design team used clean lines, bright color, and a sparse style to visually convey the American color line to a European audience."[28] In mixing visual arts with social science, they were pioneers in data visualization, demonstrating that in communicating data to wider audiences there was potential to generate "new patterns and knowledge through the act of visualization itself."[29] This is to say that communicating research was not simply a matter of portraying identified social facts about an already-made social reality. Instead, their practice of designing visual representations actually generated new public insights and knowledge about the Black experience in the United States.

These visualizations also involved ongoing theorizing about the social construction of race. While those in the United States and Western Europe continued to falsely depict indigenous and African peoples as "savages" who could only achieve social progress with the charity of whites, Du Bois offered counter images and narratives. His visual displays showed strong and resilient communities of Black Americans that had survived in spite of, not because of, white society. They also showed how the social realities that Black people in the United States faced were not of their own making, because their circumstances were shaped by continuing racism that built on generations of slavery and colonization. The visualizations and descriptions of these social realities were only the beginning.

Du Bois and colleagues began to realize—especially in the wake of new lynchings and voting restrictions for Blacks across the south—that they needed develop more political power if they were to achieve lasting change.[30] This led to dozens of leaders meeting and organizing from across the United States starting

---

[28] Whitney Battle-Baptiste and Britt Rusert, "Introduction," in Whitney Battle-Baptiste and Britt Rusert (editors), *W.E.B. Du Bois's Data Portraits: Visualizing Black America* (Princeton Architectural Press, 2018), page 16.

[29] Battle-Baptiste and Rusert, page 8.

[30] Recent research from the Equal Justice Initiative found that there were at least 4084 racial terror lynchings documented from 1877 to 1950. Much more on this historical context is provided in the report: *Lynching in America: Confronting the Legacy of Racial Terror, Third Edition* (Equal Justice Initiative, 2017), accessed at: https://eji.org/reports/lynching-in-america/.

in 1905, in what came to be called the Niagara Movement. As some leaders in the white community began to see the need for a national civil rights organization, Du Bois with others from the Niagara Movement and white activists founded a multi-racial organization called the National Association for the Advancement of Colored People (NAACP).

The NAACP was officially founded in 1909 with a mission "To promote equality of rights and eradicate caste or race prejudice among citizens of the United States; to advance the interest of colored citizens; to secure for them impartial suffrage; and to increase their opportunities for securing justice in the courts, education for their children, employment according to their ability, and complete equality before the law."[31] In some ways, this mission was the outgrowth of Du Bois's evolving research practice. His early work contributed to raising consciousness for the social realities of Blacks in the United States. The NAACP was a new stage in this practice—a sort of experiment to see *what might be possible through social action*, and therefore, to learn more about the social and political realities of racism.

As he participated in the founding of the Niagara Movement and the NAACP, Du Bois discerned that his practice was not just about convincing a white public of the need to act, but that it must also be about the *creation of new publics*. While raising consciousness certainly meant educating specific audiences, he understood that securing civil rights and protections from others who might cause harm (i.e., freedom *from* discrimination) would not be enough. The work of social and racial justice also involved mobilizing marginalized communities to contribute to the creation of a new society (i.e., freedom *to* create). For Du Bois, organizing and designing for inclusion was therefore not about incorporating the marginalized into an already-made plan or existing social reality; it was about widening and deepening the opportunities for creative participation in the ongoing making of society.

[31] Lisa Snowden-McCray, "The NAACP Was Established February 12, 1909," *The Crisis*, February 2019. See also: Patricia Sullivan, *Lift Every Voice: The NAACP and the Making of the Civil Rights Movement* (The New Press, 2010).

FIGURE 5.4 Editorial offices of *The Crisis*.
Source: Getty Images.

Toward this end, Du Bois turned increasing attention to engaging and raising consciousness among the Black community, especially through the creation and distribution of creative publications. One of his most influential and well-known publications, called *The Crisis*, was published as the official magazine of the NAACP starting in 1910. By 1918, its circulation had grown to more than 100,000 readers. Rather than focus only on politics, research, and policy, Du Bois believed that an active Black consciousness could also be nourished through art and literature. Throughout his time as editor (from 1910 to 1934) of *The Crisis* magazine, Du Bois brought together a creative community of writers, artists, editors, and researchers oriented toward racial justice—in the editorial office (Figure 5.4) and the wider network of contributors. Issues featured portraits and artwork (like the drawing from Laura Wheeler Waring (Figure 5.5) in the April 1923 edition of *The Crisis*) to uplift the work of Black artists.

FIGURE 5.5 Cover image of *The Crisis*.

Source: Beinecke Rare Book and Manuscript Library, Yale University.

The goal of the magazine was to "develop the knowledge people needed for their liberation," and accordingly "the analyses disseminated through *The Crisis* were intended to spur social action and social movements that could build a more just and equal world."[32] In this way, Du Bois saw that civil rights on the political level required a cultural revolution, which would only be possible with "a new desire to create, of a new will to be" in the Black community and across racial lines.[33] Eradicating racism, therefore, meant unleashing the *creative capacities* of people, just as much as it required legal and political changes.

Overall, these examples of visual design, and the power of art and creativity for inciting new consciousness, continue to be relevant. Many today are centering the power of human creative capacities in struggles against racism.[34] For example, more recently in a new wave of Afrofuturism there is focus on the importance of creativity and imagination for developing the consciousness to overcome oppression. This has been especially the case in social justice movements that are embracing the power of "visionary fiction" to mobilize thought and action. Visionary fiction is a form of science fiction that imagines more just futures. It is based on the premise that "all organizing is science fiction" because "organizers and activists dedicate their lives to creating and envisioning another world, or many other worlds."[35]

Contemporary forms of Afrofuturism are also relevant to technological design and transformation. Afrofuturism can be a means to "think through the sociocultural implications/conse-quences of design decision making" with "more inclusive design conversations about both user and context of use."[36] It can connect design processes to creative forms of Afrofuturistic reimagining, for making designs and technologies that might contribute to

[32] Morris, pages 135–136.
[33] W.E.B. Du Bois, "Criteria of a Negro Art," *The Crisis*, volume 32, October 1926, pages 290–297.
[34] See, for example: Reynaldo Anderson, "Afrofuturism 2.0 & The Black Specu-lative Arts Movement: Notes on a Manifesto," *Obsidian*, volume 42, issue 2, 2016, pages 228–336; Myron T. Strong and K Sean Chaplin, "Afrofuturism and *Black Panther*," *Contexts*, volume 18, issue 2, 2019, pages 58–59.
[35] Walidah Imarisha, "Introduction," in Adrienne Maree Brown and Walidah Imarisha (editors), *Octavia's Brood: Science Fiction Stories from Social Justice Movements* (AK Press, 2015), page 3.
[36] Woodrow W. Winchester, "Engaging the Black Ethos: Afrofuturism as Design Lens for Inclusive Technological Innovation," *Journal of Futures Studies*, volume 24, issue 2, 2019, page 56.

more just futures. This could range from forms of social innovation, to places where Black communities are imagining more socially and racially just forms of urban development.[37] Overall, visionary narratives and speculative futures can be a strategy to let go of the status quo, if only momentarily, and stoke a creative imagination for new ways of designing and acting.

Of particular importance here is the recognition that the socially marginalized or oppressed have a unique vantage point toward designing and making futures. As Du Bosian notions of double consciousness and second sight suggest, the marginalized status of oppressed groups can contribute to a deeper understanding of how society is structured and, based in part on struggles for survival, a richer imagination of other possible worlds.[38] Accordingly, the role of social thought, in working with marginalized groups more broadly, can be in collaborating with people to "theorize their lives" as they strengthen their capacities to "determine what knowledge is valid and strategically useful" for acting.[39]

For all of those who continue to seek imaginative ways to spark change in the present, the unleashing of creative capacities is a radical potential of human consciousness. That is, a new consciousness can enable us to work together with others—to understand the world anew, pursue a particular line of thinking, imagine the world beyond immediate social reality, and make new worlds. There is a long history of oppressed peoples, summoning their determination and courage to make a way out of no way, and this is precisely the lineage that so many draw upon as they continue to make sense of the world and act—to face down racism from Du Bois's time, to our own.

[37] Anna Livia Brand, "The Duality of Space: The Built World of Du Bois' Double-Consciousness," *Environment and Planning D: Society and Space*, volume 36, issue 1, 2018, pages 3–22.

[38] Itzigsohn and Brown, pages 42–43.

[39] See, for example: how some participatory action researchers describe their work with low-income LGBT people using Du Bois's concept of *second sight*: Michelle Billies, Juliet Johnson, Kagendo Murungi, and Rachel Pugh, "Naming Our Reality: Low-Income LGBT People Documenting Violence, Discrimination and Assertions of Justice," *Feminism & Psychology*, volume 19, issue 3, 2009, pages 375–380.

PRACTICING POSSIBILITIES OF
AUTONOMY AND COOPERATION

Throughout his life, Du Bois's theorizing moved toward a central insight about community and cooperation. That is, a main purpose of cultivating a new consciousness could be autonomy—as part of a struggle for self-determination in the Black community. As he noted in his writing on double-consciousness, the profound material, cultural, and spiritual alienation of Black people in the United States inflicted long-term harm during and beyond slavery. In his research with Black communities, from urban neighborhoods to rural communities, Du Bois found that racism, and oppression more broadly, stifles people's capacities and sensibilities for acting in the world. At the core of his arguments was that "social oppression creates cultural deficits among the dominated, thus encouraging cultures of domination to take hold in ways that stunt a group's social development and its capacity to engage in collective action."[40] This is why Du Bois saw that a renewed social consciousness, and indeed robust social imaginations, in the Black community could be so powerful. He envisioned that new forms of consciousness and autonomy develop in tandem. As one becomes more autonomous in one's own thoughts, body, community, and work there is a new level of consciousness, and at the same time, as a new consciousness emerges, increasing degrees of autonomy are possible.

Clearly white Western civilization was already in the midst of a profound revolution of consciousness and culture that began in the enlightenment. Thinking and acting in the wake of the enlightenment created a certain kind of autonomy, which enabled increasing numbers of people to actively question the laws that governed their existence. That is, in enlightenment thinking, societies began to call into question the institutions and laws that structured their lives. It exposed the social order, that monarchs, kings, and religious authorities argued was a natural

---

[40] Morris, page 44. It is worth noting here that social oppression also creates particular kinds of deficits among the "oppressor" or dominant class, as will be discussed later. Du Bois theorized about this in his writings on whiteness.

state, to be just one imagined form that society could take. As such, social thought, reflection, and consciousness emerged as active interventions in the world to challenge pre-given social orders—ultimately toward action that could begin to make a new society.[41] The kind of new society that this sort of thinking gave birth to was, in many respects, being forged in the century after the French and American Revolutions.

At the beginning of the twentieth century, the autonomous government fought for in the American Revolution—of, by, and for the people—did not formally include groups beyond white men. From within this context, and drawing on the history of African societies outside of the Western European context, Du Bois recognized that autonomy was not charitably bestowed upon the oppressed; it was taken in an ongoing struggle for inventive thought and action. His book, *Black Reconstruction in America*, looked specifically at Black struggles for autonomy in the years during and immediately after the United States Civil War, from 1860 to 1880.[42]

The academic consensus was that reconstruction was a failure. After the Civil War, the federal government sought to enforce equal rights for former slaves and prevent rebel governments and paramilitary forces from forming. But by the end of the 1870s, federal leadership fragmented and left ensuring rights of freedmen up to the individual states. By the 1930s, scholars argued that reconstruction had failed; they said that African Americans in the south were no better off than they had been during slavery because so many still lived poor and destitute lives. In *Black Reconstruction in America*, Du Bois told the story of reconstruction from the point of view of the Black experience.[43]

---

[41] This also resonates with the way Castoriadis conceives of autonomy as "the capacity, of a society or of an individual, to act deliberately and explicitly in order to modify its law." Cornelius Castoriadis, *World in Fragments: Writings on Politics, Society, Psychoanalysis, and the Imagination* (Stanford University Press, 1986), page 340. See also his discussion of autonomy on pages 16–18.

[42] W.E.B. Du Bois, *Black Reconstruction in America* (Harcourt Brace, 1935).

[43] David Roediger has more recently elaborated on the historical significance of Du Bois's arguments: David R. Roediger, *Seizing Freedom: Slave Emancipation and Liberty for All* (Verso, 2015).

This perspective showed that while the federal government had indeed failed in many ways, the government had never been fully responsible for freeing slaves in the first place. Abolition of slavery was, for Du Bois, only finally accomplished because of organizing in the Black community during and after slavery. Du Bois especially notes how the strikes and work stoppages led by enslaved people during the Civil War forced northerners and southerners to begin imagining the end of slavery. Northerners began to recognize that to win the war and preserve the union, they would need the ingenuity and support of free Blacks. This realization joined some white radicals and former slaves together in a struggle for building what Du Bois called an *abolition democracy*.[44]

For Du Bois abolition democracy was one of the most vital ideas to emerge from the struggles for Black autonomy, and it entailed a "clear and definite program for the freedom and uplift" in the Black community, which would assure an "extension of the realization of democracy."[45] That is, for a true abolition democracy to emerge, "The abolition of slavery meant not simply abolition of legal ownership of the slave; it meant the uplift of slaves and their eventual incorporation into the body civil, politic, and social, of the United States."[46] Abolition democracy, therefore, had the potential to be the expansion of the collective autonomy in and through the Black community. Although racist resistance from white society ultimately made this vision fail immediately after slavery, Du Bois looked to the ideal of abolition democracy for inspiration about what should be done going forward. It affirmed that abolition was not merely a negative project of making slavery illegal, but it was also the generative process of designing new institutions, and a new society.

Du Bois saw that, because there had been no comprehensive program to undo institutionalized and systemic racism, the Black community would struggle to build up an educational and economic foundation. In the face of continuing policies that

---

[44] Du Bois, *Black Reconstruction in America*, pages 55–83.

[45] Du Bois, *Black Reconstruction in America*, page 189.

[46] Du Bois, *Black Reconstruction in America*, page 189.

benefited the creation of white wealth, the Black community would continue to be challenged at every turn, in their efforts to gain ownership over the material conditions of their lives. This is perhaps why he turned his attention toward strategies to facilitate economic and political self-determination of the Black community. Of particular note in his writing and advocacy in this area was his attention to social and economic cooperations.

He came to realize that even when formal institutions had so miserably failed Blacks after the Civil War, they had nevertheless persisted in forming networks of cooperation and mutual aid. In their economic enterprises, religious institutions, educational efforts, and mutual aid organizations, Black Americans had developed practices of joint-economic ownership to uplift their community.[47] Du Bois discerned that "broad social cooperation could be directed into economic cooperation and could place Black Americans at the forefront of new forms of industry guided by a vision of industrial and spiritual emancipation."[48] In this sense, he argued that cooperative social and economic practices ought to be central to the struggle for a new consciousness and autonomy in the Black community.

With this theorizing, he reaffirmed a commitment to not simply assimilating the Black community in to the white United States. The goal was instead to design and build a Black "co-operative commonwealth" that could counter the individualism at the core of the exclusionary white capitalist economy in a settler colonial nation. One way he applied this idea with the establishment of what he and collaborators called the "Negro Cooperative Guild," which served as an incubator and accelerator for Black-owned businesses. Although this was not a long-term project, it was an instructive experience that generated new knowledge about how to confront the challenges of developing an economic base

[47] Jessica Gordon Nembhard, *Collective Courage: A History of African American Cooperative Economic Thought and Practice* (Pennsylvania State University Press, 2014).

[48] Chris Haynes Jr., "From Philanthropic Black Capitalism to Socialism: Cooperativism in Du Bois's Economic Thought," *Socialism and Democracy*, volume 32, issue 3, 2018, pages 125–145.

in the Black community. Du Bois would later recognize that this was the sort of project that demanded more attention.[49] In this way, through his thought and action on cooperative practices, Du Bois showed how autonomy could be grounded in a much-needed collaborative and social approach to intervention.

The project of building an abolition democracy through social and economic cooperation remains unfinished and relevant today. For example, it has become part of the inspiration for renewed calls for community-based investments, design, and development in the contemporary era of racism and mass incarceration.[50]

In this way, the notion of abolition democracy through cooperative practices returns us to the example of prisons that began this chapter. Rather than respond to crime and social disorder after it occurs through law, policing, and prisons—in towns and neighborhoods that have a history of marginalization and disinvestment—a new focus of social thought and action, in the tradition of abolition democracy, is emerging to connect top-down resources with longstanding bottom-up intelligence of communities.[51]

Kali Akuno, for instance, describes the vision of Cooperation Jackson today which is rooted in democratically transforming the economy through understanding evolving social conditions, organizing, and taking action. The program involves green worker cooperatives, mutual aid networks, solidarity economy institutions, food sovereignty, ecovillages, and community-owned production in emerging industries. The larger vision centers on advancing Black ownership, decolonization, and a just transition

[49] In his autobiography toward the end of his life, Du Bois describes how his views evolved to see that real equality, freedom, and justice would require expanding the cooperation that had secured freedom for African Americans to the political and economic realms. W.E.B. Du Bois, *Dusk of Dawn: Toward an Autobiography of a Race Concept* (Harcort Brace, 1940).
[50] Angela Davis powerfully connects twenty-first century prisons with Du Bois's notion of abolition democracy: Angela Y. Davis, *Abolition Democracy: Beyond Empire, Prisons, and Torture* (Seven Stories Press, 2005).
[51] On the role of the communities imagining and designing abolition democracy, see, for example: Allegra M. McLeod, "Envisioning Abolition Democracy," *Harvard Law Review*, volume 132, 2019, pages 1613–1649.

to an ecologically regenerative economy. Such an approach is meant to confront and defeat "black disposability" that manifests in present day high rates of unemployment in the Black working class.[52]

Overall, in emerging practices it is increasingly clear that cooperative action is fueled by a new imagination and consciousness. That is, cooperation is both a material/economic practice, and it requires relating, theorizing, and acting in ways that envision beyond the confines of present realities.[53] Such an approach to cooperation has the potential to undo systemic and institutionalized injustice, while also nourishing and encouraging collective autonomy in communities that have experienced exclusion in the wake of colonialism and racism. This might return social research and design practice to the sort of radical engagement with social realities that W.E.B. Du Bois advanced—to collectively imagine better words, and move toward what might be possible now.

ENGAGED PEDAGOGY

The praxis of Du Bois models a form of *designing and thinking as engaged pedagogy*, which is useful in grappling with continuing forms of racism, discrimination, and marginalization today. In this approach, engaged pedagogy is a way of acting reflectively that centers human creativity, consciousness, community, and potential. Such an emphasis can orient design and thought toward forms of social cooperation that might advance creative capacities for thinking and acting.

---

[52] Kali Akuno, "Build and Fight: The Program and Strategy of Cooperation Jackson," in Kali Akuno and Ajamu Nagwaya (editors), *Jackson Rising: The Struggle for Economic Democracy and Black Self-Determination in Jackson, Mississippi* (Daraja Press, 2017), pages 3–41. There is also broader attention to the related idea of "unbuilding racism" in architecture and design, as evidenced in the some of the work from a recent MoMA exhibition: Sean Anderson and Mabel O. Wilson (editors), *Reconstructions: Architecture and Blackness in America* (Museum of Modern Art, 2021).

[53] Elke Krasny, "Working Together: Toward Imagined Cooperation in Resistance," *Journal of Design Strategies*, volume 8, 2017, pages 62–70.

Although the term "pedagogy" may evoke images of classrooms and formal education, here it refers to a much broader and powerful practice that can occur outside of formal school buildings. More specifically, engaged pedagogy can be a means to think through ideas or possibilities collectively, to develop new action-oriented knowledge or understandings of social reality. This notion of pedagogy is relevant in its most radical sense, where education is not purely a credential, but a project *of drawing forth the potential* of individuals and communities. Engaged pedagogy therefore provides a model for what designing can be—a way in which professional and non-professional designers go about eliciting or participating in the knowledge and imaginations of communities.

Du Bois discovered, when he sought to generate new understandings of the world, that new knowledge may shed light on the limits of conventional policies, practices, or knowledge. It must therefore sometimes be oriented toward a world that does not yet exist (or is not yet understood to be possible from within the prevailing/dominant consciousness in society). Pedagogy, then, is a practice of clarifying, sharing, and generating knowledge, as much as it is an exploration of possibilities.

This is especially a challenge for design and higher education today, where teaching and research are often seen as separate activities, and the elite universities tend to reward research or professional practice accomplishments over teaching. Especially if research is only conceived as gathering information *about* a pre-existing social reality, then it will indeed continue to be at odds with pedagogy. As Du Bois demonstrates, however, pedagogy is not just a means to disseminate knowledge. It is a project of working with others to develop new knowledges or practices. In short, pedagogy can create spaces for the real and the possible to mingle in playful or serious ways.

An *engaged* pedagogy invites people to clarify the contours and constraints of social realities in order to transform them. At its best, this sort of pedagogy allows people to reflect on their lived experiences within social reality to formulate new concepts and courses of action. It has the potential enable designers, and those interested in social action more broadly, to consider the impacts of their own social location in the design process, as they imagine and design with people who experience social margin-alization today because of their race, class, gender, ability, or sexual orientation.[54] Engaged pedagogy is therefore potentially a means to begin to *transgress* the boundaries that make it seem as if there is only one way of thinking and knowing that must be learned from universities. That is, pedagogy can be a mutually empowering process (beyond traditional roles of teacher and student in schools) that engages people from whatever they do, experience, or make in their own lives.[55]

One particular example of this sort of engaged pedagogy in action today can be seen in the model of the international Inside-Out Prison Exchange Program.[56] Courses, workshops, and learning experiences that happen in the Inside-Out model bring students from a university campus ("outside students") together with people who are incarcerated ("inside students") to learn, as peers, behind prison walls. Thousands of courses have been offered at hundreds of universities around the world, but they all involve topics that are concerned with social reality—including disciplines from criminal justice, sociology, and design to literature, history, and environmental science. Regardless of the topic, Inside-Out style learning creates spaces where "everyone is seen as having something vital to offer in the learning process," and the instructor acts not as a lecturer but as a facilitator of the discussion.[57]

---

[54] Lesley-Ann Noel, "Promoting an Emancipatory Research Paradigm in Design Education and Practice," *Proceedings of DRS 2016, Design Research Society 50th Anniversary Conference*, Brighton, UK, June 27–30, 2016.

[55] bell hooks describes this approach to engaged pedagogy that applies and advances the Du Boisian tradition in: bell hooks, *Teaching to Transgress: Education as the Practice of Freedom* (Routledge, 1994).

[56] I discovered the possibilities of engaged pedagogy, and the particular model of Inside-Out, in my last ten years of work to design, implement, and evaluate prison education and reentry programs. See, for example: Matthew DelSesto, Diannelle Chaparro, and Allison Pyo, *Advancing Transformative Learning Partnerships* (Boston College, 2020); Matthew DelSesto and David Sellers, "Inside-Out as Humanistic Pedagogy," *Humanity & Society*, forthcoming.

[57] Lori Pompa, "Drawing Forth, Finding Voice, Making Change: Inside Out Learning as Transformative Pedagogy," in Simone Weil Davis and Barbara Sherr Roswell (Editors), *Turning Teaching Inside Out: A Pedagogy of Transformation* (Palgrave Macmillan, 2013), pages 13–25.

The Inside-Out model centers on a dialog-focused approach, where the instructor does not present a finished version of social reality for students to consume, but rather initiates a process that leads to new understandings in and through group meetings. The diversity of the participants across lines of race, class, and social status is also quite important. In the process of reflecting on their own different social realities, Inside-Out participants can come to develop a new consciousness, and practice a new way of participating in community. This is also encouraged by devoting a significant portion of group meetings to developing collective projects, which set forth some possible courses of action—in a process of designing specific interventions or imagining entirely different systems.[58] In other words, the formation of a new collective consciousness through dialog can be an end in itself, as it establishes a basic foundation of comradery, autonomy, and cooperation.

It is helpful to see the development of this a new consciousness and sensibility in light of what the Brazilian educator and activist Paulo Freire referred to as *conscientization*.[59] Much like Du Bois's insight that oppression could stifle creative capacities, Freire saw how dominant systems often teach people to be passive observers of a pre-made social reality. Conscientization accordingly counters the passivity induced by systemic oppression, through engaged pedagogies that involve reflective dialog and action. It is the cultivation of dispositions required to critically analyze unequal power relationships in social-historical realities. Such critical spaces, opportunities, and networks for dialogical reflection can be designed as interventions that enable people to actually practice a new way of being in the world, as active participants in social reality.

[58] For example, the non-profit organization Designing Justice + Designing Spaces used a version of Inside-Out pedagogy to imagine restorative justice spaces and systems as an alternative to the conventional punitive justice system in the United States. Cynthia E. Smith, "Imagining Restorative Justice, Interview with Barb Toews and Deanna Van Buren," in Cynthia E. Smith (editor), *By the People: Designing a Better America* (Cooper Hewitt, 2016), pages 124–129.

[59] Paulo Freire, *Pedagogy of the Oppressed* (Seabury Press, 1970).

In this way, it is evident that the general model of Inside-Out pedagogy—sparking social change through convening diverse groups for dialogue across profound social divisions—helps to illustrate a process of cultivating capacities for social thinking, imagining, and designing. The Inside-Out approach offers ways of thinking about social interventions that highlights the power of dialogue to reflectively act, the need to emphasize a process that builds collective capacity, and the potential of dispersed leadership. It also points to the relationship between collaboration and consciousness across social boundaries. What emerges in the Inside-Out classroom is neither the voice of privileged university students helping their incarcerated peers, nor the voice of incarcerated students teaching their counterparts. Rather, it is a different way of knowing, that some have referred to as a hybridized third voice born in the "productive tensions that arise when disparate groups unite behind a common cause."[60]

The Du Boisian tradition of reflective action similarly demonstrates that the specific content of knowledge needed to address social injustice is perhaps less important than the ways of learning and knowing that we practice ourselves or initiate with others.[61] Schools in design and the social sciences often overly-systematize the thinking and designing process. While it may be important to learn specific skills, the formalization of knowledge can also perpetuate the very problems it aims to address, as it impoverishes the social imagination, or constrains what people see as possible potentials for thinking and acting. Formal schooling gives the tools to design, reflect upon, and sustain society to only the credentialed few, who then attempt to "manage" growing social and ecological crises. Conversely, engaged pedagogy, as an approach to thinking and designing,

---

[60] M. Brinton Lykes, Martin Terre Blanche, and Brandon Hamber, "Narrating Survival and Change in Guatemala and South Africa: The Politics of Representation and a Liberatory Community Psychology," *American Journal of Community Psychology*, volume 31, Issue 1, 2003, pages 79–90.

[61] Aldon Morris describes Du Bois's approach as one that facilitated different ways of knowing through "insurgent intellectual networks." Morris, pages 187–194.

can counter this trend with efforts to distribute power through sharing knowledge or skills in collaborative projects that expand webs of learning and thought.[62]

Overall, the Du Boisian approach suggests that engaged pedagogies and scholarship do more than get press coverage for research, promote participatory design, or share project outcomes with wider audiences. In this sense, engaged pedagogy is fundamentally a disposition toward thinking and designing that centers the *process* of knowledge sharing and creation over the outcomes. The goal could be described as bringing values and action together with a deep attention to social realities and lived experiences of people.[63] Through conceiving, and practicing, design and thought as pedagogical processes, new imaginations about what is possible can emerge.

The commitment to social engagement that Du Bois and his colleagues model places value on creating communities of teaching and learning beyond traditional academic spaces. Such a commitment can be a practice of trying, and sometimes failing, to develop structured ways of exploring ideas, experiences, and courses of action that allow all involved to try out new ways of thinking, knowing, acting, and being. This requires presenting, questioning, and creating in many different forms—moving beyond disciplinary silos, physical spaces, or social barriers that impede action, from consciousness to collaboration.

---

[62] The Du Boisian tradition, especially its efforts to counter the ways that white universities and institutions were using knowledge to consolidate white power and advance empire, is relevant to the project that Ivan Illich referred to as the "de-schooling" of society to create a new "convivial" society. See, for example: Ivan Illich, *Tools for Conviviality* (Harper & Row, 1973); Ivan Illich, *Deschooling Society* (Harper & Row, 1971).

[63] Biko Agozino describes the simultaneous pursuit of normative values about how the world could be and truths about social realities as "committed objectivity." Biko Agozino, *Counter-Colonial Criminology* (Pluto Press, 2003).

PART THREE
The Choreography of Beautiful Action

In an era of high-speed global communications and detailed visual representations of society and space, design and social science professions often embrace the next, new, or best-packaged ways forward. With the urgency of so many challenges today, thinking and designing can tend to focus on the latest findings, technologies, or solutions. The traditions of Patrick Geddes, Jane Addams, and W.E.B. Du Bois model a different way of imagining, engaging, and shaping social worlds. In doing so, they also challenge the narrowing of action and specialization of knowledge in the present.

Their projects sought to clarify the social-historical context within which they were living, and accordingly, to design interventions toward greater equity, hospitality, caring, or life-giving relations with the planet. Such an orientation reveals new possibilities for making societies that might enable human potential and awaken people's capacity for shaping new worlds. In this sense, Geddes, Addams, and Du Bois are significant for more than their individual projects. They show how social thought and action can be imaginative and collective processes, through their work with people facing down the challenges of their day.

The twenty-first century is in urgent need of the lessons that these histories and contexts of social thought and action can offer. Crises we face today are compounded, and sometimes even caused, by a lack of imagination. It is easy to look at the data on issues such as poverty, migration, climate change, or racism and be confronted with a wall of information, opinion, and analysis. This leads to three common responses that we may move to and from at different points in our life and work: resignation, reform, and resistance.

First, we may become resigned to the way things are and disengage entirely. This happens after either thinking about the enormity of suffering in a particular case, experiencing a problem directly, or when we fail after trying tirelessly to solve a problem. On some level, resignation is a response to moral distress or information overload in a highly individualistic society. With so much information and conflicting views, we may come to wonder what the right thing to do is, or we may even doubt that we can make a positive contribution. Family or community commitments can also present practical reasons for withdrawal. Why bother worrying about social problems when it is difficult enough to secure one's own livelihood in today's wildly uneven economy?

Another response is to abandon hope that these problems can be addressed in their entirety, and instead embrace the most convenient or efficient reforms. A reformist approach to social change addresses a small subset of the problem, or responds to the most obvious symptoms of an identified problem. The focus on reform may ultimately help some individuals, but it fails to address the systemic roots of the challenges we face, potentially worsening challenges in the long term. This impulse to identify specialized problems, practices, and policies to be reformed happens in all types of institutions—from education and health, to environment, economic development, and public safety.

A third response is to resist—that is, to identify the people and ideas that are causing problems and then struggle against them through protests, critical debates, or organizing campaigns. Resistance is often characterized by activist refusals to participate in an exploitative system. Demands of such activism have been important when they are connected to a larger social imagination (for instance through the work of abolitionists who resisted the system of slavery), however, resistance can also set the trap of beginning with some person, policy, organization, or institution to be positioned against. If resistance does not move beyond a focus on undesirable circumstances, it can get stuck in giving energy, thought, and power to already existing realities. While activism that offers negative critiques of an existing system can powerfully draw attention to urgent issues or contribute to a public conversation, it can be less successful at creating alternative institutions, organizations, practices, and spaces in the present. This is, at least in part, because social change and activist organizations are often riddled with the same problems of power inequalities and burnout that are present in larger more mainstream institutions and organizations. How, then, can we engage today? What are thinking and designing capable of becoming now?

This final part of the book introduces the *choreography of beautiful action* as another way, or at least one potential approach to engaging with the contemporary condition. Although it aims to define this mode of action, as a way of viewing the possibilities of what thinking and designing might become, it does so in a somewhat incomplete way. That is, it aims to only provide some signposts or general outlines that point to what a choreography of beautiful action might entail—a central goal of Chapter 6. On the one hand, such an approach means intentionally blurring the lines between thought and action, being willing to try things out, to move toward that which brings us joy, to recognize all that we already know, to stop waiting for the right information, time, or place. At the same time, this approach implies a certain way of knowing and being more broadly, which Chapter 7 will describe as *contingent becoming*. How do we cultivate a consciousness that participates in what our lives are capable of collectively becoming, instead of one that stands aside to watch things unfold? The thought and action presented here offers some concepts, models, and strategies, but the work is unfinished and awaits your participation.

6   If You Can Think You Can Act

Antanas Mockus is known as a Colombian philosopher, mathematician, university professor, and academic administrator who was, by most accounts, an unlikely mayoral candidate. After winning election in 1995 to become Mayor of Bogotá, Colombia, he set about transferring his craft of thinking into creative forms of action. In reflecting on his tenure as Mayor, Mockus explained: "As mayor I assumed a fascinating pedagogical task: learning and teaching in a community of seven million people. I decided to confront the culture of the city, its languages, perceptions, customs, clichés and especially people's excuses."[1] He inherited a number of social challenges, which had made inhabitants feel socially distanced and isolated, perhaps most notably one of the highest rates of violence and crime of any city in the world. Many in the city and country were resigned to the way things were, in a despair that bred further crisis.

Mockus's approach to violence and other major social issues of the day was a "Civic Culture" strategy that involved bringing thinking into everyday life with a series of creative initiatives, public art, and performances. As a pedagogical intervention this strategy was a way of bringing people together, initiating dialogue

[1] Antanas Mockus, "Building 'Citizenship Culture' in Bogotá," *Journal of International Affairs*, volume 65, issue 2, 2012, pages 143–146.

on difficult issues, and inspiring action.[2] Some of his initiatives included:

— Hiring hundreds of mimes to mock reckless drivers or pedestrians who broke traffic laws (to curb dangerous driving habits), and distributing thumbs-up and thumbs-down cards so that citizens could express their disapproval of harmful driving without resorting to aggression (traffic deaths were cut nearly in half during his tenure as mayor);

— Asking for residents to voluntarily surrender guns, which were symbolically melted into baby spoons, and initiating "Days of Inoculation Against Violence" that ultimately had more than 45,000 people participate in dialogues facilitated by mental health professionals (more than 2500 weapons were collected, and the homicide rate was reduced by more than half, from 82 per 100,000 in 1993 to 35 per 100,000 in 2000);

— Asking people to pay more in taxes to fund infrastructure and social programs as a way to demonstrate civic pride (more than 63,000 did);

— Showering live on TV programs, turning off the water as he soaped, to ask people to conserve water (people used 14 percent less water);

— Organizing a "Night for Women" in the city where men were asked to stay home, in order to bring attention to gender-based inequality (more than 700,000 women participated and most men volunteered to stay home).

As Mockus has explained, what unites each of these interventions is not simply their creativity or cleverness, but rather an approach that seeks social change though coordinating law and

---

[2] See, for example: Carlo Tognato (editor), *Cultural Agents RELOADED: The Legacy of Antanas Mockus* (Harvard University Press, 2017). In his editor's introduction, Tognato touches on some of the critiques of Mockus's strategy and political orientation, which, although worth considering, do not detract from what can be learned from the general significance of his work.

policy with a renewed social imagination and cultural agency.[3] In transitioning his thinking and pedagogical skills into new forms of reflective action, Mockus models an approach to thinking and acting, which is at the core of this chapter.

Mockus's dexterity in mixing reflection and action calls to mind the often-quoted proverb: "If you can talk you can sing, if you can walk you can dance." Much of the meaning is perhaps self-evident that singing and dancing involve skills that are adjacent to what we already do in everyday life. In a similar way, taking action today can be intimidating. Action can seem difficult because there ae so many ways to go wrong. While we can try again if we act in error, some actions have consequences that can never be undone. It is easy to feel inadequate to the task at hand, ill-equipped to do what we believe needs to be done a context of experts and large institutions. As many of Mockus's colleagues may have assumed about their professional academic life, it can also seem like spending one's days thinking in a university creates a barrier to other forms of participation in the world. Despite the fact that he was not a professional policy-maker or politician, Mockus nevertheless thought his way into a new field of action.

This book has proposed that, just as dancing is an extension of walking, so too thinking is not as distinct from acting as we may tend to believe. It is common that people will give up on action because they sense that they do not have enough time, money, training, resources, or power. As many of the thinkers explored in previous pages show, however, we actually already have all of the basics for taking action. This chapter accordingly argues for acting as a form of thinking, or as Mockus demonstrates along with many other authors from this chapter, that thought is already in the act. Such a stance certainly does not mean we should take the most obvious or expedient action, but rather that there is potential for thoughtful action, beyond the boundaries of professional practices, around every corner and in every moment.

At the same time, because of the relations between thinking and acting, it is also the case that it might be useful for those

[3] Antanas Mockus, "Convivencia Como Armonizacion de Ley, Moral, y Cultura," *Perspectivas*, volume 23, issue 1, 2002, pages 19–37.

immersed in practice, whether explicitly design-oriented or otherwise, to also see themselves as thinkers.[4] This involves opening to the possibility of more intentional or deliberate thinking in, of, and for practice. With such an approach, of theorizing practice and practicing theory, action can use the creative potentials of critical thought to make thinking and acting more effective, inclusive, and transformative.

BEYOND RESIGNATION, REFORM, AND RESISTANCE

Here, I propose a way of proceeding that is distinct from the present-day tendencies of resignation, reform, and resistance, even as it draws on elements of each of the three. I call this model for thinking and acting today *the choreography of beautiful action*. It uses design and social imagination capacities from within the contexts of our lives, to make social engagement, reflective action, and transformation irresistible.[5] Building on the work of those who have blended forms of scholarship, activism, and practice, the approach has a foundation that can be traced through the work of many—including, but of course not limited to, Geddes, Addams, and Du Bois—to the present. It is fundamentally about a combination of skillful engagement, strategic intervention, reflective action, and creative organizing.

The choreography of beautiful action seeks to bridge social-historical location of oneself and one's community with the possibilities and opportunities to make new realities possible. Such an approach creates connections, from personal history to institutional power relationships and purposeful action. This means imagining and pursuing courses action while also reflecting on one's own positioning in social realities. It's not as if this is a linear journey from struggle against oppression to happy resolution. Just the opposite. It is to work in and through institutional

---

[4] Or in Herbert Simon's terms, to view designing as a way of understanding the world. Herbert Simon, *Sciences of the Artificial* (MIT Press, 1969), page 164.

[5] Toni Cade Bambara, who was an artist and social activist, famously said that it was her goal to "make revolution irresistible." Thabiti Lewis (editor), *Conversations with Toni Cade Bambara* (University Press of Mississippi, 2012).

norms and cultural assumptions—constructively challenging the way things are through critical participation in what already exists.

To choreograph beautiful action is to work with others in a way that generates new forms, images, ideas, practices and spaces that are deeply engaged with social realities. It therefore builds on the sensibilities of design, but it also focuses on the social and spatial arrangements of power as they appear in specific moments or sites. Those interested in social change through reform or resistance typically contest the *ideas* (e.g., challenging racist rhetoric or policies) and call attention to the *effects* (e.g., through marshalling evidence to show educational disparities) of social problems. Alternatively, the notion of choreography interrogates and seeks opportunities for systemic intervention in *how everyday environments and interactions are arranged.*[6]

The choreography of beautiful action is fundamentally a form of active reflection that is practice-led as it theorizes in, of, and for practice. It is about acting, but it also about opening up taken-for-granted social realities through reflection. It is an iterative process in between reflection and action where we may seek to make the kind of world we want to see. In this way it can also lead through example or proof of concept—where a desired world is actually discovered in practice.

At the same time, the choreography of beautiful action acknowledges how reflection itself is a form of intervention, revealing potential ideas and courses of action that may not have been tried. Like a dance performance, its mechanics can be described even while its essence is also partly beyond written description. The choreography of beautiful action is, therefore, not just about making the right case for a new approach, or intervening within a given social reality, but it is shifting the very grounds on which new social realities might emerge.

In building on foundations for reflective action described in previous chapters, the choreography of beautiful action challenges

[6] This framing is inspired by The Design Studio for Social Intervention, which argues that efforts for social justice and change often focus on ideas and effects while neglecting socio-spatial arrangements: Design Studio for Social Intervention, *Ideas, Arrangements, Effects: Systems Design and Social Justice* (Minor Compositions, 2020).

social thinking and designing to evolve. Perhaps most notably, it counters social thought's habitual return to passive observation or analysis of an "already made" social world with a model of thinking through active, relational, embodied engagement. This is even a challenge for critical social thought, which can get bogged down in pointing out the failures of an already-made society and, therefore, hamper social action.

For instance, some of the more radical movements for social change across the globe have often theorized and organized about/for *withdrawal from* institutions, which are understood to be corrupted by imperialism, racism, and/or capitalism. An emphasis on the choreography of beautiful action, however, calls for a critical *engagement with* institutions, as exemplified in emergent forms of artistic activism.[7] Such strategies of engagement can unsettle common sense as they encourage people to participate in new relationships or experiences, and contribute their own unique perspectives. The engagement with institutions in this model of action goes beyond defining and critiquing the moral failures of present social conditions, or using rational debate to achieve policy change. It is the work of convening different, and sometimes competing voices together—bringing designing to a process of social thinking, strategically as catalyst for transformations.

In this sense, a choreography of beautiful action also points beyond the objective of designing as reaching a better end product or reformed service and system. Instead, it suggests that design processes ought to aspire to incite thought and action iteratively toward new imaginations of the possible. This orientation, of using action to investigate what is possible, demands a rigorous engagement with histories that design practices are only beginning to consider.[8] Perhaps most especially, practices

[7] Chantel Mouffe, *Agonistics: Thinking the World Politically* (Verso Books, 2013), pages 83–105.
[8] Claudia Mareis and Nina Paim, "Design Struggles: An Attempt to Imagine Design Otherwise," in Claudia Mareis and Nina Paim (editors), *Design Struggles: Intersecting Histories, Pedagogies, and Perspectives* (Swiss Design Network, Plural Series, 2021), pages 11–22.

related to design for social innovation and social design require a deep understanding of the human capabilities of people involved, and also recognition that what people are capable of evolves over time, in and through practice. Such limits are not purely natural, but they are conditioned by where people are situated in histories. Encounters with new possibilities that are grounded in the social historical lives of people and places may be beautiful, capturing our attention and drawing us forward into further thinking or acting.

BEAUTIFUL ACTION TODAY

Social problems are often conceptualized as dreadful and ominous things. Qualitative social research chronicles the pain of people facing social inequality, and quantitative analysis shows the larger, often disheartening, trends of which these stories are a part. The media covers such research with narratives of suffering and destruction. Some argue that this is the best approach for social change, to compel people to act through data and descriptions about how social problems contribute to unequally distributed suffering, violence, or despair.

The larger question at stake is the kind of *social imagination and motivation* that such an orientation to danger, fear, and suffering invites. Do people feel as though they "should" contribute to social change efforts because it is "right thing to do" as a serious and solemn duty? Or is reflective social action a potentially joyful activity that can enrich and positively shape our lives, communities, and societies, if only we cultivate this capacity?[9]

Analysis in empirical social science often tells us that we just need the "right" wording of the law or policy, or the appropriate amount of prior understanding to make a change. Indeed, this was the hope of some of the most sweeping civil rights laws in

---

[9] Arne Naess, "The Place of Joy in a World of Fact," in Alan Drengson and Bill Devall (editors), *The Ecology of Wisdom: Writings by Arne Naess* (Counterpoint, 2010), pages 123–132.

the 1960s United States—that new rules and regulations would guarantee equal protection under the law, regardless of race. Yet in this struggle civil rights leader Martin Luther King Jr. argued that the transformation of society ultimately cannot be completely legislated. While he saw the need for new laws and policies to constrain the effects of Jim Crow racism (in state and local laws that restricted voting rights or allowed businesses to refuse service to non-white patrons), he also recognized that more was needed for real change. But what is this *more*, and how can it be engaged through social thought and action today?

A similar problem has challenged environmental research and policy. Since the 1980s, scientists began to observe the connection between the burning of fossil fuels, carbon in the atmosphere, and global ecological health. Over time, the threat posed by fossil fuels became increasingly urgent and the problem was publicly framed as a moral imperative. That is, human beings should and must act if they are to prevent the planet from warming to dangerous levels. As awareness about global warming grew, the language used was increasingly apocalyptic—to draw attention to the urgency of public and political action. Yet, even if and when political leaders do act, there is a question that remains important: will policy and laws ultimately solve the problem of widespread ecological destruction? What else is required?

Like civil rights laws, carbon regulations surely could have some crucial impacts on society (like restraining the amount of fossil fuels that are burned and promoting other forms of energy). Yet these legal- and policy-focused approaches to social change, which have dominated the social sciences, are superficial. They ultimately fail to address the root causes of the problem, which are deeply embedded in the cultures, imaginations, and procedures of institutions. Other courses of action are surely needed, and inspiration can be taken from those who have experimented with different approaches.

In reference to the ecological crisis, but of relevance to all contemporary social issues, Arne Naess offers a way of proceeding rooted in a form of social imagination. He suggests a move from the surface appearance of things that can be measured (e.g., through formal research methodologies) to the deeply creative and relational potential of human life. In short, he calls for *beautiful action*.[10] This sort of action is about developing our inclination and capacity to care for and creatively respond to the world. It's not only that we think ourselves into a new way of acting, sometimes we act ourselves into a new imagination of what is possible.

Beautiful action is opposed to "right or wrong" action, which has been the goal of much law, policy, and social thought (e.g., that identifies problems or injustices in need of correction). Right and wrong action is also fundamental to everyday life in the Western societies, as a moral orientation passed down through families and cultures. In his writing on beautiful action, Naess points out that when something is framed as the right or wrong thing to do, we may decide to do what is right out of a sense of duty or obligation. Right action is enforced through intricate systems of discipline, fines, courts, police, and prisons—but also through the "soft power" of people regulating their own behavior.

The basis for right and wrong action is rooted in punitive, individualistic, and calculative thinking—from the level of the human body to the national government or corporation. In right or wrong action, people are merely an object or tool—a means to an end—which is to be manipulated in the service of doing what is thought to be the right thing. That is, even if people are miserable in fulfilling their duty, or do not believe in the worthiness of the cause, the system forces their compliance. The ends of a promised personal or social good justify whatever coercive, uncomfortable, or painful means are necessary.

Yet the notion of beautiful action suggests that victories achieved with such coercion or force are not sustainable, because people will find ways to informally work around the system or create entirely new systems. Even if they do comply with rules and laws, they may do so in a way that diminishes the human potential or creativity of themselves and others—transforming living human beings into functional inputs in a technically and legally managed system.

---

[10] Arne Naess, "Beautiful Action. Its Function in Ecological Crisis," *Environmental Values*, volume 2, issue 1, 1993, pages 67–71.

What sets beautiful action apart, from this conventional approach to moral action, is its focus on cultivating our potential inclinations to actively participate in caring for people and environments. Jane Bennett further describes this kind of action when she argues that ultimately codes and criteria "are not sufficient to the enactment of ethical aspirations." For Bennett, acting on ethical aspirations "requires bodily movements in space, mobilizations of heat and energy, a series of choreographed gestures, a distinctive assemblage of affective propulsions."[11]

Because life is unexpected and surprising, ethical action is more likely when we nurture a "spirit of generosity" over time, which can respond to the particular situations we encounter in daily personal and professional life. This "embodied sensibility … organizes affects into a style and generates the impetus to enact" ethical aspirations.[12] In other words, we need compelling stories, models, ideas, cases, propositions, and experiences that we can actively live within, engage, and shape. Challenges of the twenty-first century demand new ways of imaginatively participating in our world. This is not the distanced participant observation in social science, but an active immersion in social reality to collectively imagine what's possible and try to make things happen.

The notion of beautiful action is also potentially an intervention in the culture of institutions and organizations today—which can be so focused on outputs and productivity that people come to pursue obsessive and dysfunctional doing. Bringing more reflection and intentionality to the action we take today involves making time for deep listening and presence, while creating space to more deeply understand the social-historical contexts of our work. Although many organizations seem to think that reflection is a non-productive detour from the real work of doing things, the notion of beautiful action offers an alternative that is ultimately more effective in the long term.[13]

[11] Jane Bennett, *The Enchantment of Modern Life: Attachments, Crossings, Ethics* (Princeton University Press, 2001), page 3.

[12] Bennett, page 131.

[13] Steven D'Souza and Diana Renner, *Not Doing: The Art of Effortless Action* (LID Publishing Limited, 2018).

On the other hand, beautiful action also involves a kind of reflection that is more attuned to the human experience. As Fransisco Varela puts it, "intelligence should guide our actions, but in harmony with the texture of the situation hand, not in accordance with a set of rules or procedures and experiences."[14] That is, acting in line with some normative ideal of what should be, requires a "middle way between spontaneity and rational calculation."[15] Unlike conventional design and social science practices that often view the world as a series of puzzles to be solved (through specialized design or research methods), the kind of expertise that is required for ethical action is a "journey of experience and learning ... where immediacy proceeds deliberation."[16] Accordingly, while reflection can help to orient possible courses of action, the actual process of *acting reflectively* requires the capacity to analyze situations as they are happening in real-time. This may involve both creating moments to strategically pause, reassess, and redirect collective efforts as new conditions emerge, or taking a break from thinking to actually try to make something happen.[17]

Acting differently today also calls for a renewed *courage for the beautiful*.[18] That is, the current era demands the imaginative transition from a functional approach to design, based on personal security and organizational profit, to designing as a mode of reflective and co-creative action. The *beauty* in beautiful

---

[14] Francisco J. Varela, *Ethical Know-How: Action, Wisdom, and Cognition* (Stanford University Press, 1992), page 31. The lectures in this book were meant to be an elaboration of Varela's theory of "enaction" which argues for a science that is more attuned to lived experience, initially developed in: Francisco J. Varela, Evan Thompson, and Elanor Rosch, *The Embodied Mind: Cognitive Science and the Human Experience* (MIT Press, 1991).

[15] Varela, page 31.

[16] Varela, page 33.

[17] In some ways, this approach is related to what Scharmer and Kaufer refer to as "leading from the emerging future." Otto Scharmer and Katrin Kaufer, *Leading from the Emerging Future: From Ego-System to Eco-System Economies* (Berrett-Koehler Publishers, 2013).

[18] John O'Donohue further elaborates that this is "the courage to search out where the real thresholds of life are, the vital frontiers, the parts of our life that we have not yet experienced." John O'Donohue, *Beauty: The Invisible Embrace* (HarperCollins, 2004), page 39.

action is quite significant here. Design and Western culture have long positioned the beautiful as some "thing" to gaze upon at a distance, yet beauty is perhaps better described as that which comes about through interaction and experience.[19] Beauty is a vital, gentle, and strong experience of coherence that cannot be completely manufactured. Here, beauty is not conceived as an absolute and timeless object, but as a mode of acting that initiates experiences, spaces, or relationships—bringing "the real and ideal in connection and conversation with each other."[20]

The beautiful, as a moment, experience, interaction or process, can prompt the mind "to move chronologically back in the search for precedents and parallels" and "to *move forward into new acts of creation*, to move conceptually over, to *bring things into relation*, and does all this with a kind of urgency as though one's life depended on it."[21] Beautiful action in this sense is acting that contributes to life or *heightens aliveness*, inciting deeper engagement through thinking and doing. Especially in a world so strewn with waste, ecological destruction, suffering, despair, and violence, beautiful action is about acting toward the repair of injury, to restore wholeness to fragmented and fractured relationships.[22]

In many ways, this is precisely the work that thought and design can take on today—to constantly bring ideals and aspirations into conversation with fragmented and destructive social realities. Such work also means recognizing that the end goals of our aspirations may not be perfectly reached. New inspiration and knowledge that emerges from experience may enable us to reconsider what is desirable or reimagine what is possible.

---

[19] Cameron Tonkinwise distinguishes between the "appreciation of pure aesthetic beauty" from a "beauty-in-use" that puts designers into relationship people and environments: Cameron Tonkinwise, "Beauty-in-Use," *Design Philosophy Papers*, volume 1, issue 2, 2003, pages 73–82.

[20] O'Donohue, page 9.

[21] Elaine Scarry, *On Beauty and Being Just* (Princeton University Press, 1999), page 30, emphasis added.

[22] See, for instance, Scarry's description of beauty as a "reciprocal pact" of aliveness in: *On Beauty and Being Just*, pages 89–90.

Some designers have recently called for a renewed attention to the beautiful as a quality of action—to awaken social imaginations, in a process of designing systems, buildings, services, and spaces. As Bill Morrish and Catherine Brown explain, even in what some consider the "ugliest" designs of society—infrastructures of transportation, water supply, sewage, and garbage disposal— there is potential for beauty.[23] Infrastructure is not just about function, but it can and should contribute to meaning and identity in human communities, while also enriching ecological life. Instead of focusing on the utility of public works, design of infrastructure can creatively and artistically invite people to participate in their local environment. That is, infrastructures that people rely on for daily life can aspire toward beauty through social equity, cultural expression, and replenishment of natural resources.

Others similarly argue for a design process that engages deeply with social reality—to understand and transform social-spatial realities, through the cultivation of context-specific imaginations of equity and beauty. In Medellín, Colombia Segio Fajardo and Alejandro Echeverri famously declared, in their Integral Urban Project, that "the most beautiful buildings must be in our poorest areas." Their participatory public projects included grand "library parks," with impressive community centers and plazas, and the Metrocable network of aerial gondola-lifts, in order to bring public transportation into poor neighborhoods on the mountainous urban edge.[24] The overall idea was that beauty is both a process of designing spaces, and also an outcome that

[23] William R. Morrish and Catherine R. Brown, "Infrastructure for the New Social Compact," in Douglas Kelbaugh and Kit Krankel McCullough (editors), *Writing Urbanism* (Routledge, 2008), pages 138–153.

[24] Anthony Fontenot, "Activating Medellín and the Politics of Citizen Engagement," in Farhana Ferdous and Bryan Bell (editors), *All-Inclusive Engagement in Architecture: Towards the Future of Social Change* (Routledge, 2020), pages 165–171. See also: Segio Fajardo and Alejandro Echeverri, "Positioning Practice in Architecture," *Talk at Syracuse University School of Architecture*, February 2009, accessed at: https://www.youtube.com/watch?v=7e2EwXjVynE&list=PL_RhkDiJl4OxBTWPxpUo2j2BpEnXKke2F&index=13.

expresses civic and social ideals. It is a way of working that creatively draws people into the process into remaking society.

Others argue for the role of investing in beautiful spaces and inspiring experiences for the most marginalized—from public health and peace-building in Rwanda to education and economic development in US cities. For instance, community activist and leader Bill Strickland explains that marginalized communities often "live in a world where beauty seems impossible." The intentional inclusion of beauty in the buildings, services, and spaces that his organization has designed in Pittsburg, Pennsylvania "isn't window dressing," because "you can't show a person how to build a better life if they feel no pleasure in the simple act of being alive."[25] Strickland points to the ways that material forms are deeply intertwined with people's emotional dispositions, identities, and thoughts. His practice also explores how new services, objects, and spaces can draw people toward participating in relationships and communities.

Similarly, in their professional design practice, MASS Design Group pursues beauty as a vehicle for justice. A goal of their practice is to physically manifest a new social imagination through community-centered participatory design processes. In describing a hospital in Rwanda, Michael Murphy explains that "Buildings tell a story, and when a story hasn't been told before, a new building can emerge, one that is forged without precedent, that offers a salve to the chaotic challenges of our world. One that offers new direction, a guide, a lighthouse, and with it that hope, without which there cannot be justice."[26] Here, beauty is not only something that is achieved and immortalized in designed forms. For Murphy, what is beautiful about a building is how its forms relate to the social-historical context and process that made them, along with the aspirations of human dignity they point toward.

[25] Bill Strickland, *Make the Impossible Possible* (Broadway Books, 2007), pages 13 & 17.

[26] Michael Murphy explains further: "We might say the opposite of beauty is not ugliness, it is injustice. Beauty is not a choice if we fight for truth, it is the central artery that delivers it. Beauty IS Justice." Michael Murphy, "OR, AND, IS," in MASS Design Group (editor), *Justice Is Beauty* (Monacelli Press, 2019), pages 29–30.

Beautiful action therefore proceeds collaboratively, catalyzing processes of designing that are fueled by a social imagination. It is rooted in reflection within present social realities, and also oriented toward previously unconsidered, but possible, futures.

Overall, the concept and practice of beautiful action invite us all to consider the kinds of worlds that our thinking, activism, designing, or acting envisions. To be open to beautiful action as a practice in this way offers alternatives to a central premise of Western democratic societies over the last century—the notion that more fair, ideal, or just social order can be achieved through rational deliberation and calculated reforms. Although there are times for withdrawal from the world, beautiful action demands that we join together, to sketch out and imagine possible scenarios and movements of people, materials, and ideas. It also calls for physical engagement with our local environments and everyday contexts, inviting us to consider not just what we have accomplished at the end of a day, but what might *move* us toward new ways of relating and acting in the world.

INSURGENT SOCIAL CHOREOGRAPHY

Choreography is typically thought of in the context of performance and dance, but it also has great relevance to social thought, design, and action today. This kind of social choreography imagines social spaces, interventions, or relationships that might engage, incite, and draw people into alliances for new ways of knowing and acting together. At the core of a *social* notion of choreography is that social realities are not just made through brute force; rather social orders are understood to be created through bodies and practices, in movements of people, objects, and ideas.[27] As a concept, choreography brings attention to where we physically and socially locate ourselves, and how we act as part of an evolving interactive process. It models a reciprocal and collaborative mode of working with others, attentive to the

---

[27] Andrew Hewitt, *Social Choreography: Ideology as Performance in Dance and Everyday Life* (Duke University Press, 2005).

lived bodily experiences of the groups, neighborhoods, places, or systems that are relevant to our practice.

This social/political application of choreographic, theatric, and artistic interventions is also a major insight in Augusto Boal's approach to performance. Boal describes a series of embodied practices and exercises that invite people from out of their tendency of being passive receivers of social reality, to become collectivities who investigate and act to transform their social reality. He sees the potential for people to become "spect-actors"—to thoughtfully observe realities unfolding around them, while also imagining their potential as actors in shaping the social, material, and political scenes unfolding in their lives.[28]

Choreography is also significant in that it demonstrates how "every practice is a mode of thought, already in the act."[29] For instance, in the practice of choreographer William Forsythe the lines between movement and language blur. Although choreography outlines a series of sequences, "it is never a question of formally working something out in advance."[30] That is, choreography points toward activating collective rhythms, initiating relationships among people and spaces. Movement comes alive through interactions. Choreography is speculative and future-oriented—not deliberately reasoning each possible course of action, but thinking in and through movement.

The key is to be willing to keep the process "alive and uncertain … a movement precise with training but still open to regeneration."[31] Even if learnings from practice are not written down, insight and knowledge emerge in action, which always has some quality of not-knowing exactly how things will work out. It is therefore essential to shift from designing or acting as a means to achieve a particular outcome, to design as a way to situate ourselves on the edge of the real and what else might be possible. Choreography, then, is both a potentially transformational

[28] Augusto Boal, *The Rainbow of Desire* (Routledge, 1995).

[29] Erin Manning and Brian Massumi, *Thought in the Act: Passages in the Ecology of Experience* (University of Minnesota Press, 2014).

[30] Manning and Massumi, page 43.

[31] Manning and Massumi, page 44.

social practice and lens though which a process of designing might be set into motion.

Marc Bhamuti Joseph practices a form of choreography that points to an important form of reflective action today. He describes how social science and public culture have been content to view "action as behavior." In contrast to this view, which portrays action as a mechanical response to stimuli in the environment, he describes the need to see action in relationship to movement—shifting meanings, drawing forth ideas, and nudging bodies forward. He explains that "Creative action works to prod forward the edge of what's possible, and maybe even what's normal. The creative act centers the horizon."[32] That is, reflective and imaginative action can displace what is familiar and create a new meanings, identities, and horizons from which people act.

For example, in community outreach for a multi-disciplinary performance called peh-LO-tah, Joseph created a "kinetic learning module," to spark a social imagination in young people through the game of soccer. The project, "intersects curriculum development, site-specific performance, and the politics of joy, while using soccer as a metaphor for the urgent question of enfranchisement among youth of color."[33] This allowed young people to reconsider what they may have assumed about masculinity, US history, or competitive sports culture. In addition to learning that no game is innocent (the United States is a nation founded on the premise of "passing" the other), students are sometimes surprised to find that they are becoming familiar with both artistic expression and soccer skills.

In using active engagement to demonstrate the affinities between poetic expression, artful moves of athletic success, and the physical exertion of creative dance, the intervention breaks down assumptions about immigration, sport, gender, and dance. The pedagogy—which links sports, arts, and public

[32] Marc Bamuthi Joseph, "Action as Behavior and Movement," *Creative Mornings*, August 2015, accessed at: https://creativemornings.com/talks/marc-bamuthi-joseph/2.

[33] Marc Bamuthi Joseph, *Moving & Passing Curricular Tactics* (Guggenheim Foundation, 2017), accessed at: https://www.guggenheim.org/guggenheim-social-practice/teacher-guide.

spaces through the cultivation of a new consciousness—engages students to creatively understand social reality—not only as a classroom lesson, but in the act of movement itself. As much as this is an example of creative youth education, it also shows how choreographed interventions can contribute to the shaping of the new identities and subjectivities that are necessary for new practices, ideas, and societies to emerge. This choreographic strategy, of bringing diverse disciplines and practices together—to move people, literally and figuratively, to imagine themselves differently—can open up new pathways for action.[34]

Overall, Marc Bhamuti Joseph employs an understanding of social action and change that points toward the creation of opportunities for reframing social reality, exploring connections between ideas and practices, or initiating intriguing interventions that invite people to engage. Transformative ideas, products, processes, and practices do not simply come from targeted investments with the right amount of evidence behind them. Although design, social change, and innovation are often assessed based on their replicability or scalability, the most potentially powerful ideas and practices require a creative practice that ventures to "the edge of reasoning unencumbered by replicability metrics or scale."[35] The trick is to try out ways to explore what is possible—through creative combinations of action and reflection.

What is needed, then, is a *gradual but relentless probing at the edges of the adjacent possible.*[36] In this sense, the innovation, design, and creativity that might drive social transformation is sometimes a process of piecing together ideas, practices, and spaces that already exist. The kinds of action called for today to not necessarily require some revelatory singular new idea, study,

[34] For instance, another project initiated by Marc Bamuthi Joseph and collaborators, the Life is Living Festival, aimed to imagine ecological crisis differently, and open up new strategies for acting. Shannon Jackson, "Life Politics/Life Aesthetics: Environmental Performance in Red, Black & GREEN: A Blues," in Erika Rischer-Lichte and Benjamin Wihstutz (editors), *Performance and the Politics of Space: Theatre and Topology* (Routledge, 2013), pages 276–96.

[35] Joseph, "Action as Behavior and Movement."

[36] Steven Johnson, *Where Good Ideas Come from: The Natural History of Innovation* (Riverhead Books, 2010).

data set, or design; action instead can aim to convene diverse groups of people to explore boundaries of thought and practice. Just like the sports/performance metaphor of Bhamuti's peh-LO-tah, where soccer is explored a context of poetic expression, performance, art-making, politics, and US history, the adjacent possible is that which we may have the skills to practice or the intuition to understand, but do not yet realize it is possible to actualize.

The notion of a social choreography can be a potential model that expands on the foundations for reflective action developed in previous chapters of the book, pushing social thought and design in new directions. Especially in a moment when visualizations of worlds or thinking about societies can be done from behind a screen, choreography urges us to consider where and how we might more fully step into communities and places around us. Even if our own particular work has nothing to do with dancing or choreography in the literal sense, what does this approach teach us about thought, design, and action today? How might our thinking about the worlds we inhabit or aspire toward emerge from what we do? Are we willing to try out what we are imagining with others? Will you *dance your thoughts around*?[37]

---

[37] Erin Manning and Brian Massumi put it this way in their challenge for the potential social thought today: "There is no *having* ideas. *You* do not have ideas. The body itself, with its rhythmic milieu, *is* a motional-notion: a movement of thought. Dance that thought around." Manning and Massumi, page 45.

7 Contingent Becoming

This book has focused on a number of interrelated 21st century crises, ranging from poverty and uneven economic development to ecological disaster, racism, migration, and social exclusion. These issues are deeply unsettling and have provoked much reflection in the personal and professional lives of many. They are not, however, universal challenges that everyone directly experiences in the same way. Distance can provide a certain kind of safety that puts one outside of the messiness of life in all its complexity and interrelations. For instance, watching video of fires engulfing homes or hurricane waters overwhelming city streets far from where I am, there may be a feeling of unease or empathy, but the fact that I am removed from the event can provide a sense of security. Words that describe the past and present, or imagine the future, can also create this sense of distance and comfort. That is, *conceptions* of a certain issue may become disconnected from what is actually experienced or perceived in real-time, on-the-ground so to speak.

As this book has demonstrated, activists and thinkers have long discussed the issue of bringing serious thinking closer to everyday life and action. In this tradition, which has a concern for praxis, philosopher Henri Lefevbre saw that there is a need to reckon with conceptions that have dominated the (social)

200 DESIGN AND THE SOCIAL IMAGINATION

science, planning, and design professions.[1] It's not necessarily that conceptions of events, issues, objects, people, or spaces are inherently bad, but rather that they can be mobilized in ways that perpetuate human suffering, even if the people behind certain conceptions of space have good intentions. As Lefevbre suggests, the problem is when conceptions are forced on contexts, spaces, and people as if they are coming from outside of the actually existing living realities.

More generally, Lefevbre describes how the pervasive way of thinking in design and social science professions has used thought to corral, control, and dictate bodies, or even life itself—resulting in concepts that ultimately support social exclusion or ecological destruction, even when done in the name of social progress. This is not just a problem for professionals, because Western capitalist societies operate from a worldview where abstraction holds sway over the body. That is to say that in Western cultures we typically learn to use thinking to manipulate ourselves and others, based on some rationally calculated purpose or conception of the world. This is especially evident in discourses of bureaucracies, organizational management, and self-help.

The key for Lefevbre, and in a way, for all of us today, is therefore returning to the intelligence of bodily experience, of what we can learn from people's already-existing, but perhaps unrecognized, knowledge of their lived spaces (including our own). To do this requires remembering that we always live in *more than what has been conceived*, because "what we *live* are rhythms."[2] In other words, we live in worlds that are defined my more than language and thought. The space of rhythms that vibrate and flow through human bodies (entering though our sensory perceptions) is a "lived space." There is no single past or future in this lived space, but multiple histories and futures that are always contingent on what is unfolding now. Lived space is also where the "massive energies" of human,

---

[1] Henri Lefevbre, *The Production of Space* (Blackwell Publishing, 1991), page 205.

[2] Lefevbre, *The Production of Space*, page 256. See also: Henri Lefevbre, *Rhythm Analysis: Space, Time, and Everyday Life* (Continuum, 2004).

plant, and animal organisms are constantly being accumulated and expended.[3]

As the perspective on choreography described earlier suggests, the body is an important reminder of how we are each situated in social and ecological life. It points toward the potential of thinking as/through action, or more rigorously acting as part of a systematic process of thinking. It also juxtaposes the boundless human imagination with the very real, but always shifting, limits of particular collections of bodies and materials in a certain place and time. Attuning to this possibility—getting into the flow of things—is a highly nimble and flexible kind of thought and action that dialogues with the continuously unfolding contexts of the present.

This book has suggested that designing can be paired with thought as a practice of thinking that lives more fully outside of people's heads and in everyday life. That is, critical thought can do more than react to the way things are or reject injustices of the status quo, in order to imagine futures, scenarios, interventions, and ways of organizing life differently. Paul Miller describes this approach to contemporary situations as a need to shift from a *reactionary* stance, content to "just press play" and see/hear what unfolds, and toward an *actionary* stance, that actively "plays" and works at creative ways to shape social, cultural, and ecological realities. The challenge, then, is to "always try to create new worlds, new scenarios at almost every moment of thought."[4] Such a disposition is to be attentive to the social, spatial, and temporal rhythms of our days, which are already flowing through us.

Overall, the approach described in this chapter is ultimately a style of thinking/acting that emphasizes *contingent becoming*. Ontological design theorists recognize that in designing tools, interventions, systems, or institutions we are really designing *ways of being*.[5] The emphasis on becoming, which is implicit

---

[3] Lefevbre, *The Production of Space*, page 178.
[4] Paul D. Miller, *Rhythm Science* (MIT Press, 2004), page 109.
[5] Anne-Marie Willis, "Ontological Designing," *Design Philosophy Papers*, volume 4, issue 2, 2006, pages 69–92; Arturo Escobar, *Designs for the Pluriverse: Radical Interdependence, Autonomy, and the Making of Worlds* (Duke University Press, 2018).

in the projects of thinkers from this book, suggests something slightly more specific—that designing, whether initiated by professional designers or not, plays a role in what and how people and communities are capable of becoming. Becoming as a concept and orientation to action suggests that human beings and their potentialities are constantly in flux and evolving rather than governed by some static, unchanging laws.[6] Becoming also emphasizes that designing is never only about achieving some end state, object, order, or form. It is about action that exposes and brings different possibilities to the surface—in ways that discover and realize of potentialities of materials, people, ecologies, and communities.

Moreover, becoming is a useful concept because it involves a certain contingency. The course of events or the shape the society takes in a particular historical moment is ultimately radically contingent on more variables than any social scientific analysis could ever analyze. This does not mean, however, that everything is simply relative and left up to chance, but that we can empower our thinking and acting to skillfully use all that is available within a particular moment. If "the social" is in a constant state of becoming, then it is no longer something "out there," and instead is always offering invitations to participate.

Contingent becoming then points to a theory of change where transformations do not happen by reaching a new social order, equilibrium or consensus, but rather through creating new public spheres precisely for exposing fissures, conflict, and disjuncture. This is done so that conventional ways of doing things can be confronted or reframed, and new points of decision can be reached.[7] Contingent becoming has some affinities with the notion

[6] Thinkers have recently sought to further clarify the relevance of becoming to notions of being. See, for instance: Samantha Bankston, *Deleuze and Becoming* (Bloomsbury, 2017). See also Connolly's call to participate in a world of becoming: William Connolly, *A World of Becoming* (Duke University Press, 2011).

[7] See, for instance: Mitrasinovic's notions of design as a catalyst and designing as a strategic practice. Miodrag Mitrasinovic, "Concurrent Urbanities: Design, Civil Society, and Infrastructures of Inclusion," in Miodrag Mitrasinovic (editor), *Concurrent Urbanities: Designing Infrastructures of Inclusion* (Routledge, 2016), pages 179–203.

of emergence in social ecological systems that some activists and thinkers described in recent years.[8] And it also points to the generative qualities of thought and action—to spark cascades of future thinking and acting that are often unpredictable. To see other futures, strategic points for intervention, or alternative ways forward—this requires a lively social imagination.

GENERATIVE PRAXIS

Overall, a central concern throughout the book has been praxis—the ways in which social thinkers as activists have pursued the transformation and clarification of social realities. This was evident, for example, in Patrick Geddes' praxis of transforming vacant land, Jane Addams' praxis of democracy and hospitality at the Hull-House, and W.E.B. Du Bois's praxis of social cooperation. The choreography of beautiful action embodies the spirit of these models to offer a way of conceiving the kind of reflective action necessary for today. This mode of reflective action ultimately suggests an approach to comprehending the relations between social thinking and designing/making worlds, which could be referred to as *generative praxis*.

In social thought, critique has a reputation for being negative. That is, the role of social thought is often positioned as describing injustice; analyzing social systems, institutions, and objects; or pointing to the undesirable social worlds. Yet Geddes, Addams, and Du Bois show the potential of a *generative form of critique*—a reflective and critical participation in local contexts that is oriented toward imagining and enacting what is possible within a given place and time. That is, they demonstrate a form of critique that is positioned as a conspirator to action, or even as an intervention itself. Through their collaborative social thinking they identified desirable worlds, and then set about sketching out and initiating the courses of action that might bring these other worlds into existence. They accordingly issue a challenge

[8] Adrienne Maree Brown, *Emergent Strategy: Shaping Change, Changing World* (AK Press, 2017).

to thinking and designing today, to thoughtfully engage and center compelling visions, futures, and actions for worlds yet to come. Their praxis invites us to consider: how might we envision, theorize, and practice forms of critique collaboratively in, as, or for intervention?

At the core of generative praxis is a mode reflective action that is responsive and imaginative. Built objects, forms, social systems, and institutions present constraints. Thought, however, can be cultivated as a way of being that opens to generative possibilities—a kind of mental life that is "porous, open to the air and light, swings forward while swaying back, scatters its stripes in all directions and delights to find itself beached beside something invented only that morning or instead standing beside an altar from three millennia ago."[9] It is precisely this plasticity or elasticity of thought that allows us to entertain or generate different modes of being and acting.

The systems that Geddes, Addams, and Du Bois worked within during the early twentieth century sought to produce sameness: environments that prioritized continuing industrial profits over community and ecological health; cities that sustained the social position of already established citizens over newcomers; and a society that upheld whiteness as the model identity over the "darker races." In this context, their praxis was generative because it allowed for and produced *difference*. It sparked ideas, contexts, spaces, and arrangements that creatively intervened within the socio-spatial conditions of their time to bring more plural ways of thinking, making, and being into co-existence. Such an orientation reframes the relationship between thought and design—from instrumental knowledge for carrying out a specific task to thinking as a *way of reweaving relationships*.

As the notion of praxis indicates, generative praxis also moves beyond the conventional dualism of understanding versus transforming social realities. Euro-centric social thought has long propelled dualistic ways of being. In splitting us/them, man/woman, mind/body, subject/object, or nature/culture, such thinking

[9] Elaine Scarry, *On Beauty and Being Just* (Princeton University Press, 1999), page 48.

positions society as a singular, purely objective state of affairs. It is precisely this thinking that has advanced forms of designing and making that sustain colonialism, deepen ecological crisis, or perpetuate human suffering (even if this is unintentional). In everyday life, dualistic thinking disconnects us from the capacity to get involved in shaping the worlds unfolding around us.[10] It contributes to some of the limitations of social thought and design today, from the tendency toward passive observation of the world to the divide between designers and users.

Although certainly not perfect, Geddes, Addams, and Du Bois model a more generative way of thinking, making and becoming—in and with communities of practice. While it may be easy for contemporary design practices to shy away from social realities in favor of the new, shiny object or carefully packaged service, the model of generative praxis invites us to learn how to honestly handle and work with the realities confronting people and the planet today. That is, generative praxis begins, in part, by *entering the scene* and *letting oneself be affected* as a thinking, feeling human being in a body that desires, imagines, and acts in rippling webs of social ecological relations.[11] Much like a dance, generative praxis is therefore a highly embodied way of thinking and acting. In other words, rather than trying to observe or describe various aspects of social reality, generative praxis points toward an *enactive kind of reflection*—that involves actually making or doing the phenomena we hope to better understand. This recognizes that social thought already does imagine and make worlds in which we live. As an activity, thinking can accordingly reflect upon the kinds of worlds that could and ought to be made.[12]

---

[10] Arturo Escobar explains that these symptoms of "ontological dualism" are a major limitation of social thought today: Arturo Escobar, *Designs for the Pluriverse: Radical Interdependence, Autonomy, and the Making of Worlds* (Duke University Press, 2017), pages 79–104.

[11] This phrasing is taken from Marina Garcés, in her explanation on what it means to be honest with the real. Marina Garcés, "Honesty with the Real," *Journal of Aesthetics & Culture*, volume 4, issue 1, 2012.

[12] John Law and John Urry, "Enacting the Social," *Economy and Society*, volume 33, issue 3, 2004, pages 390–410.

For instance, in the praxis of Jane Addams, understanding democracy meant actually trying to initiate and participate in the creation of new more democratic power relations. She understood that what needed to be challenged was not only economic conditions and physical spaces, but also the dualistic ways of thinking and being at the core of industrial society that turned immigrants into foreign others. For Addams, the new approach to making spaces and programs would come from solidarity and reflective action that sought to generate new knowledge in, of, and for practice. Her work invites us to consider how our own relationship to power impacts what we think and make. In what ways might we situate ourselves differently to allow for more reciprocal, and life-giving power relations emerge?

Loïc Wacquant articulates related lessons for the twenty-first century as part of his critique of methods that sever the mind from body, or thinking from doing. He argues that "performing the phenomenon" in a mode of "observant participation" can shift our attention to the "primacy of embodied practical knowledge arising out of and continuously enmeshed in webs of action."[13] This means, for example, that understanding court systems involves actually participating in the administrative processes of the court. Or trying to understand social housing would involve actually being involved in a process to build new housing and then live in it. In other words, what is needed to understand the real and the possible today is not always grand theories or interventions, but for more people to reflectively *enter the theatre of action in some ordinary capacity*.[14]

The generative quality of praxis is its *catalytic* potential. Praxis can be catalytic to the extent that it "enables people to change by encouraging self-reflection and a deeper understanding of their particular situations."[15] This might involve opportunities for stepping out of routines as part of a design or research process, but it could also involve a design practitioner

[13] Loïc Wacquant, "For a Sociology of Flesh and Blood," *Qualitative Sociology*, volume 38, 2015, page 2.

[14] Wacquant, page 6.

[15] Patti Lather, "Research as Praxis," *Harvard Educational Review*, volume 56, issue 3, 1986, page 263.

or researcher immersing in everyday lived experience of communities or institutions for an extended period of time, without a specific agenda for thinking, data collection, or intervening set up beforehand. Validity of knowledge in this model comes not only from academic communities or peer review, but in terms of how well new knowledge resonates and transfers among people's lives or everyday practices.

In this way, praxis can be generative if it reorients, refocuses, or reenergizes everyone involved. Generative praxis looks relationally at the implications of a designed object, system, service, or intervention, to trace the non-linear ripples across contexts and spaces. This was exactly the sort of process that the Outlook Tower and environmental education projects of Patrick Geddes hoped to catalyze. For example, in Geddes' generative praxis, the curation of exhibits, surveys, and dialogues in the Outlook Tower was not an end in and of itself. It was a means of developing a more ecological outlook, which spiraled into other local projects, including neighborhood transformations of land. Geddes suggests that we ought to explore how thought can get its hands dirty in growing or making something new. Are we willing to step back from deep immersion in a specific project to see the larger social-ecological systems that shape and are shaped by our actions?

The aim of a generative praxis is not only for filling a gap or puzzle in academic literature, even though what is learned in action will likely contribute or add to existing scientific understandings. It is also fundamentally a practical activity, as is evident in "grassroots cultures" of the global south, with relevance for all kinds of communities. Praxis in this sense is fundamentally about addressing everyday challenges people face, with recognition that community needs and knowledges often differ greatly from more formal organizational, academic, or institutional knowledge.[16] With close attention to the lived experience of trying to make things happen, design for social

---

[16] Also refer to the work of AbdouMaliq Simone who argues, "many attempts to 'make things better' dismiss" the praxis of "those who attempt to forge a kind of sense in the moment when all 'common sense' seems to disappear." AbdouMaliq Simone, *Improvised Lives* (Polity Press, 2019), page 124.

and spatial interventions might be more sensitive to the ways of knowing that constrain and enable life today.

W.E.B. Du Bois recognized this insight as he aspired toward an engaged scholarship and pedagogy that bridged informal knowledge and subjective experience with rigorous data collection. As he formed cooperative networks for thinking about and shaping new worlds, he recognized that forums for creative expression and social economic cooperation had an enduring cultural power reawaken people's social imaginations. For Du Bois, thought and action were judged by their potential long-term contributions to remaking society, even if an end goal (of dismantling racism) was not completed within the lifetimes of individual thinkers/ practitioners. In this way, thought is a way of better attuning to the life-giving potentials of designing and making. In light of the Du Boisian model, we might ask how what we are making and thinking can contribute enhancing people's lives in concrete ways. Will we rely on others to "apply" our thinking? Or will we allow our thinking to emerge from those who are already acting to address the issues? How might we begin forming the networks and relationships to situate our acting in expanding webs of thought?

Overall, generative praxis is a future-oriented intervention, with the goal of generating new insights, ideas, communities, or practices. It is not intervention purely for the sake of doing or understanding something. Instead, generative praxis involves participating in social reality order to open things up, put new groups in relation, point to other possibilities, move in different directions, initiate new conversations, or imagine alternative courses of action. Such a praxis positions thinking and acting as participating within flows of living social ecological realities. Reflective action in this sense both proposes and also anticipates futures in the process of designing. The potential of this praxis is ultimately for it to probe the edges of the possible, where the limits of what humans can make within a particular time and space are explored and constantly redefined.

Afterword: Social Thinking, Imagining, and Designing

In many ways this book has been about how key social thinkers approached their process of thinking and designing in their time, with particular emphasis on environmental issues, migration, racism, and social marginalization. What emerged in this project is some foundations (i.e., concepts, arguments, strategies, and models) for reflective action. This is not meant to be an ultimate or definitive foundation of connections between design and social thought. Indeed, many have sought to conceive and encourage forms of "reflective practice," especially in the professions and more recently creative practices.[1] The model of Geddes, Addams, and Du Bois orients reflection in a slightly different, although potentially complementary, way—as a blending of the *professional*, *political*, and *personal* realms of life. That is, they situate reflection in the domain of *action*, rather than only professional *practice*, modeling ways of acting within and beyond the context of professional demands.

---

[1] Perhaps most notably, many have used Donald Schön's notion of the reflective practitioner, including Linda Candy on her more recent extension of Schon's thinking to creative work: Donald Schön, *The Reflective Practitioner: How Professionals Think in Action* (Temple Smith, 1983); Linda Candy, *The Creative Reflective Practitioner* (Routledge, 2020).

Despite longstanding aspirations in some social thinking to better connect to action, a chasm has persisted over the last century and a half—between science and action, theory and practice, studying and doing. This book has argued that the gap between reflection and action is at the very core of how design and social science professions have narrowly imagined, theorized, and pursued their practice—which has, in turn, constrained the wider public imagination about what forms of social action are possible.

In particular, contemporary professionalization and methodological advances in the social sciences reinforce this gap, when they position reflection to be passive observation of the world. Many of the conventional foundations of social science point to a certain kind of knowledge—which emanates from credentialed experts, uses specialized methods, and loses sight of human creativity. Now, perhaps more than ever, there is a need to think and act from the basis that *another relationship to knowledge is possible*. Yet it is also the case that what *seems* possible and what *actually might be* possible are two different realms. Many futures do not seem possible precisely because of how the social and historical contexts into which we are born condition us to accept what is real and possible in our time.

Just as—in order to address the crises of our time—we must reaffirm that other worlds are possible, these *other* worlds can only be made with *other* ways of knowing and being. The twenty-first century therefore must be a moment to face up to the historical fact that the world made by modern industrial capitalism was also a world built by the social science and design professions, which thought and imagined present social realities into existence. It is in this sense that the book has been an attempt to point to and suggest some possible alternative contexts, histories, and foundations for social thought and design practice today. The choreography of beautiful action is a potential, if somewhat incomplete, model here that invites further engagement. It points to a transformative process of bringing people and groups together—to thoughtfully make new relationships in and through practice.

The lives, contexts, and practices of thinkers from the past, such as Patrick Geddes, Jane Addams, W.E.B. Du Bois, are especially helpful for understanding the possibilities of thinking, imagining, and designing today. Taken together, the lineages of these scholar practitioners offer a particular kind of foundation for reflective action. This is because their projects were imagined at the moment when industrial capitalism was consolidating and advancing in unprecedented ways. At the beginning of the twentieth century, society was moving ever more toward the dysfunction of obsessive doing in a modern industrializing capitalist society—so consumed with increasing outputs that it was in danger of losing capacity for genuine reflection. This condition resonates with the twenty-first century—both on specific issues like the environment, migration, racism, and social marginalization, and on the ways that new media and technology have profoundly sped up human life and information flows, making sustained efforts at genuine reflection difficult.

In their contexts and projects, Geddes, Addams, and Du Bois discovered some approaches to bringing thought and action together, which are especially relevant today. They were not always revolutionary, but they were, perhaps in small bits at a time, able to reimagine the possibilities of living through and transforming the weight of social oppressions and injustices in their time. As activist thinkers who were themselves on the margins of their disciplines and professions, they also point to the need to pay attention to all of the others who continue to be positioned on the edges of advancing Western thought, culture, society, and space.

In this context, like many of the thinkers presented here suggest, reimagining what is possible ought to be a central task of thinking and designing. Such a position may mean exploring alternatives in specific social contexts, but it also demands we reconsider what is possible for thought, design, and action today. That is, making the new worlds we so desperately need and can realize today is about also reconceiving how we go about thinking and designing. Reflecting on what it means to view Geddes, Addams, and Du Bois through the lens of design and social thought is helpful here—to clarify what social thinking and designing might be capable of today. What would it mean if we saw designing as part of process of thinking? Or conversely, what are the implications of viewing our thinking as part of a process of designing? A preliminary sketch might involve some of the following implications.

If designing were part of a process of thinking, it would be a long-term project that is capable of critique and equipped to make new worlds. Rather than rushing toward a previously specified deliverable or outcome, thinking models a process that is endlessly flexible and open to revision, even if there are products along the way. Genuinely critical thinking aims to radically question and reconsider previous assumptions, including the possibility that previous thinking could have been incorrect. This is, in part, what it means for design to realize its capability for critique, as always searching for more equitable and sustainable strategies and arrangements, or being willing to acknowledge the partial, incomplete nature of any outcome of a design process.

Although continuing a design project for the long term may be beyond the scope of an individual, this is precisely why it is crucial that all stages of a design process remain connected to the ongoing thought and action of communities most impacted by potential designs. By situating design in communities and places, designing might acknowledge its potential as an instigator and catalyst for future projects, even if there are different people involved over time. It is in this sense that designing is capable of being a world-making endeavor. That is, when connected to specific communities over time, design does not only make services, systems, spaces, or objects. In setting about to identify the gap between existing conditions and desired conditions, and then choreographing and moving into possible courses of action, design is ultimately capable of making new worlds.

Conversely, from the perspective of social thought, if thinking is a process of designing it is capable of intervention, shapes what is possible, and emerges from action. To see how thinking is capable of intervention requires a willingness to consider more than the text-based worlds of thought, and to explore how ideas are expressed in images, movement, action, diagrams, and physical objects. Images or objects can show people what a new world or condition could look like, even in speculative or prototype form, but it is also clear that words by themselves can powerfully depict that which does not yet exist. This is how thought is capable of not simply describing reality, but of shaping what is possible in the first place.

Although thought can be projected onto existing realities, to posit alternative possibilities, it is also capable of emerging directly from action. For instance, laws, plans, and policies of governments, organizations, or institutions are meant to shape a framework within which action should happen, but it is also evident that action never fits neatly into categories of established professional practices. In this discontinuity or contradiction between professional theories and practices, is there an opportunity for creating new knowledge, for building theories about how society is being made in the present, while opening toward the future?

How then, do we realize these capabilities of designing and thinking? In part, this question is entirely up to you, the reader. No matter how new or established in your work, what you do every day with others shapes the practices, knowledges, and worlds that are possible. It's not so much that we have to choose between working for a large organization and being an activist, but that we have to imagine how what we do every day can meet overlapping individual and community needs.

In other words, we ought not feel guilty because of our career or organization fails to be socially conscious enough, or rush to fill our days with commitments to the right causes. Rather the model suggested here involves finding ways to blend and hybridize different identities and approaches. This is especially important in an age where flexible, hybrid work arrangements and rapid technological change mean that we may be increasingly pursuing multiple kinds of projects at once, and may have a range of professional positions for different organizations in a life time. Such a condition demands we redefine the boundaries of conventional professional practices.

The good news is that there are models for where we might begin—for instance, the people explored in this book who blur the boundaries that conventionally (and perhaps, artificially) separate *activism, knowledge,* and *practice.* Scholars, activists, and practitioners referenced in this book suggest these *stances or dispositions toward acting* ought to inform each other and ultimately blend in creative ways. Yet it is common to think of activism, knowledge or scholarship, and practice as separate domains.

For instance, the stance of *activism* can be impatient with the practitioner who lacks vision and has given in to injustices of a system that marginalizes and excludes, and might be frustrated with the emotional and social distance from conventional knowledge, seeking to learn from on the ground realities. With leadership and trust in other people the successful activist reminds people of values that are important, and insists we do not need to settle because collective networks have tremendous power. The activist re-members for/with others—pointing to how things are, could be, or were made otherwise. In sum, activism involves a normative or ethical commitment to the possible.

The stance of *practice* may turn away from the systematic knowledge of the scholar, whose theories are often said to have little use for the everyday demands in the "real world." A busy practitioner may dismiss the activist who supposedly has no experience with the creative or administrative labor required to complete contracted projects and effect change within complex institutions. The practitioner knows that change requires repetition in daily, sometimes-agonizing iterations and small transformations, and may ask us to consider the practical implications of political or social aspirations. With concerns for logistical demands of effective interventions, practitioners in different professions orient their work toward what might be accomplished in a given day and how.

Knowledge or *scholarship* sees itself as guiding the practitioner who otherwise would act without consideration of the evidence and social conditions. The scholar or thinker may be ambivalent toward (or inspired by) the activist who raises relevant issues, but does so in a seemingly unsystematic way. An enduring strength of scholarship is the ability of knowledge to make connections and crosses scales, demonstrating that a powerful question can change everything. In this sense, the scholar or thinker encourages and elaborates until concepts have a durability and resonance that changes minds and forges new constituencies. Those who emphasize scholarship and knowledge foreground the importance of ongoing deliberation in beginning or sustaining any course of action.

Overall, to design and also cultivate a social imagination is to move, within our embodied and lived experience, through the strengths of all three of these identities (activist, scholar/thinker, and practitioner). Knowledge and activism (or even the hybrid forms of activist scholarship) have much to learn from the slow patient work of daily practice, with small everyday acts that can plant seeds of compassion or possibility. Similarly, the scholar and/or practitioner has much to learn from the vision of the activist that insists a more just and peaceful world is within reach. Many of the scholar practitioners and activist thinkers in this book have presented ways in which these identities might be blended or hybridized.

The modes of thinking, imagining, and designing that are sketched out in the book point to an approach that is available to everyone. More than a purely cognitive or academic exercise, it involves reflecting on lived experiences and knowledge, to work from where one's own unfolding life is positioned in relation to the what is emerging in now. While making time to reflect may be important, so too is the process of thoughtfully acting to form new relationships, mobilizing others to reflect, and learning to move through the world with reciprocity, creativity, and care. If only in small ways, those featured in the book model the potential of reflective action to understand and transform the pull of dominant trends in society.

It is important to emphasize the need to continue learning from social historical contexts other than the present, and what they may say about possible futures. Different times and places can provide important lessons and context for addressing challenges we face today. Not only have our ancestors sought to address similar challenges, but they also have tried out strategies of reflection, activism, and practice. This is to say that rethinking histories and contexts of the present may also be a starting point to enable and inform more effective action.

Such a lesson is especially important for design thinking, which often embraces a hyper-focus on the present. Especially as social design and design for social innovation have widened definitions of what designing can be, looking to people who may not conventionally be considered "designers" and their contexts can be illuminating. It is a reminder that even before forms of design that are practiced today became prominent, and even though designers today think of themselves as those who act today, people have been pursuing forms of designing that contribute to making new social worlds for a long time.

Positioning design and the imagination as relevant to social thought ultimately challenges tendencies toward withdrawal, cynicism, and disconnection, encouraging us to think, imagine, and act, wherever we are. It moves us away from reactionary analysis of the status quo that dominates news cycles and toward a propositional and action-oriented reflection. At a time when governments, organizations, and societies seem to lurch from one crisis to the next, it can be easy to simply respond to policies, situations, and crises in need of attention. The promise of cultivating both a design sensibility and a social imagination offers something different, as a foundation to create new contexts from which entirely different social realities might emerge. It invites us to deeply engage with social and ecological contexts of today, and to do so in a way that is oriented to what else might be possible.

INDEX